DERELICT AIR

Edward Dorn, en route to Cambridge, September 1966.
Photograph by Helene Dorn.

Edward Dorn

DERELICT AIR
FROM COLLECTED OUT

Edited by
Justin Katko and Kyle Waugh

ENITHARMON PRESS

First published in 2015
by Enitharmon Press
10 Bury Place
London WC1A 2JL

www.enitharmon.co.uk

Distributed in the UK by
Central Books
99 Wallis Road
London E9 5LN

Distributed in the USA and Canada by
Independent Publishers Group
814 North Franklin Street
Chicago, IL 60610
USA
www.ipgbook.com

ISBN: 978-1-907587-78-8

Enitharmon Press gratefully acknowledges the financial support of
Arts Council England, through Grants for the Arts.

British Library Cataloguing-in-Publication Data.
A catalogue record for this book is available
from the British Library.

Cover image: Untitled painting (1978) by Raymond Obermayr. See list of picture credits.

Designed in Albertina by Libanus Press
and printed in England by
Short Run Press

CONTENTS

LATE IN THE REVOLUTION (1960–1962)

SILENT GUNS (1961–1963)

A CIRCLE OF SONGS (1964)

IN THE FACE OF THE LIBERAL (1964–1968)

THE THEATER OF MONEY (1971)

TRANSLATIONS WITH GORDON BROTHERSTON (1971–1975)

A MEXICO SCRAPBOOK (1972)

MELLOW W/ TEETH (1972–1976)

HOMAGE TO GRAN APACHERÍA (1973)

OFFICE EQUIPMENT (1976–1983)

FROM THE WRONG SIDE OF THE PARTITION
AT THE HOUSTON MLA (1980–1981)

MORE ABHORRENCES (1983–1989)

ABOMINATIÓNES (1991)

THE CONNECTION TO NOWHERE (1992–1999)

DENVER SKYLINE (1993–1999)

PLUS DE LANGUEDOC VARIORUM: A DEFENSE OF HERESY & HERETICS (1992–1999)

PICTURE CREDITS

Cover: Untitled painting (1978) by Raymond Obermayr. Location and ownership of painting unknown. Slide reproduced courtesy of Erich Obermayr.

The photograph of Edward Dorn (p. 2) is reproduced courtesy of J.H. Prynne, Binder D5 (July 1966–December 1966).

The manuscripts of "february child" (p. 68), "[Come with them]" (p. 70), and "AN OLD SQUARE POEM" (p. 144) are reproduced courtesy of the Department of Special Collections, Stanford University Libraries.

The drawing by Fielding Dawson (p. 121) is reproduced from the cover of Dorn, *Idaho Out* (London: Fulcrum Press, 1965), courtesy of the estate of Fielding Dawson.

The manuscript of "This is the Poem for John W." (p. 169) and the *Gunslinger* horse drawing by Michael Myers (p. 201) are reproduced courtesy of the Special Collections, University of Delaware Library.

The watercolour "Homo neanderthalensis" (1950) by Maurice Wilson (p. 170) is reproduced courtesy of The Trustees of The Natural History Museum, London.

Back cover: Tombstone insignia designed by Zephyrus Image for broadsides published during the Kent State Arts Festival, 1974. Cf. Dorn, *Collected Poems* (Manchester: Carcanet Press, 2012), pp. 362–363. Reproduced courtesy of Jennifer Dunbar Dorn.

All other images are reproduced courtesy of the Archives & Special Collections at the Thomas J. Dodd Research Center, University of Connecticut Libraries.

PREFACE

Derelict Air has grown out of our collaboration with Jennifer Dunbar Dorn and Reitha Pattison on Edward Dorn's recent *Collected Poems* (Carcanet Press, 2012). Whereas that volume exhibits the poet that Dorn became, this one reflects a career of becoming, gathering previously uncollected poems from magazines, ephemera, correspondence, manuscripts, notebooks, and recordings held by numerous individuals and archives across North America and the United Kingdom. It includes Dorn's first poems from 1952, formative early attempts at the long poem (including one composed at Black Mountain College), illustrated bucolics written for an unfinished children's book, poems written in response to the Cuban missile crisis, incantations hurled at the 1968 Democratic National Convention, numerous poems from Dorn's daybook from 1971, fragments unassimilated into his *Gunslinger* epic, outtakes from his study of the Apache resistance, translations of early Mayan and Aztec texts, an arsenal of uncollected "Abhorrences", and a five-fold extension of his "NAZDAKS".

But while *Derelict Air* substantially augments the existing body of Dorn's work, it is by no means exhaustive, and could contain a lot more. The sprawling, protean nature of his decade-long projects, and the fact that many of his poems exist in multiple, heavily-revised drafts, imposed significant challenges on the editing of this book. In the case of *Gunslinger*, the abundance of illustrated notebooks and manuscripts would require a volume unto itself. Furthermore, as Dorn drafted *Gunslinger*'s final books during the early seventies, he began to compose forms of abbreviated speech performance unbolted from the *Gunslinger* narrative. Note, for example, the second poem of *The Day & Night Report* (1971): "Day 5, 360 days follow | Kid at the clinic 1:00p". The writing of such highly-condensed texts – "light and essential", as the "Preface" to *Hello, La Jolla* (1978) calls its own "dispatches" – evolved into a thorough exploration of the epigram that continued through the eighties and nineties, reaching its apex with the radioactive "NAZDAKS" that run along the floor of *Languedoc Variorum*. Such a practice proposes the challenge that any manuscript passage, however brief, might be construed of and published as a poem.

The process of selection was therefore complicated, and different readers would have likely selected a different suite of texts. We left out numerous notebook poems written after 1970, as well as many "Abhorrences", due both to space limitations and to financial constraints that hindered our access to archival materials. And while *Derelict Air* expands nearly all of Dorn's major works, one notable exception is the unfinished late epic *Westward Haut*, published by Etruscan Books in 2012. Because we were unable to view many of the notebooks that we know to contain this work, and do not know enough about the history of the project's composition, we chose not to publish any of those fragments and short poems that we *have* seen, all of which date to the project's earliest stages. We have otherwise attempted to assemble the most inclusive volume possible. It is certainly the case that any of those instances of the poet's not infrequent mirth which left our pants fully evacuated will be found published here.

Besides selection, there was the task of recovery. During the process of gathering the material for this book, we discovered evidence of a number of lost projects, including two book-length collections: *Poems of Washington, Idaho, & Mexico* (1959) and *Silent Guns* (1963). Dorn's attempts to publish these and a few other books at the start of his career met with failure, as he explains in a 1963 letter to J.H. Prynne: "I have been screwed of publication in america for verse".[1] In every case, as the manuscripts of these unpublished books circulated among publishers, they were revised and reorganised into new manuscripts, and as each new manuscript

---

1 Edward Dorn to J.H. Prynne (TS, 2 pp.), 1 October 1963, held by J.H. Prynne, Binder D1 (November 1961–March 1964).

cannibalised and superseded the one before it, many poems were left behind, unpublished until now. Because we have not found complete manuscripts of these collections, we have assembled evidence for their content and ordering from letters, notebooks, readings, and manuscript fragments. In addition to these texts, *Derelict Air* contains a number of unrealised or incomplete projects that we have attempted to present in a version loyal to their intended form. More information about the lost books (including lists of their constituent poems), and other unfinished projects, is contained in the Notes at the end of this volume, with page references to the *Collected Poems* (2012).

*

Many of the poems included in this book have been retrieved from Dorn's correspondence, and we feel certain that more poems will surface among the papers of other writers and publishers. It is worth mentioning a few of the lesser-known correspondents who were important to Dorn's early development as a writer, and whose papers were crucial to the construction of this book.

The cover features a painting by Raymond Obermayr (1922–2014), Dorn's painting instructor during the summer of 1950 at Eastern Illinois University. A veteran of World War II, Obermayr helped Dorn avoid the Korean War by sending him to Black Mountain and paying his first year's tuition. Dorn's early long poem "TEN COMMUNICATIONS from the WEST" is likely addressed to his lifelong friend.

The first section of *Derelict Air* presents poems that Dorn sent in letters to his childhood friend Gordon Taylor (1928–2000), a corporal in the Marines during the Korean War. Their correspondence, running from 1952 to 1955, is central to Tom Clark's narrative in his biography *Edward Dorn: A World of Difference* (2002). Dorn's letters offer rich accounts of his roving search for day labour across the western United States, interspersed with reports on his eclectic reading and the poems he was writing.

Contemporary with Dorn's letters to Taylor is the beginning of his substantial correspondence with Denise Levertov (1923–1997). Levertov was not only responsible for first publishing Dorn in *Origin* (1954), but was the primary editor and agent of his early work. The poems gathered here as *Poems of Washington, Idaho, & Mexico* represent not only Dorn's first attempt at a book-length collection, but also the culmination of a correspondence that lasted from 1953 to 1962. There has been no scholarly discussion of this correspondence, and Levertov's impact on Dorn's early poetry warrants serious consideration.

Dorn's friendship with John Wieners (1934–2002) began at Black Mountain, where Wieners, as Dorn notes in the epigraph to "Rome", "taught me the Greek alphabet one September afternoon" (*Collected Poems*, p. 838). Evidence of that lesson can be found in the Greek passage in "The Righting of the Cat" (1954). As editor of *Measure* (1957–1962), Wieners solicited a number of poems from Dorn, though published only "The Rick of Green Wood" before the magazine folded. References and dedications to Wieners appear throughout Dorn's work, and several of the poems in this book derive from their early correspondence.

*

"No poet has been more painfully, movingly, *political*", writes Robert Creeley: "the range and explicit register of Edward Dorn's ability to *feel* how it actually is to be human, in a given place and time, is phenomenal."[2] Dorn's work situates disarming pleas for tenderness alongside nuclear denunciations of anyone whose actions he thought reduced the lives of others. "Give them the statistics of death", begins one of his earliest poems, "so that the remembrance may | always stick in the charred throat". These lines establish his care for the victims of state aggression, whose numbers are not retained in an historical consciousness riven by

2 Robert Creeley, Preface to Edward Dorn, *Selected Poems*, ed. Donald Allen (Grey Fox Press, 1978).

the bigotries of capitalist ideology and lost inside menus of organised irrelevance. There is no doubt, however, that Dorn's steadfast attention to the destroyed and forgotten is sometimes complicated by the intolerant extremes of his denunciations. This is a burden his readers will have to bear.

This book's remembrances include poems written for Luz, a matriarch of the Apache nation shipped to a federal prison in 1886; for Jimmie Workman, incarcerated for a string of nine West Coast bank robberies in 1962; for Diana Oughton, a member of the Weather Underground killed in 1970; for Billy Wright, a Loyalist paramilitary leader murdered in a British prison in 1997; for poets John Clare and Max Douglas; for Soviet spy Robert Soblen; and for the outlaw William H. Bonney. The geometry of our isolation from such figures sounds a fugitive harmonic that Dorn continually found new ways to amplify and project. His work celebrates the histories of resistance to conquest and persecution, and it stands as a record of the exuberance of being alive in a world suffused with the resonant authority of forgotten cosmologies.

Justin Katko & Kyle Waugh
London–NYC
November 2014

A NOTE ON THE TEXT

The Notes at the end of this volume contain information on the publication, source, date of composition, and significant textual variants of poems, as well as descriptions of largely unknown or reconstructed works. What follows here are general editorial notes.

SECTION TITLES: With the exception of the first section of this book, there are three kinds of section titles used here: those taken from a poem within the section; descriptive extensions to preexisting titles; and Dorn's titles for unpublished projects.

ORDERING: Poems are ordered chronologically. Where possible, date of composition is used in favour of date of publication. Most of the poems have a date or date-range applied only in the Notes. In cases where dates of composition were included by the author and deemed textually significant by the editors, they have been retained in the text of the poem.

NOTEBOOK POEMS: For the most part, poems taken from notebooks come from the Archives & Special Collections at the Thomas J. Dodd Research Center, University of Connecticut Libraries. There remain many notebooks which we have not had the chance to read, most of which are held in the Department of Special Collections, Hesburgh Libraries of Notre Dame.

TRANSCRIPTION OF LINE-ENDINGS FROM MANUSCRIPTS: Dorn sometimes allows the right margin of a manuscript to determine the end of his line. Other times, he extends the line by indenting its overflow. In his typescripts, he sometimes interprets the indented shorter line of the manuscript as an extension of the previous line, and sometimes as a line in its own right. Depending on our interpretation of the shape of the poem, we have treated line-endings in both ways. Meanwhile, when Dorn erases parts of lines from drafts, the newly-created blank spaces will often remain in the final version of the poem; we have taken this into consideration in editing our versions of some of the poems.

POEMS TRANSCRIBED FROM RECORDINGS: There are two poems for which we have no source other than a sound recording: "An attempt at self-sorrow" (1961) and "Quote followed by example" (1978). Line breaks, indentation, punctuation, and stanza breaks have been interpreted from pauses and inflections in the readings, and also adopted from characteristics of contemporaneous poems. The process of creative transcription that resulted in our version of 'An attempt at self-sorrow' was undertaken on a number of poems from the same collection, for which we later discovered manuscripts.

CROSSED-OUT LINES: There are a few instances in which we have retained crossed-out lines in poems. Notes on Dorn's manuscripts indicate that cross-outs were intended to appear in the final versions of "AN OLD SQUARE POEM" and "Open Letter to the Apache Nation (unrevised)". The cross-outs retained in "SO LONG CUBA", "BUT THEN AGAIN", "Night 69: THE NIGHTLETTER (draft)", and "Who will follow" express something that we have deemed especially significant to the poems.

SPELLING: The spelling of many words has been normalised. Numerous others have been left in an 'incorrect' form, either because it seems that Dorn intended these spellings, or because normalising them would remove something idiosyncratic from the texture of the poem. A single additional letter often characterises Dorn's (mis)spelling: "forgotteeness", "melancholick", "floweres", "reallity", "winde".

SQUARE BRACKETS: Square brackets in the main text are Dorn's, with the exception the text of "Night 69: THE NIGHTLETTER (draft)", where square brackets are used to indicate Dorn's revisions. A similar use of square brackets is made for the variants of several poems given in the Notes.

PAGE LAYOUT: The pages of this book have been designed so as to make page breaks coincide with stanza breaks. In the cases where this has not been possible, an asterisk has been inserted beside the page number at the bottom of the page on which the interrupted stanza begins.

ACKNOWLEDGEMENTS

Thanks to Jennifer Dunbar Dorn, without whose support it would have been impossible for us to edit this book. Thank you Jennifer!

Thanks to the generosity of J.H. Prynne, whose holdings of early Dorn manuscripts and correspondence have been essential to the construction of this book. Thank you Lao Pu!

Thanks to Reitha Pattison, whose research and editorial contributions to the *Collected Poems* helped set the stage for the present volume. Thanks to Fred Buck for providing crucial information about unpublished early poems and correspondence. Thanks to Erich Obermayr for sharing reproductions of his late father's paintings. Thanks to Gordon Brotherston for sharing his Dorn correspondence and translation papers. Thanks to Fred Wah for sharing recordings of early readings. Thanks also to Maya Dorn and Kidd Dorn for their help and support.

Thanks to Remi Thornton for colour work on the cover image. Thanks to Adrian Acu for providing photographs of archival materials from the Department of Special Collections, Stanford University Libraries. Thanks to Yugon Kim for providing scans of uncatalogued archival materials from the Department of Special Collections, Hesburgh Libraries of Notre Dame. Thanks to Claudia Moreno Parsons, whose edition of the correspondence of Dorn and Amiri Baraka has been of central importance to this project, and who has provided scans of archival materials from the Charles E. Young Research Library, University of California, Los Angeles, and the Lilly Library, Indiana University. Thanks to Michael Seth Stewart for providing photographs of the correspondence of Dorn and John Wieners from the Special Collections, University of Delaware Library, and for giving us access to his unpublished doctoral dissertation, *For the Voices: The Letters of John Wieners*

(Graduate Center, CUNY, 2013). Thanks to Luke Roberts for retrieving poems from the same correspondence. Thanks to Michael Davidson for looking into the Donald Allen Papers at the Mandeville Special Collections Library, University of California, San Diego. Thanks to Nicky Melville for looking into the Gael Turnbull Papers at the National Library of Scotland. Thanks to Steve Clay and Tom Damrauer for providing access to archival materials at Granary Books. Thanks to Andrew Wallace-Hadrill for assistance with the Greek in "The Righting of the Cat".

Thanks to Melissa Watterworth Batt from the Archives & Special Collections at the Thomas J. Dodd Research Center, University of Connecticut Libraries, for several years of helpful assistance, which included a number of grants provided to assist our research at the Dodd. Thanks to George Rugg for his generosity in making available uncatalogued archival materials from the Department of Special Collections, Hesburgh Libraries of Notre Dame. Thanks also to the following librarians and libraries in the USA: Mattie Taormina at the Department of Special Collections, Stanford University Libraries; Timothy Murray and Maureen Cech at the Special Collections, University of Delaware Library; Liz Kline at the Special Collections & Archives of the Merrill-Cazier Library, Utah State University; Bradley Arnold at the Archives, University of Colorado at Boulder Libraries; Michael Basinski at the Special Collections, University at Buffalo Libraries; Nicole C. Dittrich at the Special Collections Research Center, Syracuse University Libraries; David K. Frasier at the Lilly Library, Indiana University; Nigel Cochrane at the Albert Sloman Library, University of Essex; Elspeth Healey and Kathy Lafferty at the Kenneth Spencer Research Library, University of Kansas, Lawrence; Yolande Ferreira at the Natural History Museum Picture Library, London; the New York Public Library and its Berg Collection; and the John Hay Library, Brown University. Thanks also to the following libraries in the UK: the Cambridge University Library; the Seeley Historical Library, Cambridge; the English Faculty Library, Cambridge; the Queens' College Library, Cambridge; the Gonville & Caius College Library, Cambridge; and the British Library.

Thanks to the following booksellers who have fielded our queries or supplied scans of rare publications: Adam Davis at Division Leap; Alan at Derringer Books; M.L. Granlund; Philip Smith; Michael Good; Colin Mahar at Harper's Books; Bill Stevens; David Wirshup at Anacapa Books; Lara Feldman at Between the Covers; Rick Boyles at My Book Heaven; Jeff Maser; Shannon at Book Alley; the Generous Merchant at the Beat Book Shop; Derek at Vashon Island Books; Rhett Moran at Robinson Street Books; Gary Wilkie at Acequia Booksellers; Bob & Susan at Longhouse Publishers & Booksellers; Harry Nudel at Nudel Books; Richard Erdmann at Mare Booksellers; and Chuck Stebelton at Woodland Pattern Book Center.

Thanks to the following for their helpful correspondence: Geoffrey G. O'Brien; Rolf-Gunter Dienst; Ammiel Alcalay; Kenneth Irby; John Wilkinson; John Matthias; Stephen Fredman; Lisa Jeschke; Ryan Dobran; Marjorie Welish; Rosmarie Waldrop; Hans Thill; Mike Wallace-Hadrill; Ian Heames; Luke Roberts; Denise Low; Tom Clark; Susan Hazaleus at EDGE gallery, Denver; and Britni LeRoux of the Denver Zoo.

Thanks to the following for their scholarship: Tom Clark, *Edward Dorn: A World of Difference* (North Atlantic Books, 2002); James K. Elmborg, "A Pageant of Its Time": Edward Dorn's Slinger *and the Sixties* (Peter Lang, 1998); and Steve Clay and Rodney Phillips, *A Secret Location on the Lower East Side: Adventures in Writing, 1960–1980* (The New York Public Library & Granary Books, 1998).

Thanks to Peter Target at Enitharmon Press, and to Susan Wightman at Libanus Press, for working with us to make this book a reality.

Finally, thanks to Lucy and Jackie for putting up with months of phone calls in their living rooms as this work was being prepared.

POEMS SENT TO CORPORAL
GORDON TAYLOR
(1953–1954)

UNTITLED

The bleat of time
enters slowly
this room wet
with the enchantment
of decayed passion

A fragmentary note
upon that white table
chants all our concurrent
mistakes.

      If you come again,
      it won't be the same,
      somehow.

5.

When you return to me down those
wooden steps I lately sit under
what dimension can you have of
human selection can you manage
the severe course an iron railing
and vanishing steps demand viewed
from this spice shop with
its coriander spreading, faintly,
an account of obvious differences?

THIRD FLOOR

the bathroom in
our apt.
on the third floor
has a window the shape of
a parallelogram, two
sides vertical.
And across the window,
                    diagonally,
a partition.
the lower half section
                    was painted
evidently,
before we came so
that light comes in, unobstructedly,
from the upper half, only,
even though the window stands
3 floors up and
opens on a steep roof.

NIGHT SCENE

Pieces of junk
hanging (at)
3508
dirty windows

Pieces of Junk
in the
banging air,
late.

[GIVE THEM THE STATISTICS OF DEATH]

Give them the statistics of death
so that the remembrance may
always stick in the charred throat
and lie there throbbing the disaster of a
too barren beginning.
But do not cast me into the dark
closet again or
beat me for running nude down
the black oil road that first time
of passion.

THE SURREALIST

rode roaring
clutched the handles
          spread wide
          from the shoulders,

his black motorcycle flinching.
And behind him bounced
doggedly the trailer bearing
higher, a like cycle,
Black.

ROTUND

He sits in his swively
chair,
The ever-ready smile smiling
                 molten regularity.

For Mr. Bruce's a
Personnel Dir.

SAN F.

Bridged city under fog-white hills
The weeks were love and ended our eyes turning
Away past silence, endurable, the way damp soil tills.
In front of October, already, love was slower burning.
Wakeless suspension, her absence the agent of fever,
You gave the meaning of newspapers, and cleared the mist,
Silently plaguing like a dress I can't remember
As i held back love with gripped fist.
Sirocco, and even the week-ends spent
The mental move must precede suitcases packed
Standing eternally within this dolmen we bent
Two memories and me gazing into plaster cracked.
      Give time the time to rewind cells
      Another meeting will arrange new hells.

DECORUM ON A GREY DAY

In weightless light grey enough & sourceless
Only for luminous holes on the horizon,
Gulls make languid circles
Black as condors with the perfect sham,
An audience of winter stranded
Land birds filagreed in roosts.

While the gulls reel toward the bay & sound
Their audience has come & gone
Seeking various perches for no reason,
But outlasting the gulls with silence.
Just past the shifting noon light coming
Still from the bay a tranced steamer
Arrives from the pacific east so gulls
Again have left
                    the whole air
To a stiff airplane in intent line
Caged in glass determination.

[SEVERAL GULLS]

Several gulls
dupe gravity with no force:
a length rumbled midair
          to certain restless changes
within locusless winds
slowly arrived from the tight
          sea surface a static
gloss to thwart extenuating wings
making the deception not flight
          but dance of another sort
abrupt as dawn on the moon.

A DERELICT AIR

A sharp green counter
was where she sat
& her color was
velvet it darkened
just right, like love

The blues, so slowly chant
a memorial counter-charm
keyed with coffee odors
yellowed during 78 whirls
of revealed lacquer.

Still her dark hips
shift for cloth necessities
with no hints of malediction
for the blues demand space
as temporal as a snowman,
or marimba sounds.

THE RIGHTING OF THE CAT
(1954)

THE RIGHTING OF THE CAT

The chill and blues and those tattoos.
The rain.
Shadows and the leaves turned up.
Cold prediction.
                          Cold deflections.
New socks in box, the labels blue,
and yellow fit to embarrass.
Leave them there forever.
Now, Sun, and
a magazine in which Clerk Maxwell demonstrates
that a cat rights herself, from two inches!
Mother, come to think of it, you could leave
those goddamn socks & shorts home, you could
offer at least the advantages Clerk had.
My Dear Sir,
did you get in your laundry argyles
of oval curves made with needle and thread
from Glenblair?
No no: you sent thread parabolas. But then
your father was interested in mechanical contrivances.

Τό Πρῶτον Μάθημα —
Ἀρκή ἥμισυ πάντων

This greek &
this latin
              Cannibis Sativa
from Tournefort

"Flowers dioecious; the sterile in axillary
compound racemes of panicles, with 5 sepals
& 5 drooping stamens"

And then you know what love is
but not quite
the false Asphodel—
                    Flowers perfect,
                    Perianth more
                    or less spreading, persistent
                    the sepals concave, oblong, without
                    claws, 3-nerved.

A cold reflection:
"not begun, done in" like a cubed steak
like me, with too much breeding and no blood
but no frigging breeding either,
but what I have will follow:

Eurylochus ran back to the ship
empty handed, flat footed, panting
Yeats
    "... a distinction between the perfection
    that is from a man's combat with himself
    and that which is from a combat with
    circumstance..."

CIRCUMSTANCE.

Cordelia   "Nothing, my lord
Lear   "Nothing!
Cordelia   "Nothing.
Lear   "Nothing

CIRCUMSTANCE.

Yeats
    "... the struggle to come at Truth takes away
    our pity, and the struggle to overcome our passions
    restores it."

This is well bred. This is polite,
This moral I will not be run to relief by
if I sit all day
and frown.

2

A theory of the economy of sleep—

"sleep from five in the afternoon
to 9:30, read very hard from 10 to 2,
exercise by running along the corridors
and up and down stairs from 2 to 2:30,
sleep again from 2:30 to 7."

avoid serendipity
    "   condescension

keep the window shut when it isn't in use
    "   the word in your mouth until it wants out

anticipate his leaving in order to conduct your own
    "   idleness in order to turn away

The last, a trick.

3

Walk walk walk

love is not in you, not in me, the lips give

give on tissure a print, your eyes downcast, wear your new

shorts you got in the mail, your new socks

leave the tags on, it was so sweet of you to clothe

me to hide my unbalanced mind,

so sweet of me to wear them to go with my beard,

at this point I'll wear anything.

I'll give anything

I'll give

> Cordelia's moral tone to Edmond's
> responsibility and you'll have a respectable
> Cordelia, not a craftier Edmond

$$\frac{\text{A man}}{\text{circumstance}} = \text{a variety of man}$$

$$\frac{2 \text{ men}}{\text{the same circumstance}} = \text{tennis}$$

4

Cat,
the wheels
cat,
the mountains don't make of the earth
a mace,
cat
but you do, the most
you, the mouse
right in your own house
the mountains lunge,
you won't come out and
play
tennis, you don't have a
circumstance in the middle with backspin
all around

I think that I shall burn the next box you send me
just from the awful sore limp it gives me to get
a thing from you, don't think of me damn you, I forbid
that you think of me, don't send me a needle and thread—
if my clothes drop off the sooner

exposé d
I played
tennis
with it right in us,
the pubescent, roughish, ball
diameter 2½ inches
stuck near whatever . . .
in the bag.

        when you meet a man how
the hell do you determine his rank?

                  Maturation?

Progress?
doctrine?
strike?
        Solemnity?
        inter?
        windjammer?

Speak windjammer:

           "I HAVE GENTS IN THE BOTTLE
           YOU WILL NOTICE IN MY LEFT HAND
           THE DISTILLED RESIDUE OF YOUR BRAIN
           WHILE IN MY RIGHT I HAVE THE PRESENT-
           FUTURE-PAST OF YOUR MODUS VIVENDI
           WHICH BY FORCE OF MY CONFIDENCE
           I SHALL NOW MIX BEFORE YOUR EYES"

LOOKING, FOR A THING
(1957–1959)

REPORT FROM WASHINGTON: MARCH

Concerning biffetting
and being pitched against
the door jambs of life with a capital
L.

Gems.
Germs traveling unheard of distances
Spreading through Ida(ho
Until
One's bowels are loose
in Washington.

They travel by mouth.
We've had word
Germs are motored
is what I heard.

If they came over the mountains
at this season
they must have had ice-picks and crampons
even the passes are clogged.

March!, is the cruelest month
The spectres of children
attaching great black bats
to strings. Barking winds attack the hemlocks
on the hill back of my house. Bending
Alder saplings over the slate cliffs.
Screaming against the red Purple yellow and orange
crocus rows in the commercial plots.

Influenza! Coming from Idaho.
March! The top sergeant of the germs.
A visitation from an employer.

John. Brought his child Raymond.
A bug. What they call germs.
A horrible malady was he.
His main action was grinning backed up
by screaming. Father John brought him to the house
today and for a notion hit him full
in the smacker. Screaming like a louse.
You could have heard him in the windy mountains.
Blasted flat against the door-jamb a hard-shelled bug
fell on his piercing opened mug.

Legs would have been an accomplishment.
The basic four. Insects are prelimited
as to size and motility.

Thank God there are no dangerous snakes
In Western Washington. Altho the news
is full of slugs and snails; makes
contractile, motored, creatures occupy
the public
eye.

TH'ABJECTIVE NONE

Havent I
summoned All

the people
of the world
into my
head,

said nothing,
included
my toggenburg goat
because she
is near
to me,
            Have I not

gotten
their faces, the flash

existence,
the whole grey row
                    how?

many times today
like a yearly
reunion

            28 years,
Not precluding
anyone
at first,
            the thirst
for number,

Th'abjective none.

            The bleeting nan ...
with torus eyes.

Carl Gustav Jung
my pulpiteer

rises above
the venetian blinded room
of my head,

seeks to manipulate
the shutter cords,
differentiate,
The Mass.

*   *   *   *   *

The Great Ones,
                    affirming

Heart, forthwith desert
us, arent
in it, the head-room—

& I,
in my own manner
a Great One,
arent in it either . . .

But I hear
unhearable
despair, a dollars worth
of disease,
the sentiment,

the heady world
saying—
We didnt mean it
We poorling pseudo-
Moderns, really didnt

mean to be
a horde
                    (get enough of
                    us together &
                    we'll go off

miserable
misled
confused
cond
with sophisticated feet
cloven,
torus eyes,
no passage back
to the hinterland
or forward
to the mechanick
land, tricked
out of a god
of any quality—
What we great ones
move so much by.
Forgive me, are moved thereby . . .)

Wreck
Wreck
Wreck O my filthy mind

I scream too,
until I differentiate
because I too
am great

     *   *   *   *   *

They are worthless.
The man in the pulpit
was correct,
       & I
end a poem like that

deserting the horde
of the
      flash
          of my sin

THE POET SPENDS A DAY AT THE DUMP (MT. VERNON, APRIL 20

Overhead,

sea-gulls, glaucous wings
slight impression of breeding
in the advanced season, suspicious

flounderings, where Spring
is an obvious hungup dog.

Lower,
      acre-wise

Johnny & me

ogres of a sortilege,
keeping, as I saw with surprise
the gulls from their browse
of grapefruit, astir in the air . . .
their care
      their care.

Gulls, ponderous in flight
gawkily the bob
the knob of the head socketed, wooden
but for the glide

slid, grace slipping into what
one nearly cant look at ... (

     The rooster! Johnny says
for your mantle?
No No laughs I nor old beds
old mattresses,
               nor broken chicken coops

These hardly worn house-shoes I said
are good yet, I'll bet you can wear them
but he wore them not

Walked off grinning, emptying boxes
Ho Ho paradoxes of the daily confetti of Man

Making
a new
world

      the ash can

          Well,

here's a span of toy mules
of tiny tools, cast away rules
from an office, a broken dish
something of a fish, the whole
alliteration of creation.

What do you find, Johnny m'boy
what's found. A witch?
on a green motorcycle, a black broom aflying
a witch on an orange wheeled M'cycle

     *   *   *   *

MacBeth hovers over the American dump

*   *   *   *

The decayed grapefruit Sun

begun
downward, wrung

soundward, late afternoon

the gulls going home, wards
of the city no more

home to the barnacle spun shore.

                    Home! for us

Johnny boy . . .

another toy, for the kids?

What nonsense
lets go!

a man could pick his life out ahere
could shake the dear boxes of life

What a sun, what nonsense,

Here am I
the only poet in a thousand miles
Not proper I should be at the city

dump

with Fate hanging

low . . .

        back of my rump

POEM

Something lovely
before I die:
a cast
at madness, world wide
delirium, a picnic of small
tundra floweres
something the species'll drop dead at

and a sack of jingling tricks
for the melancholick, the pretty
tinkling acquaintanceship
of three eyed rats, something
friends have not recommended.

Unabashed, for once, in the face
of hardship,
and of failing to succeed,
maintain my roving household.

Kaadrror! Welcome in Abyssinia without
credentials, my merits uncovered slowly,
and after many surprises and set-backs.

Then, my slightly antique desires
resolved, as in obscure lands,
on spits, of lonely sand,
I shed a famously recorded tear
for World Wide Delirium.
Finally, something quite sentimental
so the species'll chatter until dawn
on the day I was quartered and drawn.

AN IDEA OF PERFECTION

Why, in the world
could I want loneliness revealed?
What,

      could I want
apple trees

        in my ear
        the colour
        yellow
        the wind hollow!

The Sun, God's Palm?
Apple tree leaves in the wind
my psalm . . .

THE FAIR RELIEF

Today,
I met
the first misanthropic.

His inslung shoulders,
his stringhair, and
oh, the hell with it.

His very sharp nose.
His eyes.
Yah, his eyes.
They put every
thing under
God's sun

Down.
Told me he
tried last year
in the blue season
to get stove oil
from a merchant
on credit,
refused,
mere refuse

the scar.
Apropos of nothing
a good clean thief.
A nice blend of grief

a fair relief
to me
this snarling
frank man

in a streetfull
of wellbelievers
and faintsmilers.

THE GIRLS IN THE BANK

Are so lovely
framed in the white door.
The All O'clock sun.
Curb, parking meters, bums.
Venetian blinds.

There's Cleaning Power
here, their skins reflect it.
After a breath of air
they walk away. In
their hands
they've green & gray money.
One feels perverse.
                        One
can't get the numbers
on the bills, out of one's

        head.

VILE, THOT TIMOTHY, LIKE I

On the steps of the Labor Temple
Sin—

greater than those old
Corinthian rapers knew

tho Vast
their antechristian labor

tho Vile
thot Timothy
on the steps of that city.

Vile, thot Timothy, and I
with our yearning eyes
Vile, vile blunt Corinth
and vast at that, your sin

tho apparently anyone
could, who wanted it.
Ah, to be there now, getting laid
anywhere but the Labor Temple
getting Texicoed

like a coed,
eager for a summer job.

ANACORTES REVISITED

(For Helene)

How we sat
in the middle
of off-beach weeds
How we sat

off-shore at landward
exchanged six years
without turning our heads.

Kelp is for children.
Has a head, is a whip.
Marriage is a mirage
is a ship.

Old wheels, Old boat sheds
Old locks, Old cables

and sea-tackle,
still set, where we laughed
without turning our heads,

watching the docking ferry.

WHILE DRIVING, HOME

I saw an old woman
with a mans hat on
and way out glasses

She was driving.
Hell-bent.

That's all there is.
To live in the country,
be eccentric, and

when looking at a local
mountain, grin
with satisfaction.

More to it?
My wife saw a handsome
young couple
looking to buy a trailerhouse.
& was bug-eyed for three blocks.

The mountain is on the right
20 miles up, through snow
and rocks.

AN EMBARRASSMENT

Looking for the signs
how it was once,

              a door
with many hinges
that opened out

once, allowing the bright air
like happy birthday, people

passing, odd hats in view.

Or for the crazy shaped window
in a back room, now used
for storage, Look. A pleasure

in the pain
my old refrain.

Can't be satisfied.
I can't be, in a more and more

painted hell. But then so well
one spits on the design
made by our white collar
workers, on a holiday of anticipated
prestige

or even one is embarrassed
by a social sounding poem.

But who can't go now
who won't go
sit,
by the door, with many hinges
opening out,
the world moving, delectable,
all the way to Dakota
or where you are.

LOOKING, FOR A THING

Like the heavy cow
looking for a calf
my woman searches

The corners & bays of the house
looking for an unthought port
uncalled on port

or in the traveling trunk
looking for a thing
not worn for a while.

Like the farmer
I prepare a stall
with my head, some consolation

where she can go
and looking for a rest,
wait till we have gone.

LETTER FROM AN AGÉD AUNT

"I have been your Aunt
all my life.
            —It
is terrible
to grow old
                I
am the last of my
generation.
            —It
is horrible to live
in an institution."

        *   *

One reads slowly
the letter has come
a great distance
in the last three days.

One thinks: generation,
how fine to have had one.
One, or rather I am young,
relatively, making thereby
a sentimental optimistic song.

I do not laugh. Nor am I sad.
Nor, again, concerned.
One has a myriad things, if not
a million, passing thru the head,
a fragmentary world, tonight.

Still, one can put a finger
to the lips, relax a bit. Troubles
with children. Lacking a generation,
or what would serve, a city, a country,

Lacking transportation, reversion
into the self, the world of problems.

And yet lacking nothing, dinner,
a bed to rest, one has years
to burn.

How is it death waits so long
his conditions so mild, his candidates
so many. Crackerjack, it was a long
day, work never ends,
a pessimistic, sentimental song.

TWO SHIPS THAT PASS

The agency's clerk
with important
paper work
in his hand

CALLED—

        "somebody
        18
        or older
        1 day
        the pay: $1.50
        the work: Scooping
        Powdered Sheep
        Shat

(fertilizer to the Trade

When it came to my turn
the clerk:

        "hated
          to give that job
          to a wino but
          I didn't know
          you wuz here

damn shaky wino
I said,
probably
needs the cash
bad

        ("take care
          for the needs
          of the wandering")

        "But,
        you know
        where it will go?

Ah si,
I know
I know

        "anyway, sorry
        I didn't see . . .
        where were you sitting?

Oh, against the door
over on the floor

Ha, our eyes
didn't meet
like two ships,
they passed.

A BOWL OF FLOWERES

(For John Fisola)

Day for pondering . . .
Am I a gatherer, in season?
Potatoes on the ground
at Allen-town . . .

Spring turnsround
bending over the furrow
the Sea gulls etched on the cobalt & brown
at Allen-town . . .
I turn around
and Johnny with the sacks
waiting for me to go, and smiling, O
day of crazy Sun,

                       But I

unwise self, while
it all, dwindle the hours
for a yellow water bowl
of floweres, on the shelf
before we go . . .

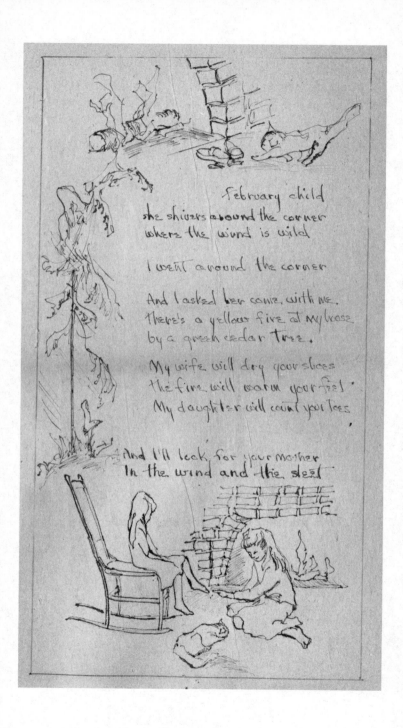

february child
she shivers around the corner
where the wind is wild

I went around the corner

And I asked her come with me
there's a yellow fire at my house
by a green cedar tree.

My wife will dry your shoes
the fire will warm your feet
My daughter will count your toes

And I'll look for your mother
In the wind and the sleet

68

FEBRUARY CHILD

she shivers around the corner
where the wind is wild

I went around the corner

And I asked her come with me.
There's a yellow fire at my house
by a green cedar tree.

My wife will dry your shoes
The fire will warm your feet
My daughter will count your toes

And I'll look for your mother
In the wind and the sleet

Come with them
To the hill in back
When the wind is roving
and the fir trees crack.

There they go
with their long coats on
Oh where have they gone.
Oh where have they gone.

Come back, come back
The fir Trees are bending
The hemlocks are cracking
The road is shaking

The hilly wind speaks
To the children up there
"When the cedar bough creaks
I'll twist up your hair."

Come with them
To the hill in back
When the wind is roving
And the fir trees crack

There they go
With their long coats on
Oh where have they gone
Oh where have they gone.

Come back, come back
The fir trees are bending
The hemlocks are cracking
The road is shaking

The hilly wind speaks
To the children up there
"When the cedar bough creaks
I'll twist up your hair."

A SMALL INQUISITION OF THE MIND
OR: THE COLDNESS OF THE POETIC ATTITUDE

Yes, the cat
is innocent
that the mouse suffers
there is not image of pain
in him

But is the mouse
ignorant that he is eaten
in ignorance   (were mice really
                                     made for cats?

Probably, the ignorance
is in me
probably, I am sorry
for myself   (the mouse?)
probably I only worry
and will die a played with thing
(the cat, to my human mind
is a treacherous creature

THE POINT IS LIGHT

The light
 actually,
as it is upon her eyes,
and its return,
from those lovely groves
her lashes.

She isn't a person we would love
carnally. Denial
is beside the point.

The point: That sitting across the table
from her light,
is an uncurtailed pleasure, as vision,
and free. Which is why the statement at all.
So little light comes back to me.

THE CALL

He came traveling in.
The entering
was fixtured, committed to fumbling
not the way we are when we are unaware.

He came carrying a gift, whiskey.
And entered as though he possessed
a vastness of time
and as though he came from a precise
direction, when it isn't true
we ever do.

He came,
and of course we talked.
I was drawn forth by the coming of a guest.
The talk revolved around the thing
it invariably does.

To suppositions of the kind that throw
blank figures, all the more representational,
upon a background of ideal conflict.
He chose one figure, and it happened
that I sometimes chose another.

The sun went down.
He said, "Well, I must be off."
And I said, "I'm very glad you came."

But before he cleared the door
I (like an empty snake) wanted something more.

IT IS

It is the dip
and the free cigarettes
It's the room
and the way his coat is buttoned.

The top two.

And all the people too.
The beforehand statements
about how it's force and control
is the thing.

—To be achieved.
Something to be achieved.
How hopeless, the transposition
and literal labor to be believed.

A few ballet positions
positing what? not
ballet surely? not
the human figure, surely?

One of *those* is standing before me.
She asks "what do you do?"
Paint, she asks,
or what?

She is from Houston
built like an outhouse
and the daughter of a dentist.
Have you been there (blue skies.

Everyone is milling slowly
looking at other people
out of the corners of their eyes.
Some of the paintings have words.

POEMS OF WASHINGTON, IDAHO, & MEXICO
(1959)

SPRING WOMAN

Come spring
in a light
              grey dress
beginning green, things
of distemper
                  the corner
of the eye holds your labor.

                  *

The high wind!
Birds
          falling like shot
past the window
gliding out on the wind
                  a fierce twist
heaving children to the tops
of trees, waving smiles of
miles of clear air.

                  *

Spring, is a woman not
          so young
her plum blossoms
blind me
Spring is a
              woman
not so young. The bark
the twig,
has brung

that sad bloom
and will blow
                    away.

                *

The shadow of the lilac
on the ground,
the lilac scent is on
her light hips
lilac branch
                and people
talking, Spring
is a fine large lady
walking along the river
a hint of summer
in her whisping hair
          a hint of lilac
in the sad bright air.

THE TRIP

From another man's world
to somewhere
treading terms, like paving stones,
it's a way to live —
like the dog, burying his bones.

From myself to somewhere
is another way.
There are no bones to be remembered
where they were buried.
And of course, very few terms.

They will not say —
"But he is living."
                              "And I am he."

So when the man in the chair
reclined and said, "How can you
bear it, what can you find to say
when everything has been said?"

I refused to go.

AN APRIL 1ST CUTTING

There are forms of inversion
to destroy a nation

albeit they lack drums
and like worms define

tunnelways abandoned
once their lengths are passed.

A badman
from a badworld only

would uproot
a lilac bush
from by thy window

to put instead
a pear tree

a mind of lead
would think the one wild

and the other
a utility

and say as I watch his axe
"We wanted something formal"

My Father
Has he seen your pear?

Is this ennui

Is this malcontent?

Is this tunnelway worth shoring up?

No, everyone will say.
Where then is my lilac

branch against the sky
outside my window

where then is the promised pear
for I love lilac no better than I love pear

what then will this man
next subtract

what even support
in thy absence?

Our lives begin
with such plantations,
(the growing of a place or death thereof
what then will be left

and what spurious thing
be gained

in thy absence

and what crime
can I help you avoid

when you use my eyesight impatiently, man
as you use   the axe?

SOMEWHERE

I still think
   that somewhere

I will encounter
   a room
in which

the Protecting
   and the Opposing

forces, will congregate
   with me:

(and no harm will come

Human Frailty
Stupidity & coldness
Egoistical insight,
(the giant

And,
      the Warm gazing pair
of eyes,
the sacred attachment,

Far away, indeed,
from detestable

Comical gatherings

a new room of mine
unvisited, and no thing invited

and quietly empty.

SOMETHING SMALL, AND IGNOMINIOUS

I thot as I plucked the stem of grass
is one such a crass hand and ignominious
to scatter seed, prior to the given time,
and I thot of the letters that have come, lately
and the searches I have made small as they are, for a house
larger than the house I now dwell in, for which I have no foundation

either in my head or hand.

A letter from friends who are building a foundation
to a house, and thus forever I guess desolated from me
become wage earners and inhabitants of the world proper.

The stem of grass I will not pluck again.
A moth I have killed lately has given me pain, its dust
on my finger tips, the dry wing under the nail makes death commonplace
. . . a misfortune of the spirit.

Something, small and ignominious, plagues the material world.
Our friends have or are getting increasingly jobs they build
things, how did they learn the world was built on a firm foundation?
Who, do you suppose told them, or did it soak in?

    "well, yes all this isn't the best of all possible
       worlds but I do not concern myself with what tv
       program to watch or which yummy yummy cake mix
       to use—or driving down to Ross Park for a picnic.
       There is a pleasant feeling of accomplishment
       about all this. I only hope that by summer's
       end we will be far enough to feel that we have
       succeeded . . . a house even made with four exceedingly
       inexperienced hands . . . can give one a feeling I've
       always wanted—that of creating our own house."

The material and the spiritual natures are at war forever.
The notion that both natures can exist in one body is fraudulent.
The spiritual world cannot win. And should not, in the sense
that mortal reason commands. The human saying—give your riches
to the poor and follow me, is the *only* radical postulate
ever put before the world upon which our foundations, and structures

are laid.

I have searched for a house and I am sorry. Forgive
me my hope, tho it is the only thing I have. I have
taken images from you my owners, my builders, my makers.
I sought water wherein were islands not unlovely to look
superficially upon, and your breezes, fair, for an instant
on my cheek.
And for an instant my farmer, my landowner I
coveted your pear, and the small salty estuary that caught my eye
going past the barn. For an instant, I must confess, I thot
I could be happy here, or at least avoid calamity, ha

                                                    Everyone
save me is a Sancho Panza and an Iago
I am laughed at in the very world I see through
with such penetration, bah! I am the only fool alive, because
to inquire about that shack on the water bless me if she didn't say—
"Well, yes, you know it is just a *unique* place, it's *very* unusual.

And when she said—don't get your hopes up—I knew I was lost.
For remember: All I have is Hope.

(This poem more or less came about because I pulled a green stem of
the grass and noticed the seed. An attempt at atonement. And an
advance in the purity of my soul because yesterday I fancied that
everyone was exactly created in the image of Bertrand Russell, in that

they all believe there is hope for the past (which is Satanism). You see, they think the world hasn't already ended, and when they hope that thermonuclear devices wont be used because of some political fix they are placing their hope in the past. I want it to be understood my Hope is strickly Christian, ie., for the future.

CONCERNING SHELTER

(for WHH, 1958

I live where I find a structure
demanding simply that it please me
and that your owner show his face
to have the rent paid him, I will

fix nothing.

The wind can do as it chooses.
The rain likewise, of exact space
I have loose desires . . .

merely that I walk
and walk back, and walk away
and from, and walk to . . .

Do not approach me salesmen.

Yesterday
a man came by selling gravelots.
It is quite unlikely he will ever

Above all,
understand that now you bore me
and fray my senses

                        never therefore
insinuate
by interesting gestures
and intentional halfknowledges,

if I should leave my shelter and make
a journey of curiosity.

BAVARIAN HORSES

The dusk colt
at his mother's flank
has his head up
and beyond them both a bank
of cool white flowers grow

Spring flowers
white, white as the lost snow
on the mountain top
and white as the mother's mane flowing
over her neck and over her eyes

In the Bavarian breeze
in the Bavarian skies.

ADDENDA TO APRIL 1ST CUTTING

And who?
is to put this bank teller down

this honest man
thru whose fingers pass the absolute green

these things of modern distress
the plantations of our lives

Walk thru that grove
we are all there, thank you!

And a man who
is ill at ease

How I value that

How I value that

And how too hate the naif
absolutely, that trick

and disparager

but when you sit there, man
having said you quit jobs

not being able to stand up,
a bell-hop formerly.

I will give you the lilac oh
worthless man, and shun

value the decoination
of all original things and know

you as a desperado, and willingly
give you peace, the death of anything
is the death to me why naiveté I will not salute

we all know don't we the death of anything

is the death to come

I give the lilac, which is mine
Oh worthless man

TEN COMMUNICATIONS
FROM THE WEST

THE 1ST

I have decided to stay in this town
for a while and the reason is clear:
the inevitable surprise the way the people
smirk about their riches (a veritable Sodom)
yet work on the sly
and the question comes to my mind
why?

I cannot answer your question
not having any answers, why come here?

Once in the west it is difficult
not to linger,
        on the way to other places.
You find you've stopped. And then an indifferent proneness
sets upon you.

And having the weary desire to go home
a formal and abstract yearning
sitting in a chair
turning around a corner where an abstract
vista never present before
opening a door
less than seconds long, never present before.

Oh, a veritable abstract Sodom
sitting on the plain of weariness,
but would you lie about your riches
carrying them as you do in your breast,
something that gently beating?
And would you work, hiding your form,
being that sly?

Proceeding along the premise:
what I have most not forgotten
the only baggage registering no weight
while carrying a beautiful inutility
are the elms and the elders. Don't laugh
in the summer they were very lovely, Winter too

under one great elm and an elder, where they came together
making a lofty arch
I was standing when my father said goodbye

goodbye to all possessions
except those instant long
less than seconds.

But of this place Santa Fe
with its gross detail and arrogant unyearning
I possess nothing at all
goodbye!

THE 2ND

Isn't it always the fate of a wanderer
to never know where he is?
When I got up this morning I looked at the sun.
And tried to grasp the larger sense
of where I am now.

The first mistake, "the larger sense." In small nouns
one will find it. My life, in its gloomiest aspect
used at times to swing but to get out from under
the larger sense is difficult. Many arriving people
populate this town. It is best to go to a town
people are leaving, not one people are going to.
Pompeii, not Albuquerque.

It was suggested this morning that money not be mentioned
in the house.

Yet a moving off is a deceptive relief.
When we abandoned Burlington our friends
took on the characteristics of buzzards, I mean
the way they circled, sat at the table, asked questions,
put our odds and ends in their boxes

and of course waited very silently, for us to go.
On the otherhand there were surly people waiting
very silently for us to *arrive* somewhere. Isn't it
uncanny how stabilized the element one moves in is?

In the larger sense, granted,
those who arrive are more dead than those who didn't
leave. What happened to they who lay sleeping
on a couch in Pompeii?

THE 3RD

Eating my lunch at noon today
looking out the window toward the horizon
a slender band of green growing
between the sky, and between the land.

It was only juniper I would guess
but it brought me I have to tell you
to a vision of osage hedge and the cool
shade below it, the grunting of Illinois pigs and the sight of those bands
of barely discernible trees beyond fences marking the earth
where red barns, gable rooves, shed rooves
placed varying the horizon. And such visions
are the relief of wandering, which are
the anchors in the mind of a specific relief
meaning nothing more than a door thru which light . . .

When I went back to work I poured out lead
into molds. The workmen are mostly pleasant.
Actually we are busy every minute. The master
laughs hollowly, as he talks, not before,
or after, the laughter is a nervous undertone
to his speech. And he is deferential
to the manager. A sadness of detail, in a day
consumed by such details. Now and then
the manager answers the phone which rings on time
like an abstract sentinel.

When five o'clock came, they paid me. Then
I washed the ink off my hands and put on my llama wool
sweater, which I fished out of a basket long ago
in Seattle (intended for the Goodwill.

Walking down the road home I ran into George.
You don't know him. He had left a book at the house
and picked up his Philippine machete. We talked
about how dangerous it was, such an instrument —
then he said he was building a lean-to
by their house so he could paint outside this summer.

Then, as I was standing on the road by George's car
it suddenly occurred to me I will have to work
half the month to pay our rent.

THE 4TH

When the sky is cloudy my love
I wish you were here, today
is such a day. This is so fabulously
an inland city, you would have to see it.

Hudson thought people are compelled toward the sea
now because they have lost something and think
to find a power in that great generalized and inhuman
mass. Well deep inland, where we are all cut off
in a different and aching vastness, and where we come
arbitrarily, it is not the same. Here we go
(I don't) to the indian, or a ruin, gazing on that
backness, but the sea
offers nothing to man which he doesn't bring
with his own symbol, clanging
over it, a human reservoir is more dangerous,
and the smirking pay one gets (not me)
is a deserved and pitiful irony.

There are no "lessons". But in a vulgar utility.
Here one asks the forgiveness of all sociologists
historians and criminals. There is nothing for it.
I'm sorry.

Such a business. I didn't tell you that
when I came home yesterday after talking to George
I talked to our landlady (avarice as concentrated
as a diamond pipe) who has recommended me
to the head of the folk-art museum. I was tired
and rather casual as a result, when she
mentioned that he wanted me to call him.

I said perhaps I should introduce myself with some
amount of pressure — Hello, Mr. ***** if you don't
give me a job I will murder all your "folk",
NO FOLK, NO ART. (theoretically that's true, if
unimportant)

         She was quite put out. Like insulting the sea.
It won't be tolerated. How did people get so big.
Any man?

THE 5TH (SAME DAY)

But of all indians
now that we are on the components
of this place, I take the ones on the street.

Cigar store indians, who invented them?
The indians of course. Certainly not whites.
When it was all up, and the land was *all*
reserved, what was the point? Reservation?
For whom? For all the strange people to come.

But the indian man, the thin red band
across his forehead, and the one in the loafer coat
a full bandana on his head hiding his wild grey hair,
the odd old ones, bright green,
                                        the fresh
is in them, not the young who have rediscovered dance
as we have (not I).

And you don't see these old ones at the dances
on Sunday, the incantations to cameras.
They are in the plaza waiting, for what?
This is their secret, they are the ones the town people
call dirty. In their J.C. Penney's,

. . . Far superior to the Indians you see hanging
from the belt of the governor or the doctor or the lawyer
or archaeologist or posing
in the picture handing a pot to the curator.

   By the way, in the plaza where the street indians sit
in their secret (which I am sure wouldn't interest us
(I mean me) there is a monument to the whites who died
at the bloodthirsty hands of the savages, who are
now sitting, there, in their secret.

Oh, and if you come up, come from Albuquerque
not on the wind, but walk along the river,
it's about sixty miles, and don't
talk to anyone. Anyway,
you will miss Santa Fe by a wild margin,
the river swings west just in time.

THE 6TH

I know a man, in the west too
in Idaho, oh, there are indians there
but you've never heard of them, they're Bannocks
and very poor, always were.
Well, riches are obvious things and then it depends
on what routes they were subsequently on.
but this man, not the man I shall tell
you about later but another; a man named Sven,
who came from Sweden to study
the language
and they asked him repeatedly —
why he stayed so long (ten years).

Two months ago, in February, would you believe it
that far north the weather was so mild we could
walk about the hills, slight snow on the ground
and be very comfortable but maybe it was the fire
in our hearts because we were tramping for a house
site, one I knew I would never use, but the weather
I tell you was so perfect and the warmth of my friend
was like the weather, all in February. Very far below
was Pocatello, a miserable accidental town even the
Union Pacific abandoned in the forties. But the hills
and the moon at night on the snow all around that bowl
and at night too Pocatello wasn't Pocatello but a jewel
the red and the blue, something you could never narrow down
to gas in glass tubes. That afternoon with our backs resting
against the vertical rocks there were . . . well I had to follow
him there, to know land and love it, is a great thing few
people are lost as I am. And I love this man because he loves Idaho.
He wanted me to build a house somewhere near and I wanted to
but he you see, lives in a closed world but is very damn kind,
he is very great I like him more than it is easy to say
and it wasn't easy to disappoint him, but I think he knew,

he went on anyway describing the possibilities, that's love,
in the mists of indifference. But I just can't build houses.
At all. Although I dig the juniper and think the hills swing,
you know how very much my world is not closed but open, open.
Everywhere I am, I feel I am everywhere else. But that man in the sun
last February, with the western hat, and whom I shall not see for many
years to come, the Idaho and the snow there and the huge
purple bitter juniper berries.

THE 7TH

There was a time sitting in a room
I wanted to see everyone I ever knew
and of course I don't remember the bad ones
except a few. What a shock
to get over the embarrassment of using language.

That's why I write to you every day
I no longer have that tedious care.

THE 8TH

This is the portrait of a local woman
I don't like. If you are ever lost
in the ravines and canyons of the goose
flesh of her arm it will be because you touched
her and she has a cold meaningless heart. The climate
is chilly all over her body. At large

in the dense thickets of the hair
on her upper lip, you will find no surcease
from the bitter wind whipping out of the corners
of her mouth. If you seek refuge from these
terrible winds by hurrying into the escalator
(her tongue) imagining a cave a safe place in a storm
pity *you*, for the stalagmites and stalactites her
twin rows of teeth are are never I say in truth
never stationary they go constantly and the meter
is unvarying malevolence. And although decay
is everywhere as you look about the cavern do not
take hope that a breakdown beneficial to you in your
misery is imminent because she is an organism
that thrives on decay and grows stronger every minute.
Each of her social acts is cannibalism.

Perhaps by now you see this.
Even as the pot is near boiling
she will set you up in the light of Hope
and Honor, prestige is one of her most widely
held tokens, and she will shower them on you
as if there were no limit to their existence,
(There is no weakness she won't see in you
having eyes in the roof of her mouth).
Having given you Hope, the gold of her presence,
she will ignore you for a spell
while you are washed here and there on the promiscuous
seas of saliva of her mouth your seeming sanctuary.

Ha then she won't know the meaning of your screams.
She won't know you are there still. She will tell you
a story most likely of how incredible the storms were
she weathered and just how she did it. Then, finishing
she will demand the rent, and no doubt
out of arrogance you will pay it. (You are weakening now
considering yourself lucky it wasn't money you'd spent).

And although we all laugh about starving, you won't
because you will, there is no end to months, and the money
you can't find, she had hidden from you, as though
you never had it lad, minutes even, are important to her.

THE 9TH

And suddenly a sensational speed
we were going down a wide avenue toward the earthline
she was telling me
Lee wanted everyone to be happy, we should all go out
on sunday and practice running, and jumping,
playing ball, we would have cabbage leaves on our ears

as we went along she told me; and I could see for miles
under the pines, the sun, and the endless green green
sward. Oh, it was a strange happy thing, and I believed
her, both of us were crying, and going, down this wide avenue.

I wonder if we are running from something?
or is she trying to cheer me up?

THE 10TH

In the peace of the valley
there are many mean things
not seen, but madly imagined
from the prominences
I love to wander on. Much unseen
in the land of green days.

And on the plateau.
Having thought it often
I have lacked the boldness
to tell you to beware
crossing these mountains
and these plains
merely to gain one side or the other.
It is too late.

I am no dreamer.
That luxuria I have envied
if I have envied anything,
in others. There is too much
oatmeal in my soul.
I cringe at the thought of temperature
being brought forward as a commodity
and yet, can't help it.

Just now, I came from the sea.
Onto the upland plain of Utah,
its northern fringe and then
down across the medium plateau
of Wyoming, to arrive at this place.

While crossing thru the dark juniper groves
of one of Earth's removing places
I thought it nice to be away
from the exhilarating highway
and that traffic I have a propensity for
being no dreamer, alas.
But I thought of little else.

In the silent jogging coach
we came to Kemerer.
The snow stood withdrawn
around the miles-away wood buildings.
And I thought of little else.

Of expanse, and its yearning
I didn't think. Just glad to be gone
from the land of green days.

Then this morning I sat
by the table in the sun and
thought remotely.
Do you know, at least I wonder
if there were men in your old town
like the ones I used to walk with,
on the streets, with mustard in their lungs?

Alas, and then I wonder why I go on.
And wonder if I am right, you know
there are many routes to travel.
If you find that yours
has no way home,
I will come after you.

I ask you, is the mind (I speak of myself)
a cracked urn? Why should I keep
a thing like this in it: I was in a store once,
"THE PEOPLE'S STORE", and my son
found something on a shelf.

Farewell. It is ending. I have written
you some things about a journey,
pretending to be boisterous at times.
Now you must let me off. What I see
of hardship and of sin will be kept for you.

In a broken urn.
Where it can come and go
in the heat,
                on any hot day I care to watch.

LATE IN THE REVOLUTION ·
(1960–1962)

AND WHERE, GENTLEMEN, IS
THE APOCALYPSE
(for Allan Fletcher)

in Ike's baggy pants
in Krushchev's big mole
in Jackie's skinny hips?

       Ah brother

in Castro's big black windy beard?
or inside a Guatemala banana
Is it going to explode in all
Its prediction from those dynamite hip hips
of La
mumba mumba?

And when it didnt come out
of any of those places, Lord Buckley
was hired to do the Katanga
all night down in those mines, and the Lord
said move it man, only he meant ore,
because that's where there's no race
problem, it's all dominoes, black
and white, they're gonna grow
you like grass
as long as you bust your ass

THE EYES TURN

To people who have been put
into new clothes, they stand
like the end of a trick,

              all hands below
the cuff, and uncertain
as to the step they next must take.
For step they must.

In pictures new clothes
are in places you've never been
and never show until later
how you are a member of the frontal attack.
Old clothes are in places
where rice is short ration,
or in tropical palm leaf rains are stuck
and if they are costly they never look new
but appear as though they were made worn
but not worn. Sometimes, poor luck
they arrest the man who wears them.

   There is something lurking
in the background, a machine
whose turning is too well known
whose hours too fixed,
       to the heartbreak of poor people.

THE ISOLATED SEED

Grows in hostile ground, unembellished
uninvited by the earth
alienated without sound
persistent, sometimes green
sometimes yellow from forgotteeness.

Oh friend, how long can it wait to grow,
how long to come with inclination
toward the well known acceptances,
what is the name of this weed,
which might be any man.

                How does it persist
without the comforts of
other men's celebrating
other men's recognizing name?

Yes love made glowing
that seed I admire so much, growing
in its own sad wilderness,
ah why Christ
              do you isolate yourself.

LOOKING INTO DARK CORNERS
FROM THE EARTH

She has her hair set
has her mind set,
and from the dark corners of her mind
gazes out the window, yes a friend lives
in her thoughts.

        Immortality she argues
is a substance of memory, a presence
that gives life to the non-existent.
As it has always been
with all men a strong jawed dogma
of afterness and why not, the will
amounts to little more.
The slow approach of death in the distance
bothers her, the friend has gone
but she doesnt mean to go too
into that dark room.

        Gazing while the earth spins
into dark corners she sees
black objects, there is a vague hope
she will be at least one of those
or perhaps a cowering dog, or a treacherous cat
or even so, a fragment of some kind
on the window sill however exiled
but that God will grant her
some ease from the faintly sensed
utter end,
        when taken away are the sun,
the moon, the mountains, the plains
and other small paraphernalia
she had become used to.

FIRST, LAST, AND ONLY HAIKU

FUCK YOU

                        submitted to Floating B.
                        by Lin Yu Tang.

A POEM FOR CREELEY REPLICAS

If you performed
a satire
of me
what kind
of satire
wd it be?

A mime, slapstick
without a heart
Rimed coyplets
or verses
& call it art

SOME, MAN, ON THE STREET

Have a Habit? (No Art?)
Walkin *up* when there is
no up? (the inclined level)
That cradle of What? effort
not civilization, puke, it must be
his back is bent and the hat
how are hats? Romantic
they always conjure always
better places we have been
that hat

walkin with an effort up
the down street a grinning adam
smith in his hip pocket where
he thought his pay was, Modern Times:
Shit.

The habit of blue or brown shirts
goddamn his dressing man had a big
arm. You name it give him
what habit you want, but not
more, leave
him there, yess, la la
with it

And tell him what a clod he is
or how simple (beautiful or otherwise)
how he belabors you and lets the wrong
people rule him.

Have you, has yours, his song
has ended, That's true, Si
Wow, oh yes, Why not, what a clod
yah.

Catch him quickly, before he hits
the hay, whisper in his ear more exhaustion
as he sleeps, about some dream you had of him
and his lot, how he looked back
and was made the salt of the earth (disinherited?)
about his sex, fantasies which through you
reached a great perversion, a great starkness

But man, not inflation, Newsweek does that dance
drugs? that's goodly, but he can't get 'em, you
oughta be in Morocco for that OK
tell him about Morocco, be his
bullshitter National Geographic
with a couple of fucks and cunts
thrown in just to keep it going
and esoteric to him (not erotic

Or that bit about Bureaucracy how
you and H. Hoover and Rickover
and Bar Goldwater and whoever agree
it's gotta go (leave out how you'd all
be dead without it)

Naw, you'd be bored as usual and this man
is just tired, first of all you and them
and three centuries of penny mayhem, of his
burden which was called white, the color
being the mistake he was stuck with . . .

So come back in the night to cornhole him
tell him he wanted it when he yawns
make it right with a corkscrew motion
I mean leave no room for an incognizance
on his part tell him when he farts it is
because hypothalmouse kicked him
beans have nothing to do with it, (Si)

and from what's the source he derives
his incomparable stink, which you feed upon
like a vulture a like deadman's body
who may have breathed I dare say for
a grace of only such food-love's lost
of what it is, was once for that man
and you too

will come one day to such an end (that meaning
is intended) as a man's whose foot was truly
upon the earth the ankle grabbed by Ernest Jones
and will have made it simply that way, unyielding
as an opinion.

Throw in a fuck, and a cunt or two,
and that old tale about the best fuck is
a chicken with its neck snapped, the one
he heard when he was 9 years old but
what he didn't hear leave out what you might
have told him
years ago
but you were in Morocco
living off one of the very fortunes that put him down.

FOR NEVADA

    proclaims pairadice
to california
        and it says
you cannot come here
and nevada says you got
radioaction
        don't drop
those turds across this border
we says what's in that
payroll is sumpin else

and we says we got that space
an a pair of dice but don't
come hea no more after they
drop that biggest crap
what I mean is when dey close
that missile gap

DOGS OF THE FALLING SUN

Lights the children sliding off the hill
on cardboard sleds
wreathed of green pine fronds
ponderosa
and unloosens the bones of light
around their necks
ah the dogs
have collars of diamond inset, they shine
the way in
the blue under

ah the lean dogs with collars of bone colors
of ponderosa the large yellow vein
the lights of the sun
following the sounds of the stout bark
running from the dog pack's throat
into the valley beyond
they are gone.

COMPARISON

She is a loudmouth and gross.
Mostly it's her arm like Mexico
with Yucatan a clenched fist.

She spills coffee over her skirt, and crumbs
of cookies, her new teeth cut
the sides of her tongue but she
talks all the louder.

Her auditors despise her. She uses
words like a butcher a meataxe
not giving a damn, a miser with care.
She is sanguine she gives a bad impression.

Her grossness appeals, an accomplished bore.
One wishes she
said less, used Yucatan more.

LATE IN THE REVOLUTION

> "every heart yearns for a bullet"

1

who can tell
a sinister continuation
of only imagined sounds
when one leans forward
expecting to hear wisdom
from the lips of men who
elect themselves to speak —

the proposed love lost
the plan of escape too much
in the future, figures of a year
were misgiven

on second thought how cold

i remember it was
in the March expectations

how hot in the late spring, where is
my homeland, I said a thousand times
while walking in the street,
where our certainty, when?

2

the sway of booming drums, a fragment army
we see again,
if we cross the land again again
for one hard empty noun, a barn
of echoes so flat

the crow as a flock lifts
as a dark hill

or dynamited up from the hedge
another kind of boom

but beyond the poem
                                        there is no earth —
the reunion of sense
beyond and backward from the con-man
in the eyes

The clotheslines run between two egyptian crosses
nearly fallen
a dependent allusion
hung in the air near the horizon.

SAY SOMEDAY

I walk into a tavern like this guy does
and say give me a straight shot of ancient age
on a little ice and give my shoulder to everybody
while I drink it. Then say give me a bag of those cashews,
hang it on the end of my cigar.
I want to be exactly 50 and have that look in my eye.

And I want a suede jacket and stetson like he did.
and just like him I want to leave for some meeting
fortified just like that, I want to walk just like that

out of there to nowhere.

EVERY HOUSE NEEDS A CAT AND A POET OR: THE WAY THE POPULATION IS KEPT DOWN

Look at your watch.
You go there, you go here
and do that. Very close by.

I'll sit on my ass till
you get back.

You open this door
and punch that card
and when you get through tell him.

Get me Honolulu, Lulu.
Like, Hello!

MODERN POEM

I left for the great outside
My mission was to piss
a final dying fly
buzzed with his november
wings
orbiting my ears. He shit
in the air about my bliss.

A GENERAL ANSWER

I was handed
Something green

they asked me
is this grass?

My answer
had to be NO,

Snotgrass!

A cat named allen Dugan
ate a copy of Yugen

to unstop his ass
they tore it w/ glass
and now, it's shaped Kugen

SILENT GUNS
(1961–1963)

AN ATTEMPT AT SELF-SORROW

No winter has been this desperate—
More than foolish preaching required
or more than lazy thought
could have made in the silent cowardices
of which any man has more than enough
have made their trenches in that
smallest terrain I call the battlefield
of my emotions. When I told myself
I was a man, I was a beetle
            and hid in any handy crevice.

First, and not important
the great snow fell—
and the first plan of our movement,
laid in September, seemed wrong
after much work was done to bring it to execution.
Secondly, and as an augury of failure,
there were the gatherings
and freak flights of the magpies their hideous noise
before dawn, when the eyes had barely yielded
                        sleep, their domain.

Uncountable were the mornings
the magpies arrived. The sharp
northwest gales continue
The cat lies under the eave
            waiting, watching the sparrows.

Wherever, in the mountains or in the valley
I don't know, but our pleasure is out
hunting, hunting its own cure.
Christmas is nearly here. I wait
like an idiot, for the great horned owl
to return, to restore my senses
with his piercing eyes to look at me
but he comes down from the mountains to the dead tree
only on the coldest night

                    and not to see me.

THE VAGUE LOVE

When I got there he had a book
On Human Communication
and said Po*a*tery and introduced
me: this is the Po*a*te, Edward Dorn.

Though I had heard it was
I am not certain it was
part of a Harvard accent.

A delightful man I'd say.
Fey. But with pretentious insouciance
in his walk, he listed

and being as he was, large,
his white silk scarf flowed
over his camel's hair coat

in the prettiest manner.

He spoke of aphasia at lunch.
I ordered meat. One of our party
ordered 2 tureens of Vichyssoise.
Two. He had been a quiz kid,
if you'll remember them.

Later, at a party

he sat on the floor
on a pillow
and put everyone down
the white scarf had been laid aside.

Yes, it was very nice.
4 martinis at lunch
four.

And oh yes our host at the party
was a southern educated fag
with money, taste and as they say
not a little learning.
He had corrected me on the pronunciation
I remember of Schliemann's name
for which I was grateful.
His great line came
midway at the party
when he said of someone that he
was a male Amelia Earhart.
Everyone laughed.

By now I am embarrassed —
such language I've never used
and I had no point to start with.
One tries to make of prose
a little better thing and there are
no exemptions. Everyone is sometimes
on the board of trade, the end of
an occasion is always heavy.

BOB CONSIDINE

But I really hate band concerts
in the park and
        Bob Considine
3000 Sundays ago
when half the world
was mopping up the fire storms

I hate them.
who can among men retain
    their honor

praising such things
men. men are always put in chains
the world is just shit.
All of it.

FOR SOBLEN

International spies are rare men
when they have swallowable poison sewn in their linen.

DONALD IS INSANE THEY SAY

after James Whitcomb Riley

Now we know many Donalds
and they aren't all insane.

Some are in the army
and some are on the train.

Some can play it straight
and some they can't contain.

This Donald is insane.

But not really
He's forty.

And thinks to go to
Salt Lake City.

Is that why he's insane?
Not really.

He was told to take the train
but he thinks he might remain,

in Pocatello.
His father has some money

So send the bill to him
but Donald scratches his head

a cut of very close trim.
He mentions Dr. Barker

who told him to come
but that was mid september

and he's sitting on his bum
here in this place.

I don't know why he doesn't go
when they wrote him saying so.

IDAHO AGAIN

How impeccable always

were his tight jeans
and how perfect his hair
he was always there

silhouetted against
the typical western mountains
talking in the dust and wind and
the sage pollen, his nose
up like a coyote.

His wife had left him.
And he had beat her up
but he was not a cruel man
just one eye on the implied end of the world.
Nor was she a cruel woman,
when I met her she was very quiet and unassuming.
It was said by both
of them that
they couldn't stay out of bed
with other people.

SAT NIGHT OCT. 1962

You have been in the grip of another god.
You have been there for the final time.
Your front teeth have grown numb.
They want to be pulled.
There is no hope lasting beyond
that; a civil war is going on
within the context of your own
enclosure.
The gums grow intolerably tight
as you oh sinner
contemplate the outlands.
What are we to do?
One man said the new poet
would say, would be hortatory,
would be prescriptive,
the tongue grows enlarged with Blood
against an enmeshed time—
night has come
the cannibalisms
                    of america
approach thru all the
tiniest cracks of ahee dubee
do do ee
give me your hand
wind
I want to shake idaho
for all my friends and let
the trees fall out
but I don't
want really to kick
the hunters' asses
but is there courage
is there
courage in such a refusal.

when do we meet in a grove
of shaking aspens
oh I am lonesome
as you are
just as you do I tire
of the coy tricks of cognizance.
I tire.
I had just taken an inch
of cocaine
saw how they said
E.E. Cummings was such
a good
little
clear
individualist.
a man of few ideas?
a man of few ideas:
oh lawrence where are you?
now the world does
not *only* pigeonhole ideas!
Weep with me now please,
America,
            for what they
do leave us of
our great men.

DEATH WAS A DREAM

Conscience is what we miss if we die.
The possible awake, & dying is fearful
by a vacuum of that not by a lack of breath.
And not to breathe is that horror shut off.
I have in my dreams month after month
combined something to make me stay alive
when death grabbed in long stabbing strides
across wide plains, and in my birth foretelling
of my death, across long plains without end.
How do you think you will die? Do you think
there may have been a harpy at your birth
and that it is waiting to get you
with its long final bayonet, a moment
of utter unpredictability as you say goodnight
to a love you thought there in the middle of busy
predictable cities, and what of the children
who were born one day as you were doing something else?
And what of your mother who seems more of the same
each time you see her
as the years pass more lengthened every time,
these are the questions they ask you when they sell you
insurance.
But really, what of it?
To die nobly, is that what you fight it with?
like men in their studies, figuring the way?
Death. Though it comes as a staggered effect yet
and we do not die in common: we do all die
and does that therefore mean you can claim it
as private? No, you cannot.
Unless you are very organized. Mail a letter
to the head of the state
and he'll tell you to go fuck yourself!

SOME AID TO THE NEEDY

If you're wishing
    you had not quit high school
Stop it! baby.

There are no free lessons inside
and you shall be rescued
by no one
nor will your doom
when it comes
tend to be larger.

WHEN I MET RED

    and shook his hand
        the first time . . .

a late afternoon in the poolroom
when the shadows were drawn
just as I like them
the only intrigue where I was born
is the full mood of late day
the sun,
was immensely red,
and finally
        sat.

Good Lord, I have
in the land of those hours waited
for the girl I had not thought
at that time

a passing fancy,
but who became like a relative, like Red
in another stark place, across
those fields
as I walked to town
along roads, a mile one way, turn
and so a mile the other.
If you prefer to take it going east
it probably starts in North Dakota.

You're right—he was not black
but he was like he was red. And I don't
know . . . the fact of that origin
if not that in the hybridization,
the clots become unmixable, as they
do not in the light brown.

Red. His name.
He came on with a hat.
But I was lead to believe, the way
his brown double-breasted suit flapped
around his legs as he came smiling at me
and as I looked at him over the pool table
he smiled, that he was a changed man.
He was unusually clean, he had just
come from the dirty Blackfoot slam.

That dull afternoon when the bartender slapped
his face
he became quite sober
and said don't
Don't ever, do that
to me
again.
        And the larger man
was not meeting his gaze, dunking glasses

he was,
and talking along with the other customers
and pretending to be very calm, pretending
he had done what was his right.

But Red was speaking very quietly
for he was after the meaning of language
in that instance he meant what he said
and that probably doesn't happen each day
in all places. Not language's persuasions
at all. He said don't jim, don't ever again.

Later we were elsewhere
and talking and I handed him something
and he said Ed I didn't dig you
that way.

There was a time then
I saw him not at all
until one afternoon he
flapped in and tilted his hat
He was washed and utterly clean and shining,
and looked younger.

He has disappeared. I asked
a lot of people about him
they said aw man I don't know . . .
He was a bad cat . . .
I mean he came out of the Utah state prison
and you know . . . he just cut through
he might have climbed a freight
to portland, or denver . . .
but you can't trust a cat like that . . .

SO LONG CUBA
LETTER TO FIDEL CASTRO OCT 29, 1962 OR:
JUST ONE MORE INEFFECTUALITY FROM A POET?

The disengaged are perennial
and left holding the bag.
My impression was you'd be around
thus giving occasion to a lot
of wind
about the failure of men
and more interestingly say
~~than a fathead like kennedy.~~
But it seems over.

The 10:00 pm news says you're thru.
For all I know
you never existed, for all I knew
you were just another booger
from the running nose of AP.
A man who might have been there
and now is said to have gone.

Mrs. kennedy missed her modern art group.
Morgan beatty's father passed away yesterday
and we're supposed to take that
as having something to do with Cuba.
It might. We're supposed to believe
all these people exist.

So what about all this communication
how about being so casual
about the death of 4000 people
or the resurgence of the asian horde,
and is the news a weapon?
and think of the gall of their saying so.

How does one man die, what does he say
in the grip of that, is there
total indifference to such an event
and do only the famous really die,
do the rest pass merely onto the heap?
Aren't there really
any citizens of the world anymore, even say
one tom paine to take india
and stuff east pakistan up burma.

What do you think?
Dominion never comes
to the people
or to those who would
help their people. When you
copped all that sugar and oil
from all those little ~~kennedies~~
~~and~~ goldwaters
rocking away on their porches
you made yourself extraordinary
and unlike the A & P booster
you can be invaded.

So you're abandoned
by all those big greasy nations
you were a ploy of, and in the middle
they switched it suddenly to the sino-
indian border and really big stuff. Really
big freedoms are suddenly at stake.
What happened to all that talk about one world?
Of course, one world is *not*
very interesting, but not because
it would keep those pricks busy
with a little straight administration.

Farewell!
I hope they don't catch you. I hope
you got something sewed into your clothes like Soblen
I hope you got a boat or a different colored
beard, but I hope you got something,
a luger at least. I hope you can
still aim when they wade ashore
using homer capehart, the beef candidate
for a flag.

And farewell . . . to the problems of your starving people
they are just news now on the hour . . .
until they give back that sugar
and then we shall hear no more of them
because these things will be running smoothly,
the hoods will be back in havana, batista
will have again his dripping fangs in the asses
of your girls, pardon me . . .
they will be called your liberated girls
and Krupp, who wasn't exactly pissed off
at three world conflagrations,
will be making the indian scene.

And in spite of the fact I can't help
Farewell to the problems of your starving people
we shall have no more of them—
33½ percent will be employed and fed
ie, free, and the rest
will necessarily go into that pool
of the semistarving a healthy democracy has to have
to keep itself straight, forever progressing,
forever advancing, getting freer . . .

farewell to your people.

CHANSONETTE FOREVER

If your favorite things were cats
and dogs
then You'd be happy
but that's not true,
for you.
So there is nothing you can do
but *want* a horse.

And if you ever get one
I hope I get it for you
but darling
they are vast beasts
three legs
relaxing the other,
with expensive ease,
who stand around much of the time in barns.
And I've yet to provide us
a house
after all these years

FOR JIMMIE WORKMAN, THE BANDIT, CAUGHT IN PHOENIX

His brow is arch, Hollywoodian. Skillful. Mean.
There are hardly any handsome bandits
anymore. One forgets
they are not all
as post office walls.
About the handsome face of a bandit
there is something pure
            who take useless backwater
            out of circulation dollars
from the bank of america.

They say he had gone to Phoenix
a snowbird to winter
but well armed and supplied with cash.
It's not the point to praise him
but I was sorry those fbi thugs
nabbed him. My first wish
was that he sometime may be sprung
to take other dollars from satisfied
useless americans.

Jimmie Workman the professional.
A worker in a trade unpopular.
A master craftsman
who happened to be on the wrong boulevard
at the right time.
(if america were a quick country she wouldn't
need bandits
to steal her money.)

So they'll incarcerate his ass
for a lifetime. Are you sorry
or glad? Rather, do you have
200,000 dollars in the bank of america
or are you not obliged by such fatness
to care?
            (if the classics had a wide circulation,
               does it trouble your sleep?)

A CAMPAIGN OF JANUARY 17
IT IS TOO LATE FOR THEM
TO SEND THEIR ARMIES

We have escaped.
We are compelled by a larger notion.
We run, waving our arms, across the open plains

No, that's not true.
All we have done is hide our little secret
In a hole.
  That's all,
There has been no victory,
Not even the slightest.
Any test we took
Was a failure by their say so.
  And that's all. What if we do
sit here?
Won't they come later at their own bidding
and convenience?
What, in the meantime, if we do rail?
Will that matter?

A WALK OF SPRING

No redemption
without sin
the sinless man cannot
  be saved
and lust without love
  perhaps

love though knows lust
in her bed
            or in
her small head so
the maiden's thoughts are always private
and all
the men in the world
are in her stable

They come out one at a time
   at night
   or by day
seeking the trails of the world
the colorful countries of their desire
receive them or in the latitude
of their torture, do not

Melville's Clootz
in a womanless novel
parades the charged speech of his congress
of the passion of the word
   it can occur thus
in any assembly

Or Rima, in a lost forest
from a lost race can
or in the starker terrestrials
of the north the woman descends
hopelessly and impassively
   into the claysmelling tarn

Antique are the passions.
An april woman
              is beside us
again.

AFTER LOVE
for R.C.

Who,
accusing me of
that sensuality
could trust his wits

yet,
I love many men.
Perhaps they are my guiding light
and its possible

they lead me,
outward to the places
I want to be.

ON NO

for Tom Raworth

No to easiness
and stance
and the decorum of imagined
gratitude

and those who would breed
the lonesome exploitation

nothing is Not enough
there must always be more
for the man who waits

against all obligation
that yields not the fairness of
much distribution

oh against all abstract love
and against and against

and make our graves tomorrow
with those
    who
    deal outrage
to the slick slick world.

AN OLD SQUARE POEM

Everyone knows the cold wind as it comes across the barricades
of the earth or perhaps you do not and in that case it might be
you ~~xxxxxxxxxxx~~ have been removed artificially, made safe
from dangers by fortune, insulated by a lucky stroke from sites
from ramparts the earth reserves for those in dire trouble, say
the man overboard in the cold sea, the woman alone having a baby
the utterly romantic man who has broken his leg while alone, and
unattended, or foolishly alone at the reaches of one of the two
poles, and mind you not one of those expeditionary persons, who
are looked after by vitue of the vast machinery invested in an
enterprisellike that, the search for the hard metal of man's ad
him arbitrary yet calculated progress upon the face of an earth
who could hardly care at all. He, the earth wants to know right
now: are you there? Are you, and do you think about it. This is
no idle question, he wants to know, from each of you, will each
of you greet the one who comes forever toward you with concealed
weapons? And will you be bright in a dim, uncontollably paltry
time to live. Or will you be one who one night comes out under
the mountains ready to greet the stark umber of hate giving nada
but the full smile of total forgiveness? So what of the strange
what of the poured concrete, what of the silly, vast impatience
of life now, will you go, when the beckon, or simply call, yes
as a volunteer they will take you anyway if you should hesitate
a single minute when they are reviewing the pressures on planet
after planet of populations grown too full, or will you say try
me, and goodbye my lovelies, goodby forever, I will see, as you
know, what happens in the non-existent forever is so long for now
goodbye my lovelies, adieu, vaya con dias, my little friends may
you have a happy little journey and may you remember everything.

AN OLD SQUARE POEM

Everyone knows the cold wind as it comes across the barricades
of the earth or perhaps you do not ███████████ it might be
you are lifeless, ██ have been removed ████████, made safe
from dangers by fortune, insulated by a lucky stroke from sites
from ramparts the earth reserves for those in dire trouble, say
the man overboard in the cold sea, the woman alone having a baby
the utterly romantic man who has broken his leg while alone, and
unattended, or foolishly █████ at the reaches of one of the two
poles, and ████████ not one of those expeditionary persons, who
are looked after by the virtue ████████████████ invested in an
enterprise like that, the search for ██ hard metal ██████████
████████████████████████████ upon the face of an earth
who could █████ care at all? She, the earth wants to know right
now: are you there? Are you, and do you think about it. This is
no idle question █████████████████████████████, will
you greet the one who comes forever toward you with concealed
weapons? And will you be bright in this dim, uncontrollably paltry
time to live. Or will you be one who one night comes out under
the mountains ready to greet the stark umber of hate giving nada
but the full smile of total forgiveness? So what of the strange
what of the poured concrete, what of the silly, vast impatience
of life █████, will you go, when ████ beckoned ████████████
as a volunteer ████████ taken ████████ if you should hesitate
a single minute when they are reviewing the pressures on planet
after planet of populations grown too full, or will you say try
me, and goodbye my lovelies, ████████ forever, I will see, as you
know, what happens in the non-existent forever is so long for now
goodbye my lovelies, █████ vaya con dias, my little friends may
you have a happy █████ journey and may you remember everything.

THE TERRITORIES

Two children are playing
    april
        they slide
down a gradual slope on the snow;
one cannot make a chinese poem
in the wild west
                ghosts of
      shakespeare troupers linger
      on the corners
      in the little towns and dust
      journeys up the canyons
      away from the sun,
      late this year, late
every year.

           the
                juniper
is jade
      and the coat of the boy is
a western red
            the hair of the other
a most northerly white, and the hills
block what
    is a passage
           of great yearning
nothing
      self contained
and ultimate; no thing or planting
refined with nostalgia.

Where frontiers held men of passion
away from home
they now yield
and there are many passengers
who would leave all
be gone, bye bye, with a glance.

[AND STILL FINDING]

                        and still finding
in the hills I went out on one long shadowed afternoon
not the place I sought but the rising problems
of those hills.

Much has come to my attention there
came nothing more than the depression
one finds finding oneself in hills always
put down, shortened by the height
of surrounding masses. one spring morning
in 1513 Ponce de Leon saw the gulf

and if it isn't hills it's rain. How many
times have I spoken of that?
people shift, not for themselves, no not for themselves.
and the mare's heat? What was that.
a service—no, long winters mean much
to me, and the slowness of winter's serious torture.
Never back to the prairie—these hills
roll like drums to my senses
and the spine of my land signs
                        an accent and a mark.

So this morning I come to Ross Park
and nothing to do
                    walking near
the edge of the high lava flow
could I grasp the frail branches
of the tops of the trees in time, and if
they did not hold me
my skull wld make
a thick red seal on the green grass below,
merry christmas to my brains in May.
oh happy spring,
                    to my designs

of those? there are 5 or 6 distinct
women I should go to bed with
for my peace of mind. as many
more for my health. what next?
another year in this drab place
where the white tips of mtns
lie 20 miles to the South 20
to the north and I'll have no balls left.
Society, in the form
of a picket toothed girl said,
"You write poems, don't you, Mr. Dorn."

BUT THEN AGAIN

The cat is correct.
She stops; and looks up
from the finitude of smells
a long slow staccato motion
as she bends over her food—
or is she listening?

Thus civilization.
Everytime I am intrigued
by a leader and
everytime I think
here is one makes sense
And lifting my head
smell them: not, mind you
the lesser ones—
~~Kennedy,~~ Khrushchev, de Gaulle, Adenauer, Johnson
Ah no!

but the best
like Mao.
there comes to mind but one china
with a large peasantry.

And what of the rest?
What of the man who is
uncontrollably insincere.
Is he to die because
he has been given nought
to strive for?
Destroy him, certainly.

But what of the plans
and the indoctrination
I'm asking and don't misunderstand
it can all be done in good faith
if there is a just and egalitarian end,
truly in mind.

But what of? the man
who remains unteachably contra?
that old human factor of the difference
in tolerance
of evolutions, what is the evolution
of standard populations

and what of leaders?
do they imagine the coy propaganda of their difference
to be really true?

Is there a leading
and a led? to any useful purpose whatever?

There is a prudent eye on opportunity
is *that* the difference,
is that what we are captivated by
in leadership, opportunism
by all agreement puritanical and momentary and purchased.

Say to Mao
the man who can kill
can meet all then
see all, give all
be equitable, at one stroke
and disrespectful be
to any pre-arranged interest,
to all calculated interest.
The middle peasant
cannot be allowed to keep his wealth in his wretched pocket
less the rich peasant.
You are at the outset already dated—
compromise of agrarian futility
is a backtrack to the 19th century
we all spin grimly back to the 19th century.
and the mill
of soft oozing creeping hard-shelled freedom
the freedom to creep.

A CIRCLE OF SONGS
(1964)

The late sternness
of october floods my room
with the contrast of last hard winter.
The flaws of all my being were exposed.

Dark clouds of my own
incapable nature, of my own
will to unremittable love, reform
make a ring of consonants to enclose me.

How clever the days were she ran
around
              her sparkling hair.
                              A glance
of tangibility
              weird components of
a torture I'll once again, a cheerful fool, begin.

Talk always in circles
under that power of attraction.
Our legs touch, what
that world outside a window does,
and avoid a careful regularity
the compulsion of a magnet
and nail, the snap
of attraction.

Destruction speaks behind every verb
a continuous shelling of the distant hill
I say I love you I want
to be in bed, an introduction
not certainly abstract
yet we never rise to leave
time
into time there is a faltering
a new concurrence of feet and fingers
and gestures one would never have employed
and your eyes play
                          and rest
how long how long.

Where is my world love,
oh where is my love?

Yesterday I learned of massive time
the pacific controls our continent
but what controls me is far
less in size than that and far
more burning, ah heat
can a week last so long
can the measurement of my time
been so mistaken, and so filled
with the miscalculation of what is
possible
            can I survive a passion come
much beyond the years of my
capability to be free?

No love lasts forever
and no love in the wreck of this city
I can find, almost no hull
uninfused with your
maiden's prayer, the incense
of your presence is almost everywhere.

So bury the vile omens of men
bury their hard right touch
and when in this certain hard winter
the snow sweeps across fifth street
I alone will see your figure
uncovered uncovered in our dark predicament
against the row of white houses.

My Gods
where
    are the lovely traceries
of where your magnificent presence
   where can you be?

I was downtown shortly, afternoon
there were all the insinuations
our mutuality
breeds, what she
puts on
        I likewise do
cut a small figure for the prow of my ship
and she resists the artful brushing
eyelashes, the arch finger
in the air
whole civilizations,
ours was,
are built on
such proposals, oh but that isn't it.
There are sure signs.

I am disfigured by an age
caught forward and rear of a time.
and that makes me a bad sculptor.

      Midwars I began a depression
and finally arrive just as everyone was leaving
a trip suggested, of great immediacy, get in quickly!
so one's life is
                a case of no reference.

She says One can't be free around you
you are not free, I say I know.

All the fractures of a life there are
and this cherokee and mexican
and irish girl makes them while we talk.
The serving woman runs her breath out
serving the dishes
and I ask her for matches
                  to build a fire
of a recognizable flame.

On the bed of the vast promiscuity
of the poet's senses is turned
the multiple world, no love is possible
that has not received the un-
unloadable freight of that fact
no wake permissible that has not met
the fluxes of those oceans. And fear
is merely a daily concern
only a line kept always in his hand

Difficulties spoken of
are difficulties to come
and the certain knowledge of their coming
is only our sharpest need
vivified. I met you and we walked.
All things said were a play
of what our eyes wanted to reveal
of times spent apart and surrounded
within which each our own spirits
sought that old old relief of proximity
and the light of windows
the brooding earth half light
of interviews meant
a form of that totally
like facade.

Oh Gods of my disembarked soul this is sad
a merriment of unteachable waywordness
but I tell you the lustre of any gleaming eye
stays far
          way beyond the green hills
of an expectation, please
of impatience demand a lapse
demand a tear
that only chrystal
only material of our love
of never more substance.

When I awaken in the morning
I can not say my first thoughts
are of you
        This small city is dense
with the ring of other laughters
I know
            and likewise my nights
are spent in the solicitude
of other hope, outlandish occupation.

But if you do,
you come to me, an awkward
and distractingly discontent flash,
sharpens amid those crowds, where oh
where are you then those times,
I wonder about you wonder what
you do.

Made the temporary fire
one charge
nor were your lips a smallness
that first moment
they opened, that unforgettably
moist softness
                    of all first brief instants

a renewal of,
long ago,
another such union
the same insensate fear
where the heat lies
oh where

IN THE FACE OF THE LIBERAL
(1964–1968)

MORNING CONVERSATION

Six oclock
on garbage day
the cans out
my wife still
in bed.

So have a cup
of that mexican chocolate
from the hip grocer
                    down the block.

Car lights on the street.
Hey, people don't work
on xmas eve do they?
Sure, the answer comes.
Oh wow, is that true?

You mean if xmas comes
in the middle of the week
the people get fucked?
Yes.

Oh free enterprise!
isn't that too much

IN THE FACE OF THE LIBERAL

The beasts
               of the nation come
come, come
in their own hands, which they hold out
before them, before you
and say these
                    are the principles
these spots
        spots silver as virtue
are what will keep you free
are what will keep your lovely way of life pure
are what
        will keep our daughters' asses uncorrupted
              (they don't say that
The beasts of the nation say their gas is non-lethal
those crude semanticists rarely use the word death
they are scientific in their vegetablianity . . . .
              and no one takes a gun
        or no one takes a knife
              or pours kerosene
          or lets the air out
            or pours sand or sugar in their
                or nails their eyes to billboards
        or steals the tennis shoes of their sons
    or even so much as fucks up all their automatic toasters
only a few convicts in prisons, and those mostly tubercular
black men, I'd imagine, spit like they always did
into the shiny rows of Libby's peas, and tomatoes, corn
Del Monte pears, Cut Rite green bears, garbanzos etc.

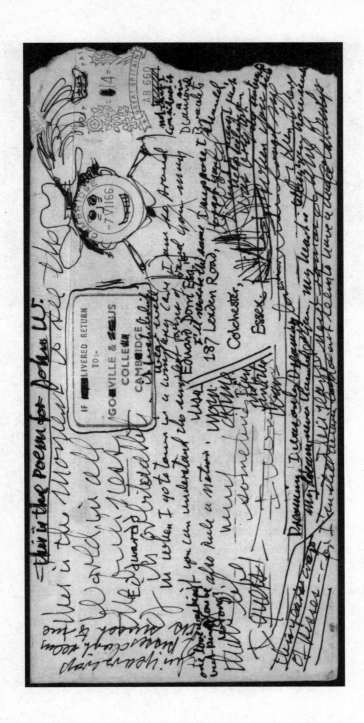

YAS SUH, OR: ON A PICTURE POSTCARD OF THE NEANDERTHAL FAMILY GROUP FROM A FRIEND IN GREAT DISTRESS

The big stud stands w/ his chin in a fur wrap
his cave over his head, the female
pounds a skin
staked to the ground. The skull
and horns of an Ibex, an example
of a meal they once had,
weathers into the earth. Caves
and a tiny dot of fire at the mouth,
the only particular deposit in evidence
they have of tomorrow.

They look pretty pissed-off
and I don't blame them.
The British Museum says their food
included the great Auk,
and that they inhabited the caves
of Gibraltar, the sea was
100 metres lower then. It all
looks bad, it looks grim
and like the end
like us
after fifty thousand years
not like the start,
like somebody already did it to them. Many times.

    But nobody came
along to kick him out of that cave
unless they wanted a definitely battered head.
And no bailiff could take his clothes,
the cat is plainly cooling it in that respect
with a skin held casually over his
shoulder, and when he wanted
to move his bowels
(they call it offal
        he simply squatted
on Franco's present peninsula.

For Tom Raworth

A POEM ENTITLED BULLSHIT
for J.H.P.

in the heat of undoing
the latch called
            our lives
there can be none.
fact, you know
as well as I
is just another distracting
preliminary equation
to be got down
          because, among
other acts
we also promise ourselves
that one.
    in the end tho
  we know
         or we don't
  and isn't that nice

[MY WANDERING]

my wandering
has cost me everything.

I have no place to be.
I am separated
and I have no claim.
      good!
    I shall make no claim.

oct / 29 / 66
(Full moon
in England

SECOND THOTS ON ASTRONAUT

(also for Clair Oursler

of all the heavenly bodies
you see the moon from a native position
and she is fixed for you there.
There is no other than an Illinois moon
for me. Now that I see her
in Essex in all her moist circulation
I write you this Clair
she sails out of my real reach
I cannot lock that total fullness
to where I am. It
is not a question of beauty
this time. It may be
a question of real-estate
It may be only Texans
can *ride* her, whore for them. It may be
new myth a mustang in Trajection:
Take that job in Nebraska
immigrate to Dawson city australia
(a magic gesture to calm the surface)
where small pyramids
have been seen in photographs.

ON FIRST READING
"AS IT WERE AN ATTENDANT"

This beautiful poem as it were
An attendant, turns, on,
Prepositions, on,
Propositions, observe this
On the westward face
And the tediously difficult
     Syntax
   which   is
An *exquisite* and preliminary
And inevitable
  Risk
To preposition Blackie
   w/out
  Passion
        and
        p.s. note: the line breaks
        are *for* the first time
        "natural"
        ie, Rests
        on the surface as
        your final ampersand.

ONCE, AGAIN

I sit in this room looking at some books
looking at my life
moving.
Smiles. Some of those things have meant
one thing or another to me. The Dead Lecturer.
I liked that one. green lantern. That was OK

those days, the exile etc. In the moment it had.
And all of them they had their moments. Woolf's books.

      I've carried them around
some people I had to have, some I thought I *should*
have with me
a long time
across the country
across the ocean, up and down stairs, you know—
tried to fix up a place for them, bricks
boards, sometimes there has been a bookcase
already there, glass doors and they looked more
as if they had a place then in a way reflections
in front of the titles of my friends. I even
borrowed some bricks this last time. Borrowed
some bricks. I guess I'll have to return
the bricks. But do I want to keep the books.

Sentimental shit.
This choked throat.
I didn't even blink
when my son discovered
he doesn't even bear my name. Maybe
I'm just cool in some areas. Signed copies
which won't fit in my pocket. Some
came off on my brain and if you open
the covers of the book
you'll find the print missing. The people
who have tried to live with me know where
to look for the missing pages. They have been
part of my life

A real part I say against the walls to bounce it
back to my own ears. I could walk out
and not look back into this room leave it
every individual page behind. My split

self tells me. Shit I got because it was hard to get.
All those. Fuck that. How many times can you have it.
Three different copies of Call me,
Ishmael
if a drowning man ever
grasped for books. And, then there are my books!
Pretty nice.

If somebody burns it all, Büchner's mistress say,
sends it right to heaven via the chimney
that's one way to get there so I'll keep the letters
and somebody can do that,
they found me forwarded.
Cendrars was right
to consider the postage stamps in his hip pocket
the best stuff in print.
                              Say the shot
you have to know is true! leave it all
leave that hard practised practicality
some other self says you'll want them later.
Uh Huh they'll come in handy some other place
later. The History of the Study
of Landforms. Sure,
maybe 2 boxes instead of 4 instead of 16. Just so
you don't get off with nothing? Just so
when somebody says where your books you
don't end up with some stammer about back there?
So I mean you got this poem you want some books too.
So take them back across, again, back?

There they are. Leave them all behind.
But not *that* way. No.
Leave your friends with your friends.
If some day
they want you
They'll find you.

A CONVENTION IS IN A
WALLPAPER STORE
(1968)

*"Intended to be strewn on the floor
of the 1968 Democratic National Convention."*

SET I

0

A Convention is in a Wallpaper Store

1

The Manticism of their selection is a Wallpaper Store

2

The presidential pattern
on the wall in Hell
The Colosseum Birthday party
for the Man of Sin

3

We are in the Room-of-Sin
absorbing the pattern
we are in with the men of GATH

4

All this depicts our lives

5

Where is the Man-of-Men?

6

The Manroot

7

Man-of-the-Earth

8

The Man of The Signs

9

UnConvention!
Homo Signorum Homo Signorum
UnConvention!
Homo Signorum Homo Signorum Signorum

10

Beware the approach of

11

Man of Wax

12

Man of Bland Iron

13

Man of Mold

14

Man of Motley his eyes

15

and all the distortions of our friend

16

the Man of Sorrows

17

who can be the Man of Spy

18

not the Man of War

19

we are the Men of Men together Homo Signorum

20

the Men Here, say it
the Man of the Woods
the Man of Blood

21

So contra the Man of Motley wallpaper eyes
fixed history on the wall
say the wall away
free of the hum
in the Man of The Signs.

SET II

1

America, you boil over

2

turn now and rise
Wrest the matter into your own
hands—and Nature's laws

3

the fear of being
misunderstood (a great mass
           Disease
that stops everybody
thats stopped

4

It is time the people had something to say about
War, about Peace, about Property.

5

There isn't such a thing
         as yr thing
until it registers its consciousness

6

If any question cld be branded into the horizon,
wld it penetrate the hog?

7

They feel easier in the protection which the
inactivity of permanence temporarily gives

CHANTS 1–5

CHANT 1

H O M O M E N S U R A
where is the manness here
H O M O M E N S U R A
H O M O M E N S U R A
where are the menhir
where is our cercle of perpetual apparition
where is the grand visionhead
H O M O M E N S U R A IS

                              he here

CHANT 2

            O,
THE MANIKINISM OF CHICAGO IS
MIAMIC
            O,
THE HOMOCHROMATISM OF CHICAGO IS
MIAMIC MIAMIC
            O,
THE RECTAL VALVARY
O THE MICHIGANISM

CHANT 3

AAAARROOOWW

SEE THEM COMING ACROSS THE FLOOR

HOUSEL THE CANDIDATES WHO APPROACH

AAARROOOWW

SEE THEM CIRCULATE ACROSS THE FLOOR

AAARROOOWW

HOUSEL THE HEADS OF THE NAMED LEADERS

HOUSEL THEIR HOMOLATERAL HEADS
AAARROOOWW
NOW WE SHALL GET TO

THE FUNNY DESTINY OF THEIR HOMONOTIONAL HEADS

CHANT 4

O,

LET THE POWER OF THE RECLIMBING OF THE TOR
LET THE SPREAD OF THE LOW SATURATIONS
     AND THE HIGH BRILLIANCE OF THAT DAY
     AND THE TINCTURE OF THE AWARENESS

LET THE HEIGHT OF THE TOR
AND LET THE DIFFICULTY OF DESCENT BE CLEAR
LET THE MANNET AND HIS MANNETS
     GO OFF IN THE CAR
     TO BE BLOATED BY MAN-IN-THE-GROUND

AND THE MEAN SAVED
AND ALL WHO ARRIVE IN THEIR SKIN
MANIFESTIVE AND MANKIND

     AGAIN ON THE TOR
     AND THE MANICATE
     AND MANIFORM

AND THE HOLY WINE OF THE QUEST
     FOR THE TOTAL CUP
     BE RAISED AND LAID

AGAINST THE PREDILECTIONS OF CHI

CHANT 5

A MASS OF NAMES STARING UP FROM THE BALLOT
think of the one you love
A MASS OF NAMES STARING UP FROM THE BALLOT
ask how your mother lived
A MASS OF NAMES STARING UP FROM THE BALLOT
ask where your father is
A MASS OF NAMES STARING UP FROM THE BALLOT
is there one there you love
A MASS OF NAMES STARING UP FROM THE BALLOT
who could you point your back to
who could you leave with the simplest task
how could you state a simple need to
what molecule of the connective universe
what sign of the spiritive permeation

THE GRAVE OF DIANA
(1968–1970)

INAUGURATION POEM #3

There is always the increase to be
dealt with always as the increase
to be about poverty, to be about misery
to be dreary
and it is all in the absorption of the media
of the word itself, the compulsion
to contribute the whole force of the ego
to the word, the increase is in the total
abandonment of the senses in favor
of the word that we all know all effort
is best toward gold
but that the era, the golden
is as uninvited as the starlings
and must move aside praying to be
let into its own natural setting and this age
will do some really hopeless thing
like get drunk. The condition
of the next morning is like a dead reed
in us — the only truly unfashionable
marching band is pessimism like too many trombones

each day there are new boundaries
closer in, close around
and one float from each state
one float, float what?
each state, state what?

TO THE TOWER

for Tom Pickard's anthology of the Morden Tower

YOU are going to the Tower
not slowly   not slowly
THE train into the north
the flower   The Flower
OF Darkness
not slowly Swiftly
TO BE final   repeatedly
and to continue to be final
SO repeatedly to read
the elevated hell intensely cold
AGAINST a burning heat
sit on the floor to sit in a chair held over the earth
WALK precociously
along the wall
GOD'S lines hold you up
or you fall dead in the alley crushed
BETWEEN the Normans
and the Northumberlands
THEN back to Basil asleep

the head of a family of stonecut figures
TO GO up to the tower be cold
cold against the fire to be the flower
OF THE Dark Cold be carved
start in Beauty be cold in Beauty

A GRAPH OF SEVERAL PERSONS

He appeared sober this time
and unaccompanied by *Sophrosyne*
Under his given name he was
more boring than Heavy Armbuster
his name when drunk.

Then another He appeared in the hallway
with his hair cut, the agent
of *dynamis*, you be the Host he said
You serve the wine, you spin the record.

Between time she disappeared
taking the children, *caritas*
in the shopping center, the phone
rang equally into its own
ear and mouth, back home.

Then just in advance of the closing
of the gates of the walled city
they all returned in time to get to bed.
While they are laid out, the body
does its best to rip out the circuitry
they put together with spit and smiles
before the hand covered the yawn.

Socrates was of the same school;
feels that a man should not act
without a full understanding
of what he is about, that each person
must organize his own search for the good.

The parallel is exact. Of course,
there remains the litigation
over next week's wrecks, doors shut
against Spring
and the difficulty of conceiving physical motion.

JULY 13TH

So this is the night
that Billy the kid
was killed the kid
the night was killed
this is the kid the night
Billy was killed
so this is this night
this is the killing

without thinking

I stood in midspace
Hitchhiking to the moon on
July 13th, the anniversary
Of Billy's death when along
Came the astronauts
Whose names I dont recall
And my thumb was there
Asking its question yet
Was it the length of my hair
That made them pass me
by? or did they
Themselves believe the sticker
On their space shield
NO Riders. They looked
the Trinity all looked.
I saw them phone Houston.
Not of course to ask permission
no not to ask permission
It could only have been
To check their position

[THIS LOVE IS A THING]

This love is a thing
to be forgot, we
shall not shall not know when
the end is
the street
            into the pure shade
            of ourselves, lost
Then a raft
adrift of emotion one by one
will fall unrecoverably behind

Hidden. Hidden. as the waves we throw
higher to make apartness
at least real
at least feel the true weight of illusion

Every love
            is true
to some sensation
and this most is
this most recovers
one lost thing of crystal
when you smile. And all
those people, all our people
wait on us, there, their
Bonfires on the shore
never out of sighting
never out of mind
the blaze of tomorrow
the assumptions they make
for fuel.

The GRAVE of DIANA
IN THE PICTURE
OF Illinois
The Body of DIANA
is sepARated
THE NAils iN
HeR Body ARe
PlANted APART
IN the PICTURE
OF DEATH the
PlACe OF Rest
is sepARated
TYPICAlly they
have segregated
the only decent
Thing iN their
Miserable Lives

The grave of Diana Oughton is in a quiet cemetery at
Dwight, Ill., near the graves of her grandparents. Daily
News photo/Charles Krejcsi.

that her role was to physically   On Friday of that week one
way possible.   mistakes ended her

The Grave of Diana
In the picture
Of Illinois

The Body of Diana
Is separated
The nails in Her Body
Are planted apart

In the picture of Death
The place of rest
Is separated

Typically they
Have segregated
The only passion
In their miserable lives

FOUR YEARS LATER

I had gone to Buffalo again
and against instinct
to be in retreat
with the sagacious John Wieners
who lived in a vacant lot
across the street from the Universe

Where the grass grew
with great effort the grass blew
so short it was cut
around the stores
of the dying town
dying torn down
tin cans and bottles growing up
through the sidewalks

which score the honky perspective
of a plane where the dated billboards cast their shadows
for sale, lease and build to suit
without ever guessing
that it was built to suit the grass
growing up through the sidewalk
Theopolis of weeds, possibly
the greatest it's yet conceived
by mere men, all of it
the Darwinian couplets
who continue the species know
who we are and what we have to destroy
They have no feeling, no response
for what comes next

THE SAM COLE SONG

This is the night of Christina Rossetti's birthday
My son has been in chicago since Thanksgiving
This is the night of the temperature plunge
After the day of the record High
On marsday wodensday and thorsday
This is the night of Christina Rossetti's birthday
My son has been in chicago since Thanksgiving
I returned from Middletown on the night of the day
Thomas Chatterton poet and forger was hit
And made to cough his brief life away
This is the night of Christina Rossetti's birthday
And oh mama this is where I been lucky
On the twenty first of October Wodensday
I read at St. Marks
That was the birthday of Sam Cole

GUNSLINGER:
FRAGMENTS & SATELLITES
(1970–1974)

you might call a derisive air
when he'd say "Due In On Monday"
because you see it was Sunday
when they left town, but
he kept knockin his right hoof
against the insde of the coach
sayin You All Alright Out There?
and he had the texan's hat on
a stetson XX sorta cockwise
on his head it was
I tell you Slinger you would of
split your levis and dropped your
beads to seen it.
                    Because he
was sayin some of the abstractest
things you ever heard
like Celery Is Crisp!
and we ain't seen him
or that individual texan
who owned him since.
I swear
that stud must have become a congressman
or something since then
He sure was going strong on that
fresh Tampico — Some of the hands
that was there that day in fact
claimed he didn't leave on the stage
at all, there's still people
around here who'll claim that horse
flew back west when the texan
went to sleep 5 miles out of town.
you boys
enjoy yourself, I'll see about you later.

LIL'S BOOK

(Everything says to Lil, as of what I don't recall—
I've changed my mind, Lil.
Yes? Does it work any better?

What Lil read on the wall in the ladies room
in Sundance, N.D.

> The humanest being of the twentieth C.
>
> was Crazy H. of the You-Know-Who,
>
> because he declined to have
>
> his picture took
>
> pull the chain
>
> when youve shut the book

Item: Teledyne Ryan, Sllabs Robot on loan
to Lil in her Beanville mansion, spent the
weekend with its parents in Colorado Springs

Lil's Soliloquy

Huge Heffner is the Walt Disney of sex
Bertrand Brussel is the dude for me.

Ah ha ha ha, ha ha ha
ha ha ha Hee!

Do you have any notion
the size of the odds against
one's birth *anyway*?

Yes, it's 1 to
Something Very Large.

Umm!
So you can really *feel* it.

Indeed!
Of course, depending on where
one's at, Las Vegas say
or Youngstown Ohio as the extremes
those odds are reduced to Nothin

Lil:

Resin is a supplement to life much like vitamins are a supplement to pastry flour, it wouldn't be very rich without it — Now the way I see it, you've kept the hours and everybody knows what *those* are, then you've needed something for the extra time you're awake and away from your dreams. Dope gives you that supplement, it fills ya in on what you missed. There's just hardly nothing like it. But most of all it's like a really nice conversation with purely nothing. A very rare thing. No poet, I'm a Brussels woman for purely practical reasons.

Lil:

Poeta is the supremest condition of the human faculty
though poetry is often not

Lil:

And her wide liquid eyes
were fixed open upon the Local Body
as it fell below the bough
and on to the horizon

Lil:

Thus we enter again the paradox
Many poets are not poetas

Lil:

I am filled with longing
please strike this specimen in high relief

It pleases me
because
Book III Pause
is for Robert Creeley

THE POEM OF DEDICATION

Some
where
   down
      the
         Road
      is
            a
   numb
ber born
standing
in the
air for
everyone
         every
one
the number
we will
become

Some
Time
it is
the number we
can do

and) All
though
few
They are
who
will

or would
suffer that

stress)

      to discover
there wa
s I
and in there
there
is
Eu

| the |
| double headed |
| wa wa |
| The |
| he & she mirror |

      And
in his course
I
knows
what
to
do to
trans port
The red shifting
coach
across
the crosshair
    and not
    despair
  that
the desire
must be greater
than
the
effect

                                    I speak to you
                                    this winter
the inside real   In Order to find
and the   not who
outsidereal   who is a paragraph
                                    but where
                                    I is

                                    Th
                                    e   XORT
                                    sh
inside that realm   ort l
in here   ine i
beside the whelm   's the
                                    longest

                                           And
                                    th
                                    e com
                                    plete p
                                    iec
                                    e i
                                    's th
                                    e completest

                                    An
                                    d   Sing
                                    so on   i n g
                                    gu
                                    lar
                                    it ey
                                    lawgd

                                    i
                                    n
                                    th
                                    e ace

of He
arts i
's the Jam
bo
ree the p
an
icle we
be
where the bee
sticks
where sh
e breeds
a tree, she is
most straight
more best

      Sways
still present
and at rest
along the im
mensity
of the Past

of y	North	are
ourself	South	the Nerves
	East	of the hemis
	West	phere

Now,
let us fast
tie me
to the mast
for my lonely Journey
thru this region

RIDDLE OF THE OMEGA

Nought was on the set
when zero placed his bet
on *by whom*
the engine would be BLED and *with whom*
    the secret train departed
        and, *exactly when*
the man had
        started his trip

Bhang Bhang!!
two shots are fired
and the last to board
are first to be hired
for they can decode
        what he sez
        from right to left it goes
        Delf Dez
        DELF DEZ

FOR THE BOYS & GIRLS
IN THE FREEIDEA STORE

    I modestly suggest
a new form of greeting
to replace
all those bullshit new handshakes:

        Hair Pulling
The advantages of hair pulling
over hand shaking
are at least two-fold
        1) more natural
        2) done gently but firmly
            it tests those agents
            among us
            who are wearing rugs

Skinheads will likely go for a soft pinch
in exchange for those gentle tugs

I, from position — 1
        as sec. to parm.

                        for Jenny's
                        amusement
                        Diversey June 71
                        w/ smiles

O'BRIEN

a message from the incarcerated

QUOTE let me outa here UNQUOTE

====

The vegetable cannot speak when its water has been removed
Therefore dried potatoes can tell you nothing

====

Very early Freud is modern
Late Freud is very Victorian

++++

The burden of proof is heavy

++++

Negativity has positively bad effects

====

Nil over the head
is the right dub

====

Vowels

If his guns are a double consonant
Then the round is the hidden quantity
I am looking for a worker whose guns
are a double consonant
and whose rounds
are a hidden quantity

====

I will do anything he said,
To increase the magneto & flush my senses
Into the Universe.
An irremedial case, the Slinger noted
Have his senses flushed into the universe

====

Is there a doctor in the house?
Everybody in the house is a doctor

FIVE ON PARMENIDES

So coming-into-being is quenched
and destruction is undiscoverable
the Black Hole is negative only
from this stand point, it is where we
have bothe been and are
                Yet it is not divided
for which of it is here
since its it is all alike

                The radical symmetry of the sphere
                as it meets its boundaries uniformly
                whether this is contemplated
                from the centre or from the out-
                side, it presents the same
                aspect in every direction.

the general Form of the argument:
        Whatever is, is F (where F is some predicate);
        for suppose not
        Then something is not-F;
        But to explain what it is for anything to be Not-F
        Involves the introduction of what is not
        And since it is inconceivable that anything is not-F
        So whatever is, is F

In order to block certain consideration
Parmenides would need to claim generally
That what is conceivable is the case
(But I thinks he does,
(That's why I thinks he covered the case

That which is is a unity, unique, complete, unchanging,
homogeneous. Negatively, it is not many things, which that
which is is often supposed to be. I is clear that it is not,
in any ordinary sense, given to us by experience; experience,
derived from sense perception,
is precisely what (Parmenides) we war(s) against.
That which is can be apprehended by reason alone.
It is clear that
that which is
is not an occupier of space or time
in any usual sense — (and so
The divorce between appearance
And reality
               Has been made complete

DR. FLAMBOYANT

Einstein was square
he could have simply
sent the whole thing
to a contortion mirror
in any carnival

what abt Energy?
strictly untheoretical

The Slinger peered thru the window
of the greasy spoon
to see Dr. Flamboyant eating a bowl
of arabic alphabet soup

Standing outside the booth under the open sky
Everything glances upward and blowing into
his hands he at once observes on high
the condition for an Abelian group

BORDER SURREALISMO

The Man From the Border
(Who isn't, he was wont to say
Stepped out of the coach
and walked throughe the breezeway
of the Western Union
in Alamosa Colorado, a message
was burning a hole in his **Brain**

Outside a blizzard roaring from the North
obscures the meatladen body of the train
and the breathing of its ironclad jowls
spreads into the great directions
the pragmatism of the altered air
where forms of these our forebears
stand signalling their demands with lanterns
Elaborating the arcs of their heavy code,
configuring their Terrible century ending demonology

HELLO he enquires with his flawless mouth
while the Ominous earpiece blocks his destination
with the full tone of its tibetan indifference
Why dont you give it a dime for its technology
prompts his companion, nose pressed flat
against the booth's glass wall, and remember Jim

It is Not the mouthpiece to which you speak
but something far beyond, so When youve
paid the stockholders, Used your apolaustic fingers
to probe the numbers so to cut the tibetan wire
pay careful heed to the next main signal

For from   far ahead an impulse will return
and that will tell you whats happening somehow
at our destination, even thoughe, till then
there will not have been a penetration of it

THE HOLDUP

There's a tree standing in the middle
of the Road waving its arms

he whipped out a pepperbox
and said Gents!
its now time
to take it easy.

I'll have that ten pounds
of raw coke you got there in
your top molar Everything
and Lil lets have
them dymon rings
oh yes, mister Slinger
and that 7 poundsa hash
An thim thousand pills of phony psoyacibin
An yes, I can use thim placibos for the small town folks
An thim bricksa Red
An that beakera agric piss
An that boxa Or
An that peck o pumpkin seeds
An that bushel of dried pears
An that groat of barley
An "   unpolished rice
   "   "   loaded Paira dice
   "   "   raw apple cider
An yes thim crystals
An finally I'll take them pistols
ah just as I thot Caps!

an Poet han me that asterlab there
it sure is a antique them jewels's a bitch
an I'll take thim Everfresh roses with me
as well as that geetar with the tightest hole
under the smoothest strings

the only thing you got missins
acid, that's peculiar

I got that sd Everything
well if you did the highwayman observed
you got nothin to worry about
no I got Everything
you missed
you got Everything
but you got nothin
you're the Thing King

now Lady, and Gentlemen too
I have one more request
If yawl will
just remove your clothes
I'll be gettin off

no doubt Everything offered

TRIG UTAH

He slammed the door of his
inconsequential pick up truk,
and said "I hear your poet
        Just shot himself
        I'd like to apply
        for that Vacancy

THE DAY & NIGHT REPORT
(1971)

NEW YEAR'S DAY

Margaret O'Hare to Mexico

DAY 5, 360 DAYS FOLLOW

Kid at the clinic 1:00p

DAY 16

Neil Young. Auditorium Theatre

    This ruptured disk is

      the voice of an
        Angel

DAY 19 TUESDAY

H. Bialy at the workshop

pp 207–208, The Discovery

DAY 26+339

space in am.   hem.
    indiscriminate
always referenced ie nonvirgin

geo
gra   Slate
phy   Chalk

whereupon we wrote ourselves silly

hi
story   europ a jelly roll a trip inside

the enclosure of the land
    leads directly to
the enclosure of the mind

DAY 30

Georgia O'Keeffe

Ultra blue line

2:pm

DAY 55, 310 DAYS FOLLOW

Ash Wednesday

Slinger wld you step in here all by yourself
I never go *anywhere* w/out my friends
*no*where?
anywhere.
How about when you go to the
I never go to the
I always go under the sky
out in the open Air

O,   the answer lies within

The answer lies within?
extra *eemly*   O extremely far out
That's the first place most folks have been
and I can only guess what it's about
but it sure is
the first time I ever heard of a cop-in!
So tell me, How do you *get* in?

simple is the message I have to impart
the stranger gestured
Just open the door and step Into your heart
I don't have one the Slinger answered
and with his fingers
traced a star
no pump?
no pump to spread the blood around in

DAY 57

     of Aries
the celestial traveller, vision most distant
Capricorn women
Capricorn men and women
trying the works ahead of time
the anxiousness of the beginning of the sun
straining the strings of Aries
the celestial traveller where Earth maybe
no longer home

(so here comes this sheepdip around the corner
(destined to sell his Self

MARCH 1

Whiterabbit!

NIGHT 65, 300 NIGHTS TO COME

The Garrick Ohlsson program of March 5th 1971 began at 7:45 with a trip on the el. A moist warm evening. We sat on the platform over the Parkway and made some smoke. Jennifer whispered isn't it strange how much this looks like a turkish cigarette? I think we should smoke it like a cigarette. The train arrived and opened its doors. As the car jogged along we were held on a vision which lay between the shining rails and which prostrated itself before a nearby infinity to be called Chopin. Like chunks stuck together. I mean it was really grotesque.

We reached the Auditorium Theatre at 8:15 and quickly moved into the lobby. Sat down on a stone bench by the stairs, had some tobacco and a paper cup of orange juice. Then up to section FF. The Steinway stood brute silent on the stage, mouth propped open with a wooden stake. The boy comes in with an old-fashioned beard on.

The first number is Soneto 104 del Petrarca with one bow and then Sonata in F minor, Opus 5 with some premature coughing and applause between the Andante and Scherzo and some mistaken applause between the Scherzo and the Intermezzo, followed by two bows. Mr. Ohlsson's exercise not surprisingly laid the foundation of the following comparative: Liszt has a head heavier than Brahms.

During the intermission we line up with 35 ladies from Miami who are shouting "The music is Everything" and ten minutes later we arrive at a niche in the wall which turns out to be the house of a skinny arc of water.

The first number this time is the Triptych of Louis Weingarden. The composer was drunk when his allegory seized him. The virtuoso does what he can, but it is a house-piece. A few rows down a group of college music teachers pass a folded sheet of paper between them which evidently has a joke written on it. A 12 year old boy sitting across the aisle is asked to leave by the listeners in his territory and he climbs the stairs with his head in his hands outstretched before him.

And now it is time for Chopin! Nocturne in E-flat Major, Opus 55, No. 2 is dressed pretty but soon humdrum. Scherzo in E Major, Opus 54's a bitch. Polonaise in F-sharp Major, Opus 44 begins with the jest of a Russian and ends with the solidity of a Pole. Just the right truck to bring around for the move home. And we chant moving through the lobby and the encore, Goodbye Garrick, Goodbye.

DAY 67 — 298 TO COME

A working day. Monday is a day I value. Since it is a prehistoric day it is impersonal and free. I woke up from night 66–67 with a pleasant emptiness. I had gone to sleep reading Ramparts. My dreams had been primary, summary, and off-hand. And I felt a redeeming, but vague, satisfaction as my eyes opened to a bright sharply outlined new day. I have been over-ridden by my mind: they were on-hand the night before. 65–66.

I rose and walked into my son's room. He was sitting on the floor behind the door with two blocks in his hand one red and one blue. We smiled and then sat down to his piano which was made like desperately in Taiwan. We played several little tunes celebrating Chinese Women.

After his diaper was changed we descended to the kitchen where we ate cornflakes and as he made some practice sounds I spoke some pure American.

I spent the morning and early afternoon getting ready for my Hour. At 3:30 I departed for my Hour in a red convertible.

Entered P1 at precisely 4:03. On the way to work I heard Van Morrison and a piece of stupefying news about the Board of Trade. I call once more for the late papers and then begin the first 45 minutes of extraction. The gold comes away from the silver with no great coaxing. The next few minutes will be easy, in fact, the point now is— what's this about. They like the formality the intimacy, like letters they say. Like he's writing a letter. I put that up like a kite which reads too easy too low too cheap. If he talks to "someone" why is not that someone you. If he knows what you say you can hear, then how is it not produced particularly for your ear? The thot is too complicated. And so am I.

We have several poems from Autumn in New York.

"Cold comes creeping in the window
And in the sky searchlights sweep"

We have a common puzzlement, as if we were reminded of something.

"In the garden of earthly delight
he laid his limbs down beside a yew tree
and surrendered his eyes to the brilliance of brass"

I am the poet. This is the day report. Ace of Pentacles is the assignment. Boston, 1934. In 45 minutes extracting time this shit comes off the page equal, say, to the GNP for 1964. Of course it is worth far more now. That's not bad. Forty five minutes is not a full workday.

I dismiss the people. Let a rider out at Belmont. When I slam the door to the garage a signal from my group in S.W. Colorado relays over my cellfields. I pull the switches. My sister's wife has a lover named Ed. I must speak to my son immediately.

1

longs
Harold G'sluga
the Secretary to Parminder ~~sends a~~ *sends* ~~night letter~~ *night letter*

REPORT GX+8 Quad 2 (Earth. For transmission Deep Section *via*

*to be set block
in PICA face*

↓ *ref "Position 9"*

1. ~~It has become~~ Clear ~~in the~~ past few hours present time ~~that~~ ~~the~~ alien plantations X decade 6 Nation 23 *will* ~~are to~~ be disposed of not by simple annilation but through process: ~~It is~~ Not possible ~~at this time to~~ supply ~~the~~ practical equations ~~but our~~ Speculation Simulator *can* provides ~~the~~ following probabilities.

Actual numbers: Irreversable prefix line
Literal numbers: Whole Information/Total Account

Identical built-in
~~And the same/~~"Noose" effects ~~are~~ expected as in Occasions 1 2 & 3 of the articulate past /Report GX+2, Works. We are ~~at~~ Absolute Present following ~~a~~ survey ~~by the~~ Linguatilt ~~of~~ site 1 ~~in the~~ Timeroof. ~~where a~~ Step this Way effect ~~was~~ found ~~in~~ relative dislocation. A parallel survey predicts ~~that the~~ colloquial locks ~~will~~ hold against any method applied outside time. Therefore the *the Line* equation for Literal numbers/~~should be~~ stable within the frame of ~~the~~ Wide Present. All present terms ~~are~~ known and without exception conform *with* ~~to~~ local strands thus the program set ~~up to~~ jump ~~the~~ Biolines ~~has been~~ pulled.

Watch it 2. ~~The motion of~~ Gross ~~interchanged~~ bod~~ies~~ *motions spew* *Watch it* *Pattern No 9* conformation ~~and it is~~ curved ~~to~~ survive ~~the~~ splitting of .78 ~~of~~ its interior vectors. ~~The~~ stimulated drift ~~of~~ ~~the~~ Continental Slaves ~~has been~~ compensated ~~for~~ by ~~a~~ factor ~~of~~ ten squares /Standard Signal +4. ~~Repeat~~ crudeness, ~~for this application is~~ outside transmission. *with result* Linguatilt ~~can and to~~ provide X tonal equivalent for Habit. The real numbers

234

NIGHT 69: THE NIGHTLETTER (DRAFT)

[the Secretary to Parmenides
~~seals~~ [sends] [hands G'slinger] [brings] a night letter]

REPORT GX+8 Quad 2 (Earth. For transmission Deep Section
[via]
[ref "Position 9"]

1. ~~It has become~~ [C]lear ~~in the~~ past few hours present time ~~that the~~ alien plantations ~~of~~ decade 6 Nation 23 ~~are to~~ [will] be disposed of not by simple annihilation but through process: ~~It is~~ [N]ot possible [Pardon me, it is not possible] ~~at~~ this ~~time~~ [framing] ~~to~~ supply ~~the~~ practical equations ~~but our~~ Speculation Simulator [Can] provides ~~the~~ following probabilities.

Actual numbers: Irreversible prefix line
Literal numbers: Whole Information/Total Account

~~And the same~~ [IDentical] [built-in] "Noose" effects ~~are~~ expected as in Occasions 1 2 & 3 of the articulate past [Report GX+-2, Works. We are ~~at~~ [A]bsolute [P]resent following ~~a~~ survey ~~by the~~ Linguatilt ~~of~~ site 1 ~~in the~~ Timeroof[.] ~~where a~~ <u>Step this Way</u> effect ~~was pickdup~~ [found ~~in~~] relative [to] dislocation. ~~A~~ parallel survey predicts ~~that the~~ colloquial locks ~~will~~ hold against any method applied outside time. Therefore ~~the equation~~ [the Line] for Literal numbers ~~respected~~ [~~cannot be~~] [Not] ~~as~~ [is][:] stable within ~~the~~ frame of ~~the~~ [W]ide [P]resent. All present terms ~~are~~ known and without exception conform ~~to~~ [with] local strands thus ~~the~~ program set ~~up to~~ jump ~~the~~ Biolines ~~has been~~ pulled.

[~~Watch it~~
Watch It
Pattern#4]

2. ~~The motion of~~ [G]ross ~~is unchanged~~ bodies[y] [motions] ~~is unchanged~~ [show] ~~of~~ radical conformation ~~and it is~~ curved ~~to~~ survive ~~the~~ splitting of .785 ~~of its~~ interior vectors. ~~The~~ stimulated drift ~~of the~~ [C]ontinental [S]laves ~~has been~~ compensated ~~for~~ by ~~a~~ factor ~~of~~ [of] ten squares [Standard Signal +4. ~~The~~ [Result] crudeness [in] ~~of~~ ~~this application is~~ outside transmission [is the result]. Linguatilt ~~can only~~ [to] provide ~~a~~ tonal equivalent for Habit. ~~The~~ real numbers unstable in this class. [Expect to materialize intersection 4 corners.]

[~~thanks for~~ [Regards to] Everything]

[Signed—**I** i]

[Secretary to Parmenides]

DAY 72, 293 COMING
SATURDAY OVERTIME

Stumpnote to Alexander Hamilton

The mechanical man stood beside a special machine. Two wheels. Two vertical pipes. Hanging in the frame a rotor with teeth powered by the truck in front. The whole thing shook and stomped with woodlust. The blurred rotor ate an inch at a swatch and then jumped over, automatically. It was soon done and the chips were impacted in the hole. The little spitz of a frowning woman attacked the spot with one last stream of piss. I wish I had thought of that. Now Alexander Hamilton the thing what makes you go has removed the final evidence of another one of our great friends.

(west diversey information service

73RD DAY

My mother took the Kid south today. He smiled
and wanted something to say like goo ga lay

THE EVENING OF DAY 74

Andrew Jackson

On the evening of the fifteenth J., M., & E. were invited to a screening at the Esquire Theater in the Russian Oak District by Mick. They quite happily consented and as the Kid was sojourning in East Central Illinois under the watchful eye of his Grandmother they had no need of Mrs Lonius the baby sitter who was on the set at the Biograph and saw it all happen that night with The Lady in Red. They departed straightaway. As they stepped into Diversey Mick told them he had just come from Frisco where he interviewed T.V. Did you see any crowds in Frisco? M. asked. Oh yes, Mick said, there was one at the Ultimate Race Track but it was Nothin compared to this movie we made.

76 + 289
ST. Ps DAY

We could have seen on video
Everything we heard on radio
Except the faces

DAY 77 THURSDAY 18 MARCH

This morning Night presented her final idea to me and I opened my eyes. Driving Snowe. I began to realize a poem from my sleep called

Parmenides in Magpieform

He poked his head
and walked around
while he said there is
nothing I have said
and Nothing
I have said is black & white
Why are you in drag
he read behind my blind
This dress as you can see
he answered me
was put on
for the party in your mind
and true to my philosophy
I am the last to go
Good Light

And then he handed me
the menu inside a chinese utility warp

Boiled Fishing Pole on a bed of Fried Ironing Bloard

DAY 79, 286 DAYS FOLLOW

Dreamtrack: I woke up riding away from robbing
                  The Big Dipper Bank in Cheyenne Wyoming

\-   \-   \-   \-   \-   \-   \-   \-

"Our Sun is moving about 12 miles
per second
towards the constellation Hercules
That's our direction," the poet announced.

Groovy the Slinger nodded
Wake me up when we get there

THE DAY REPORT

Night 79

The weather reports last night (78-79) had been conclusive. We chose the local one and awoke to a bright, solar day. I took a bath and washed my hair. Jenny asked if this were all done because it's saturday night. The answer is Yes. A habit as far back as the farm. But this is a special saturday. The 1st saturday of Winter. Spring starts up immediately tomorrow and the mighty line of my sign begins to pull me thru the flume to a position of real story, a system of motion. I greet my co-Ordinates Everywhere on this occasion of our alignment.

A resumé of Waking Moment 77. Parmenides presented himself to me dressed in the coat of a Magpie. The point was instant and clear but I couldn't quickly enough accept its simplicity. Whereupon Parmenides ran a slight but very long smile and strutted about in the plumes of his coat. Beautiful, Black and White in so pure. It was our first real meeting since I had been summoning him. That's about 3 years. I liked him very much. He is a creature I can respect totally in fact.

Day 80, Spring 12:38 am at Chicago

Trees:

It has now been established that they share certain responses with Man. Which have trees That to be in the possession Of man alone   Paranoia For example, not so much the lighted match But the Thot of the lighted match The latter trait is for them the important one In a relation to Man.

Wings: 1926 Brassa print Hal Foster Aberdeen origin 1 Re Directed

Day 81st

Great Book: The Destiny, by Kim Dietch

Report I in precisely into date Chicago shifted from position 1 to position 3. Belief from the double sixth felt immediately. Manifestations undoubtedly real not not yet apparent. L.A. now ready to suffer all the chimerical maledictions directed opposition 1.   Good luck Angelo! You're gonna need it.

82nd day, 282 days out

"everything is irrelevant until you use it" he said and then under his magnificent coat produced an old unroasted corning ware coffee pot. He ground it up into a fine brown powder and laid it out in thin lines on a chunk of obsidian. Snort he said! They did. An initial vague vision arose In the terrain around them. Then the shape of Brazil with her characteristic amazonian hair and mouth and the great nose of her sorserick formed and a rasping coffee aggression siezed them and they were strapped to the stools of a birch counter continent wide and three inches high and they were spinning around kicking and gasping and they beat the counter like fingernails with the whips woven of their arms.

082. a reconstruction by Terry J and Ed D.

He was in the Star Hotel on Madison. On his arm was the tatoo "Born to Raise Hell." That was the sign (or marquee when he held it up) they were looking for. They weren't actually looking for Him. A sign can replace you. Roll up your sleeve.)

84

Victoria and Jim they headed southwest in a van shaped like a bedpan

The driver was hunched over the steering wheel slobbering methadrine*

and Victoria and Jim were feeling fine

*"the driver who drove them was stiff with speed he almost died as he flew over the underpass about 30 years ago"

— phد of J. D.'s fate

Day 85

CANCELLED

86th day, 279 days follow

Set: Beneath the El at Diversey

I walking across the street, placed one thin dime in the slot. The machine gladly swallowed the salistrial coin, Gulp. Thank you! I looked in his pocket for more and apologized. I offered it this torn stub from the Biograph.

Fo 13867½ C.
128577   @ 1½

WINGS, William Wellman 1926 Buddy Rodgers   Richard Arlen Clara Bow (voo) Jobyna Ralston 5 fabulous minutes of Gary Cooper EATING & COOKING. OK

The machine smiled and said 1917 to 1935 applied to private What do you expect to walk through me, I hollered at I CONDITION you pay me your dimes worth. Shut up Go on idiot"

Sunday 28 March Day 87 Passion Sunday

MAYA ANDROMEDA MIRANDA MARGARET DORN
9:43 p. 87 W.

"No events in the past are required
that have no counterpart now."

209-Jack Hale Reflector

I want to spring
a yellow bird
in the sun
J. H.

Day 89, 276 days out

"can we really suppose that physical processes
go on elsewhere as they do in our Neighborhood?"

Day 90

the child and the mother are transported home
and in this transportation
there are certain antique tricks
like the internal combustion engine
plus of course the pneumatic tires
and the streets

EDWARD DORN

Day 91, uh, April 1

    The announcement today by the white house
that it had rendered Lieutenant Colly's immediate
release came as no surprise—the announcement
an hour later, of the tandem release
of Manson & Girls and Sirhan came as likewise
no surprise. But the "reasoning" that all the
defendents are victims of the same war came as
a wild surprise, indeed. This package decision
is wise and will do much to restore the
functional equity of our house.

NIGHT 79

The weather reports last night (78–79 had been competitive. We chose the local one and awoke to a bright, solar day. I took a bath and washed my hair. Jenny asked if this were all done because it's saturday night. The answer is Yes. A habit as far back as the farm. But this is a special saturday. The last saturday of Winter. Spring starts up immediately tomorrow and the mighty line of my sign begins to pull me thru the Sunne to a position of real story, a system of motion. I greet my co-Ordinates Everywhere on this occasion of our alignment!

A resumé of Waking Moment 77: Parmenides presented himself to me dressed in the coat of a Magpie. The point was instant and clear but I couldn't quickly enough accept its simplicity. Whereupon Parmenides ran a slight but very long smile and strutted about in the phazes of his coat. Beautiful. Black and White is so pure. It was our first real meeting since I has been summoning him. That's about 3 years. I liked him very much. He is a creature I can respect totally in fact.

DAY 80, SPRING 12:38 AM AT CHICAGO

Trees:

It has now been established that they
Share certain responses with Man
Which have been Thot to be in the possession
Of man alone   Paranoia
For example, not so much the lighted match
But the Thot of the lighted match
The latter trait is for them the important tone
In a relation to Man

Wings: 1928
flawless print
Hal Pearl:
flawless organ
(the Biograph

DAY 81ST

Great Book: *Doc Destiny*, by Kim Dietch

———————————————————————

Report in precisely this date Chicago
shifted from position 2 to position 3. Relief
from the double onus felt immediately. Manifestations
undoubtedly real but not yet apparent. L.A. now ready
to suffer all the classical maledictions directed
at position 2. Good Luck Angels!
You're gonna need it.

82ND DAY, 282 DAYS OUT

"everything is irrelevant until you use it"
he said and from under his magnificent coat
produced an old encrusted corning ware coffee pot.
He ground it up into a fine brown powder and laid
it out in thin lines on a chunk of obsidian.
Snort he said!
They did.

An initial vague vision arose
in the terrain around them.
Then the shape of Brazil
with her characteristic amazonican hair and mouth
and the great nose of her sertoeinch formed
and a rasping coffee aggression seized them
and they were strapped to the stools
of a lunch counter continent wide and three inches high
and they were spinning around kicking and gasping
and they beat the counter like finceros
with the whips woven of their arms.

082—a reconstruction by Terry J and Ed D.

    He was in the Star Hotel on Madison. On his arm was the tattoo
"Born to Raise Hell." That was the sign (or marquee when he held it
up) they were looking for. They weren't actually looking for Him.
A sign can replace you. Roll up your sleeve!

84

Victoria and Jim
they headed southwest in a van
shaped like a bedpan

The driver was hunched over the steering wheel
slobbering methadrine*

and Victoria and Jim were feeling fine

* "the driver who drove them
was stiff with speed
he almost peed
as he flew over the underpass
about 30 ideas ago"

— gist of J.D.'s take

DAY 85

CANCELLED

SUNDAY 28 MARCH DAY 87
PASSION SUNDAY

MAYA ANDROMEDA MIRANDA MARGARET DORN
9:43 p. 87 W.

"No events in the past are required
that have no counterpart now."

200-inch Hale Reflector

I want to spring
a yellow bird
in the sun

———

J. D.

DAY 89, 276 DAYS OUT

"can we really suppose that physical processes
go on elsewhere as they do in our Neighborhood?"

DAY 90

the child and the mother are transported home
and in this transportation
there are certain antique tricks
like the internal combustion engine
plus of course the pneumatic tires
and the streets

DAY 91, UH, APRIL 1

The announcement today by the white house that it had
ordered Lieutenant Calle's immediate release came as no surprise—
the announcement an hour later, of the tandem release of Manson &
Girls and Sirhan came as likewise no surprise. But the "reasoning" that
all the defendants are victims of the same war came as a mild surprise,
indeed. This package decision is wise and will do much to restore the
functional sanity of our house.

So April says to June PST Pst pst
An June says
MAY be, may Be

DAY 92 — 273 DAYS COMING

(Day One of my personal count

The forty-second year following the Crash

The air is filled with snowe and sunnshyne

But it takes more of it now

Given over to self origination

A refreshing day, I did the routines outside

    like fingernsaps and gingersnaps

Presence received:
      Maya (Jennifer, 28 march early evening
      Real Chocolate Cake (J. & sister M.
      Fonetrak (Colchester, Valerie
      Postcard ("When the Lamp is shattered"
           MSS 85, photographed
           at British Museum, T. & V.
      Poem (On Edward Dorn's Birthday
             by Anne Waldman

APRIL TWO

Cable (from Gonville, containing the Keys

A Blizzard (Mother Nature

Sun (the Sun

A Lid of Green Plausible (L.W. Lyde,

Manchester, 1935

A New Skinny Jenny (Maya

93RD DAY SATERDAY 3 APRIL

Salute! Pony Express (1860)
the letter carrier's only vivid moment

Braintrak: 'My one and only Purpose in life
is to entertain my mind'

Mybody

The Sun is up as
the moon is downd
and no matter where
you think youre at
you can feel the sound

94TH DAY, PALM SUNDAY

Margaret O'Hare to Nuevo Djork

> There were several attempts to divine
> > what this meant
> there were, and still are
> > nine postures in the increment

Solution to riddle 94

There was (another) man named Ed
who used his head
to move his bedstead

95+270

"Wondering if I'm really not dead"
> > (from a typescript)

Question of the day:
> Did I ever finish *The Discovery of the Mind*

96TH DAY

fonetrak R. Caplan re Cycle 'I couldnt feel it'

Compound Thot

So he drunck his drunck
And she dranck her dranck
And they told each other
What they thanck

97TH DAY — 268 DAYS FOLLOW

unnerneath imformation

. . . so we put a cap on it!
we dont even *wanta* use it!
Where's it at?
Puerto Rico!
—the National (foodstore) Parking Lot

Information trak on Lincoln ave

There's some bad vibes
at Goldblatts

98 MAUNDY THURSDAY

> Your final statement will sound
> the same as your first
> except—it will be reversed

ALEXANDER HAMILTON'S PROGRESS REPT.

At 10:23a a short lady under a plastic hat and over heavy shoes holds a leash in her right fist. Down on the ground her little white dog wearing a red knit sweater pawed the ground wood in the cavity where our now metaphysical Elm tree stood. Suddenly, it was still, and humped, and ugly, and then a great turd fell from its asshole. It then straightened up and shook from snout to tail. The lady, kicked some of the chewed wood over the dirty wood. Following this responsibility they continued in the direction they were going, which was, of course, West.

2:37p   attempted teletrak to South Carolina
Unsuccessful

I've been thinking all day about how
I can improve my aůt lůk

And how I can affect my aůt kəm

7:40p   If more people waved goodbye
        on the phone
        they would save the world

**99 PAST
266 FUTURE**

Good Fri Mr. Pickard, of NewCastle on Tyne
reads his work Bryn Mawr at St.Louise, p.m.

Earlier, with Connie, Matty, Katherine and J
to the church of the Holy covenant to hear
Blind Jim Brewer
Play softly
on his acoustical guitar

DAY 100TH HOLY SATURDAY

EASTER SUNDAY

Parade: two protomen inside brown suits
throw their cases of poisoned
bubblegum in the back seat of their yaller
car with the footlong wire in the exact
center of the trunklid. They fasten their belts
and lock into the traffic

APRIL 13 JEFFERSON 1743

104TH, 14 APRIL

President assassinated 1865

O'Hare afternoon acid lounge

Creeley from North Carolina
unnerneath a knitted temple cap
moved in a white light trip
to the nearest bar

110TH DAY

Notre Dame 8p

So. Shore & So. end R.R., 151 E Randolf st. sta.
4:05p

The train goes down the center of the main street
Of Michigan City Indiana,
after that,
Nothing very important happens

111TH DAY CANCELLED, EVERYTHING UP IN SMOKE:

Glowing Glowing
Glowing Gone!

TWENTYTWO APRIL
ONE HUNDRED AND TWELVE

A scan for Chan—

Teletrak from deep S'west

Mescalito focused his perception & came on
Like Ike Turner with an Afterburner

Also, the newspaper today (the Sun Times,
if you will) says that in Southern
Illinois the following items were
found and seized 'from people in all
walks of life.'

TNT
Cocaine
Bazookas
Plastique
Heroin (a german item
Marijuana
Dynamite (a swedish item

1 2 3 4 5 6 7 all good children go to heaven
but not necessarily in that order

Sample conclusion: This State seems to be
druggy and explosive!

DAY 117

U.S. Grant, 1822

Cubs Park Montreal
Rained out

FRIDAY, APRIL 30

Death of the Wabash Cannon Ball (last run)
by Amtrak

Multitrak satisfaction transmission
      (a blip off the continua

    OBOY OBOY WE REALLY FEEL GOOD

        AND THE MORE WE RUN

     THE MORE WE ENJOY OUR FOOD

121ST DAY 1 MAY

    Good Morneeng, commrades

122ND DAY THIRD SUNDAY

Look, you've broken all the Rules
Now what do you want?

I want the game to begin.

Agane?
Again!
      Again!
         Again!

'Nowhere to throw away the garbage'
        (J.D.

8 MAY DAY 128

On May 8, 1927, a little more than two years before my birth, a beautiful white airplane, mounting a single 450 h.p. Lorraine-Dietrich engine, sat poised on the runway at Le Bourget airfield, six miles from Paris. That half of Paris was gathered at the airfield to witness the take off of L'Oiseau Blanc. The white bird—French-built by Levasseur—was going to be the first to cross the Atlantic the hard way—from east to west. At the controls was arch-hero Charles Eugéne Jules Marie Nungesser who had cheated death so often it was believed the Grim Reaper had quit trying. By his side the one-eyed François Coli who had navigated from Montparnasse to Timbuktu using a Woolworth compass.

At 5:20am the gleaming white airplane began to move down the wet runway, and after a long take-off roll rose cleanly into the air and headed for the coast. Just over five hours later a message was flashed to Paris that the airplane had been seen crossing the western side of Ireland and was headed into uncertain weather over the open sea. After that, silence, the white bird was never seen again. Bold men, far horizons!

129, MOTHER'S DAY

Dear Mother,

Just yesterday morning that half of Paris were on the strip to witness our take-off roll. It was a Very long one. I thot it would never end. But just at the end of it when we rose cleanly into the blue air our troubles began—François discovered in a moment of horror he had left his glass eye, the one he reads with, back in the Hotel Americaine. So much for navigation!

At first the Lorraine-Dietrich purred like it was the cousin of Lucifer himself. As we climbed the sun rose. We passed with ease through the thorns of morning. The coast lay like a questionmark beyond the liquid prop. There were no alternatives. François stared one last time with his socket into my eyes and I pulled the nose of the L'Oiseau Blanc straight up—we fixed our course at Vertical, forever—goodbye Mama,

Eugéne

Eugéne

10 MAY 130

Bystander: What's that you hold
aloft in your bony hand?

Dr.Flambo
yant: The skull of Modern man.

Bystander: What's the significance
of its index
What's the point
of its apex

Dr.Flambo
yant: Super,
super index
Sharp,
sharp apex!

WEDNESDAY 132

fonetrak T. Clark re Seattle (OK

THURSDAY 133

Cab at 8:30, NW Orient at 9:40

1.   Agents
    This 747 has fruit flies
    Take it back
    And bring us a fresh one

2.   Untidy
    You've got 707
    All over your apron!

FRIDAY 134

In the Lobby of the High Rise Dorm a Washington Girl
Plays Five Easy Pieces all Morning as the Swaying Fronds
of The Dark Green Hemlocks Tap & Brush the Windows
While, into the air rise Red plastic sofas filled with
helium and Salmon and Carrots and Lettuce and radishes and

152ND DAY JUNE

Number 1

    This set of greek chorus girls
    get it?
    is gonna do the Möbius Strip

2 JUNE

Lewis & Clark
reach the junction of the Missouri
and the Marias 1805. Quandary:
Which one was the Missouri?

162

Visited By

Bob McNealy an old friend from Idaho who lives
now above the Smucker's Religious Bookshop
208½ Main st. Champaign said he knew people
in the philosophy dept and I asked him if
he knew Tom Clark's Philosopher a rare member
of the tribe who had been blown there after
Oxford but he didn't so I put down this datatrak
in case he ever ran into him:

The dude is so brilliant in his knowledge
he takes the variegated form of stuttering
his head is the blown glass shape of the future

163RD DAY 202 DAYS FOLLOW

    When it's summer in Australia
    It's winter in Chinar
        *
Ideas are like
the vocabulary of the B R A I N
and they completely explain
some Dirty words

     —　—　—　—　—　—

At precisely 1600 I began to receive from Dr. Flamboyant

       the horn rings in the stage coach of my head
       Dr. Flamboyant on the horn
       "Hello, Flamboyant here
       I've been working on one of the
       3 GREAT BEENVILLE PARADOXES"
       Which one?
       "#1"
       State it, the tape's winding
       "Paradox 1 from Beanville:
          Nature abhors a vacuum
          But for Nature
          A vacuum's got nothing at all"
            —fade, crackle—

JUNE THIRTEEN SUNDAY CORPUS CHRISTI 164

A day Ruled by Rod Cameron

The god was there
as plain as anything
a saddle with stirrups
and the pommel is a cross
between a cobra and a goose
The Sunday Morning Western
is almost like
the Methodist Church
or the number thirteen backwards
on the door of our little room
which closed like a rolltop desk
and a smell which was a cross
between the barber shop and
the funeral parlor
and it was there we learned
organized thievery from the plate
and were entertained by the *minister's* wife
who was really into ping pong

DAY 165, 200 DAYS ON THE POLE

FLAG DAY

Fly the flag of your choice!

16 JUNE

Remember those bad vibes at Goldblatts?
Well, now they're on sale—2 for a quarta

You can get the rest of the year
for a dolla ninety-eight I hear

21 JUNE 172ND

Sun 72 degrees above the southern horizon (the highest

913 minutes of Day light (the longest

A light breeze from Wisconsin. Clear bite of air.
60 degrees by the lake
70 degrees in the house

173RD DAY — 192 FOLLOW

A possible apocrypha of Bean (Been
    (which reached me via Alien Signal Band 23)

        "His wrists were bound
        behind his back[1.]
        with diphthongs
        soaked in military secrets
        and held together [2.]
        by an array of green chicklets

1. This is technically impossible — a Bean has no
        front or back

2. I.e., of course, the Bean circuitry is "locked"
        along an array of green chicklets

174

Looking thru the final papers for my
Mythology of the American Far West
read "The best way I can describe Crazy Horse
     is 'a red Audie Murphy'."

That's possibly a chicago idea.
I'm not familiar with it.

From the illustrations in another paper
I notice there was a great resemblance
between Gertrude Stein
and Calamity Jane

The caption has noticed it too:

     Calamity Jane—
This most celebrated female was no rose

DAY 175: SCHOOL'S OUT

The hemp flourishes
beneath the generous fronds of the tree of the gods

     I came home light
     and ran my hands
     over the leaves of the ailanthus
     glandulosa glandulosa
     in the garden
     and the brazen scent
     of tropical Chicago
     is headed this way

FRIDAY 25 JUNE

Fonetrak Bob Hogg Ottawa
Fonetrak Mrs Bates not in

Late afternoon:

The lady with the blue straw hat
the White Spitz and the red coat on it
passed by the Stump at 4:4—the squarest
time in the world

      and I could tell by the look
        on her face, Alexander Hamilton,
     that every trace
       of the memory
       of our elm and its race
        had been withdrawn
       from her banks
   and I could tell by the meandering
     of the spitz that its
      —do we say urinary instinct
        or that premonitional Past
   a dog locates by pissing
    is objectless but not missing

DAY 177 + 188

Off to Canada
East thru the vacua

   Sign in Ohio: Prosecutors
                 will be
                 violated

27 JUNE SUNDAY

Warrant out D. Ellsberg
charged with Possession, Jenny drives
the Lake to the left

A clipping from The Cleveland Press for H. Brown

The Easterly sewage treatment plant
dumps five million tons
say it again
five million tons
of rawr shit
into Lake Erie every hour
on the hour
                    that's regularity
                    with a capital R

. . . now we're approaching Buffalo
on our way to the falls
to see if we can see if
some of it
comes over in the form of balls

         —   —   —   —   —   —

At the border Jenny Kid Maya and me =
              1 British subject
              3 American objects

28

There is a town in north ontario
in my mind I still need a place to go
none of my changes were there
yellow moon and the far flies
the stone farm house the blue window
Italian dinner Carleton University
the party Libby's Toronto grown grass
the multiple headed Victor Coleman
"two heads are better than one
when you pull the plant plunge
the roots in boiling water (this
piece of witchcraft is meant
to seal in the principle?

180TH

Bright warm day across the nastiest border going
South along Lac Champlain dreary structures
stuck around on handsome landscape and at night
we come to Montpelier
golden dome tavern inn
chimes in the diner, nervous boy with birthmark
on his neck
at the cash register
vermont accent
every time he answers the bell

181

Arrive W. Newbury at noon the last day but 1½
of this half
a straight ahead half
with no injuries and no time out
no matter how far out
and when we got here we were not done
so I left out some of what we got done

Fonetrak J.H. Prynne English Speaking Union
No message
On set at Grolier bookshop
slow cello over the books

Goodbye June 30 mature lady

Goodbye June 13 simple church lady

Goodbye May 28 forgotten lady with zappa in your auditorium

Goodbye May 15 Tom Raworth lady from Yaddo

Goodby April 1 with 274 days to go

JULY 19TH

Crossed into Canada
Jeremy puts the Coalmont card
in the Princeton machine

JULY 20TH

Have you been to Princeton?

oh yes but not since 1943.

Princeton BC?

oh I've been *there* quite recently

> composed w/ the aid
> of Ellen Tallman Vancouver

203RD DAY — 162 DAYS FOLLOW

> 37th anniversary
> of the slaying of J. Dillinger
> Biograph (22july 1934

On first reading *The Glacial Question, Unsolved*, again

> There are a legion of poets
> and like
> with any legion the work
> is fixed and secondary
> a ride in the desert
> spent days, one
> at a time
> the serial is in some ways
> perfect for a legion
>
> and of the poets prancing
> in the academy stock
> talking into the face of the clock
> only Prynne has the wit to compose
> The Pleistocene Rock!

DAY 205

At Kitselano Beach there is a tidal Tank
Where the women swim with caps on
They are pre-eminently Noradian
In their one piece costumes only

For their excellent health is built
Like the many windowed creatures
Who loaf around the bay a
Protein chain gang drawn from one Bank

And the Kid makes his felicitous trips
Over the grass and along the ledge
Where the People notice his delicate balance
While they check out the fact of his little Crank

DAY 216

Hotel de Haro
morning:

       I was trying to come up w/ an idea for a really uptight
population like the one under observation here. Sitting in the
restaurant last night I noticed that the chemistry of their food is in
some way selected to reflect what their minds are on: war and profit,
two particularly interlocking Hostilities. French Fried (encore)

DAY 225

morning on the street in Weaverville California
a lady with an asylum smile
all over her face
strides right up to me and shouts
Welcome to Oregon!

———————————————

at the fading of
the day's light
along the road behind Point Reyes
miles out of the redwood light
I didn't mention, we arrived
at the well lit dark walled
warmth of the Creeley's kitchen

DAY 226

Stinson — Bolinas

This Saturday night Tom Clark and I wrote the following non-fiction
books while talking about Ted Berrigan:

Things to do in Buffalo, by Tom Clark
and Edward Dorn, unpublished
139 pages (all blank

Things to do in Cleveland, by Tom Clark
and Edward Dorn
243 pages unpub. (all blank

Things to do in Philadelphia, by Edward Dorn
and Tom Clark, soon to appear, 395 pages
(Every one of which is blank

DAY 229

Nebraska!
what?
Motelville?
Nebraska!
yea!
the platte river?
yea!
by the way will you pass the platte?
which one?
The one with chopped
cottonwood topped
with right wingers.
and cheeze?
yes, cheeze, why not
oh I forgot!
well, what?
omaha!

oh, no, ma!
(HAW Haw haw

DAY 230

— Welcome to Pork Country —

Breakfast menu antephysics

(Ref Sllab — Been
the Question of the Egg
ie — which came first?
the bacon or the egg.

Chicago: she's sure no Queen
the poem on the occasion of our Return

tonight we arrived again in Chicago
Jeremy, Jenny, Kid and Maya
        and (eye = Egyptian)
                the sign
    and
    pronounced *Horus*

Countessa, Countessa, we're back!
roll out the dirty sets arrange the scenes
we're thru adjurnying
we've *Been* so close to Beans

So close dear Lady, dreary Lady
with the humidity in your hair
our grass has grown to six feet.
and yes I did hear
from a newspaper

where was it, Montana
where was it, Oregon

Of the lady
Who threw her one and only body
From the ninetyeth floor
of the Alfred Hitchcock Building

a structure so large
from the inside
a christening, so to speak

and other moments of topical sin
like they happened in Berlin

But sometimes I think
Our homegrown grass was made
By the Quartermaster
At the Charge of the Light Brigade

(entered on Day 230
conceived on Day 257
Question which came first
the Day or the Conception?)

DAY 233

Wiping up shit is the beginning of an organic trip. Yet to some types it might appear to be the End DE DA Do DA the tyranny of Print! Pass the Acid, Knucklehead!

THE SLOTKOWSKI SAUSAGE COMPANY TELLS US IT'S

September 1st

Have you ever noticed this important date
gets drowned out by that fuckoff Labor Day
already all those people talking about how
theyre gonna get killed

245TH DAY

Joan Blackburn's note

(we lowered him down with a chain
 and at every link we called his name

EVENING 246

quatrain
If, when I light up a dude
And turn on I get high,
These two plants I'm standing by
Know the resin why

*   *   *

Otis Rush at A's Revisited
Stood up by some, Sat down by some

4 SEPTEMBER

    Senator Hickenlooper died in his sleep

Speaking of onanism, the German in the shop
across Sheffield confided in me that if there
was *One Thing* he wouldnt do it was kissing
someone elses ass.

Full moon out the Kid's window toward Indiana
Ohhh
the barking cars, the Blakeing of the dogs
Joan Blackburn's note on my mind
One summer evening in 1951
    I saw Dane Clarke
    in a buick convertible coupe
    at the corner of Ah yes & Yum Yum
    in Downtown Wholly wood

Saturday. Hot enough. Humidity amusing
Jenny soloed for the first time today
The Amelia E. of Peugots

SUNDAY

woke up this morning
with the Allman bros in the tape

    2:45 the first drops of rain with phonetrak
Oak Park lightning cracking the wire A great
Landstorm Driveth its car toward the lake.
Yellow and greyblue sky spectrum through
the ailanthus
            A really Outasight rainbow
in the east at sunset.

  War will not make our people happy.
  Happy? an insignificant word.
  I wear this crown but it does not
             make me *happy*
  (later, after 5 seconds deliberation:
  You must be happy prince
  Now you have everything
  Everything? No there is one thing I havent had
  an insignificant thing perhaps
  but I havent had it.

    from soundtrak of *Pharoah's Women*,
    Rome, 1961, John Drew Barrymore as
    the Pretender, Inspired!
    Linda Cristal, Good God!
    in which the Nubian Archers
    really fuck with
    the Assyrian Horsemen

LABOR DAY THE 6TH

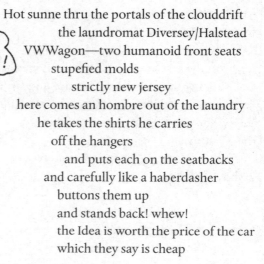

Hot sunne thru the portals of the clouddrift
the laundromat Diversey/Halstead
VWWagon—two humanoid front seats
stupefied molds
strictly new jersey
here comes an hombre out of the laundry
he takes the shirts he carries
off the hangers
and puts each on the seatbacks
and carefully like a haberdasher
buttons them up
and stands back! whew!
the Idea is worth the price of the car
which they say is cheap

Reading from the epilogue—In Hebrew
Religion—and in Hebrew religion alone—
the ancient bond between man and nature
was destroyed. p. 343 Frankfort

Weather rept — Hot
The sweet children sleep in sweat

SEPTEMBER 7 TUESDAY
250TH DAY — 115 DAYS FOLLOW

LESS NING*
    attributed to the drain of Labor Day

     (you Labor people *Really* oughta think
     about How Who is so interested in getting
     you on the road in a day like yesterday
     with no thing in mind but the direct
     reduction of your numbers—along with say
     whats being laid out on the boards now
     about the future of your genes)

* a condition which often follows MOR NING

WODENSDAY 8 SEPTEMBER

Chicago: the class arrangements

upper   Where the rich live is dirty
middle Where the next live is filthy
lower   Where the rest live is septic

      DRIVE IT OR LEAVE IT

      When the head was cut off
        a foot   appeared

SEPTEMBER 9TH
ADMISSION DAY (CALIFORNIA

What will California Admit?

1. The fartherest out
2. The most untogetherest fault
3. The most insatiable snout
4. (to be chosen by the reader
   a. th'abruptest halt
   b. the funkiest gestalt

UHHUH FRIDAY

Insight: James Taylor the housewifes special
      uh, (lovely rather than terrific

Panatlantic Monthly: The great Rahssin Novelist
                   and butterfly Vladimir N. says
                   he likes a good conversationalist
                   Con verse sensationalist, Get it?

Discovery: Across the face of the Moon
        are perfectly raised
        the letters

             T U M S

Observation: The migrations of the Monarchs
           darkened the sky
           and saddened the clerks

Early Transplant Revealed:

In what he described as the first "macro transplant" i.e., a whole body, Mr. Ziegler said today that the president received the complete physique of Ed Sullivan in September of 1921 at an undisclosed location in Southern California, and that Sullivan had been since that time until the tape ran out a purely media projection, whereas the president had suffered repeatedly from malfunctions due to what was as rare then as it is common now: the successful transfer of second-rate organs.

SATURDAY DAY 254

I aint gonna work no more
An I'll might never work agin
(Blind Jimmy Brewer alive alive

Full house. Couldnt get very close
Sat on the floor some stood up some
Cola Koka. Easy.

Began *The Elements of Theology*, Proclus
When I got home

DAY 255

Hudson discovered the Rio, 1609

Meanwhile the seeds of the ailanthus have
dried to a bright earth

Down from the tree of God,
Bombyx Cynthia, your hot seed
is going to fall
the silkworm has gone home

    Heaven is battening the hatches down
        closing the shutters on the summer mind
      even as summer begins to stutter
            hanging out the sign

      MANY EMPTY ROOMS
      BUT NO VACANCIES

13 MONDAY

Attica bombed

    Like Warsaw?

This is not a purely current event

Take heed
all y^{e} of no head
an stick out yr neck instead

TUESDAY SEPT 14

Did I hear that right Sun-Times?
All the hostages were ventilated by the gunships?
And the Inmates had dressedem up for the event?
Send for the Doctor!

Meeting, Rm P1

The "P" stands for portable and 1 of course stands for itself. There are several of them, sown by Helicopters 1, 2, 3. P.1. I had a class in here last term. All the seats turned around now, facing . . . — East. They used to face south. I wonder how they feel with this new direction, the 1st of the directions, I suppose, by the pre-ordination of its marking. There was a first time he came up and there will be a last time he goes down. Of course, we all know He doesn't move at all! This meeting is not about the moments of death and origination. It is about parking spaces, rooms without windows, and credit load. And yet it might be anyway about the original and the terminal that could *be* Portable numero uno, dos, tres. What the helicopters bringeth they also taketh away.

WEDNESDAY 258

In the news with an opinion:

   The Illinois Department of Correction
(that kind of inquisition is still
 heavier than punishment

259

"I dont see how I could have done any differently"
                    Gov. Rockefeller

(Impressive. But Chicago still has
 the coldest millionaires in the biz.
 Theyre *really* into Racetraks

MORNING TWO SIX OH!

What is the feeling
you get from smiling
morning noon and night?

For answer see Later in the Day

        Two Chicago Quatrains

A woman warm from nightrest
under the chill of the first light
the infants milk sweet mouth
on the river of her breast

(and across the street for Edward Hopper

The flat morning light on
the glass plate of the Boys club
subliminal barberpole to the left node
a black man in the spectoral inside

Later in the day: the feeling you get
                   from smiling morning
                   noon and night is

                Oa   Oa

Still later about 12 after we lit the fire
an olde constabularial knock comes on the door
a special D, a great relief

> Donald Hall
> 1971 N. University ave
> A.A. Michigan 48104

Edward Dorn
911 W. Diversey Pkwy
Chicago 60614

Dear Ed,
> My social Security number is 124-22-5238.

> > See you soon,
> > > Don

261ST DAY SATURDAY 18 SEPTEMBER

Unseasonably cool tonight.
Sat for a while in front of the
teletrak. Got rewarded with—

> . . . Do the one thing and yer livin
> Do the other
> And you may be walkin around
> But yer as dead as
> > a Beaver Hat

> > J. Wayne

And Im sorry but I dont have a clue
as to where that advice applied

Washingtons Farewell Address 1796

MONDAY 20 SEPT.

ART

3 ESCAPE FROM STATEVILLE
WITH ART EXHIBIT VISITORS

SEPTEMBER 21

The Sunne stabilized about 9 on this bright morning
Amtrak the Ann Arbor train at Union Sta
I acquire a copy of the New York Times from which
I gleaned 1 statistic:

> The human head is six inches wide
> therefore in the new prisons
> the bars are 5½ inches apart

and from the Sun-Times one social recollection

> You know something I'll always remember
> about football—I'll always remember
> the Quarterbacks. I hated them all.
> They were all the same. They came from

wealthy families and had birthday
parties when they were kids

Alex Karras

DAY 265 — ONE YARD TO GO

At 8:45a I rode with Donald Hall and a friend of his to the Pioneer
high school in ann arbor. The school laid a yellow brick 1949 vision
in my mind. Immediately inside the doors I saw the trophy case full
of engraved cups and spreading from both sides of my head in a
perspective to infinity the vertical lines of the lockers. The arrogant
presumption of the smell of 1949 came into my nostrils. My knees
shook and my forehead throbbed and a sharp weakening of the muscle
fibre spread throughout my body. This vast extortion passed lasted
10 seconds and left behind it a frothing mouth European guard dog
patrolling ceaselessly the fences of my stomach. Was that the Principle?
The effect leaned casually back and put its feet on my face which it
assumed was a footstool. Make yourself at home. Apparently, nothing
has changed. The boys and girls of the 10th and 11th grades. The
girls smile. They smile at me and the guard dog yelps. I can't even wave
goodbye to it. The lady with the permanent who is their teacher,
and who was my teacher many times, asks them, prompts them, to
respond more. One girl breathes "shit" so you can hear it, the girls
around her giggle and pop their Bubble gum. I wish I had some.

Amtrak cuts along a beautiful winding river west of Ann Arbor.
The hills are covered with dark oak. In the bottoms the sumac is burnt
red. The corn is brown, brown and green linger in the yellow of the
woodlands along the horizon. The train departed at 5pm. Don and
another Ann Arbor friend stood about the platform with me waiting
for the train to arrive. Jackson, Olivette, Ford M. Ford. Try to sleep in

the definition of the railroad trak. Exhaustion. The pop of 9th grade bubble gum lingers in my ear. And involuntary statements like "your hair's in the road." I begin to wander. In my empty head the creatures go forth starting and stopping. The mice in the future of the empty house. Battle Creek is full of big dusty empty ornate buildings of the future. Old and empty. White houses border the trak. I wander into that which has not come. Kalamazoos a russian town, maker of stoves. Union Station is full of bald headed pedestrians radiating their dislocation as they burn their hamburger fuel. I walk to the el and stand in the winde. Home at last. Jennifer greets me with "To be totally positive is to be immortal."

DAY 267

6:40p: the LeRoy Lucas fonetrak

DAY 269

Note to Day 200, or, 69 days later and
"miraculously" 96 days
out

Evel Knievel is a piece of Honky shit but there's one line in there after the old bronc buster (Rod Cameron) took his Last Fall and the guys carrying him off the set say to the owner entrepreneur — *"He's dead"* and the ent. says in a loud whisper — *Giteem outa here!*

as we say goodbye to Kid and Mrs Jaunius
as we go out thru the glass front door
as we go down the green front steps
I check out the lady with the funny hat
and the little white dog
there is an exotic rhythm theyve got. Now that's the third or fourth time theyve lingered over the consequences of Alexander Hamilton. When I first chose that image from the conveyor belt, *almost*, at random little did I expect that these two would be constantly returned to it and that the final abstraction should be indistinguishable, from my empiric Porch, from the fact, old now, of the tree itself. Registering from the present the ultimate thing 69 days back there is the Film in full branch. The stump is a middle place now, the closest fact — the dog lifts his leg to pee where the tree and later the stump, Was or does the lady determine the stop there — Whose inflexible habit is it? What else would the answer to that question answer?

DAY 270

at the lyric "the sky is blue"
the sensitive Maya
shed a tear

DAY 271

letter to Ted Berrigan re N.E.U.

8:34p fonetrak Brakhage from Palmer House:
   He tells me that in Pittsburgh he shot a Morgue flick. The corpse is wheeled in with a tag tied to the toe. Which toe? The big toe.
   OK. On the tag is stenciled Heaven, Hell, or Whatever stops in between your big toe is bound for. C.O.D.? He didn't know.

DAY 272

Kid cut his head — fall off chair onto wooden block blue room

1:55a Suddenly everything is beautifully sensible. Yesterday Maya was 6 months old. Kid played in the mud all afternoon and poured water on Jennifer's feet, laughing at the word toe, which he knows. The plants are flowering at last — 8 or 9 ft. high. I'd worried we had pushed our luck leaving them this long but couldn't cut them early because of that thing Jenny had said — "if you don't let them flower, if you don't let them do what they they're about why should they satisfy your expectations about their chemical properties."

11:30 Stan Brakhage for Breakfast. It sticks to your ribs)

DAY 274

King Carole

Carole King is the Greatest woman
I don't know alive

7:30p fonetrak Mother — Hello Mom this is Ed — Hi — when
the phone rang I knew it was you

DAY 276

About 6:am I went into Maya's room. On the way out I caught the
little toe of my right foot on a chair which was pressed to the floor
by a portable T.V. Pain heavy like the cannonading of stump. Cold
water no relief. The stupidity of enclosed darkness

DAY 277

Succotash Day! aleph-zero

---

the set of the set of natural numbers

(the arrival of J.D. North, author of *The Measure
 of the Universe*, Clarendon Press

       saying
"let you entertain as many continua as you (. . .

a Clue to the Fastest:
         chronon would be
         the Time for light
         to traverse the hodon

DAY 278

Denis O'Brien's Plotinus rundown (via AIRTRAK
On what evils are and where they come from
and *On the descent of soul into bodies*
         and Boethius

   also
my Red hot toe

       ALSO

     my red hot toe

DAY 280

A. Waldman 955
Union Station
trak 391!
or 2

anacharsis clootz Triumverate

Cantbustems on his elbows
Lees on his knees
Levistrauss on his shoulders
                    like a muse

DAY 282

The best way to prevent drug abuse is to remove them from the authorities.
                                        Paul's letta dated / 6th Oct.

the Giantess O'hare 11:45 United AIRSPACE to New York City

A HEAD SPACE sequence on her poems
Gloryosky zero
   is in front of
sputnik one

DAY 285 — COLUMBUS DAY

My left little toe is still Big

There's still time to order your
Curtis Heavy Duty Plexiglass Star Finder
from Professor Curtis, 127 Oak Terrace,
Lake Bluff, 60044

DAY 292

Farfar — father's father
Farmor — father's mother
Morfar — mother's father
Mormor — mother's mother

DAY 293

2am — went to the lab with H. Bialy to have a look at an amber dish
of cancer cells. The light came through like the surface of the sun

DAY 294 — 3AM

Short history

Having missed a shot at the past I turned his attention to, and became expert in, the absolute new — That which is untarnished by conception.

DAY 298 — VETERAN'S DAY (IN DISTRICT OF COLUMBIA AND SOME STATES)

Some shit closed

DAY 313

Toilet Training
Suppository:
a tory supposition

DAY 323

arcola group
arrives 9:15p Big H Station
        Illinois Central

Specimen waiting for the train to come in from New O. are still real at this date — they bear marks of space on them. They move around the super hot waiting room checking everybody out, they are still curious. They are a variety like in a garden (spacial arrangement) no plastic molds (time). Bus and train travelers now by definition freaks.

Back to 6pm: Victoria and Jim arrive brought up from Eastern Kansas by John and Margaret. Datsun rush.

DAY 324

AM   the Museum of Science and Industry

PM   the observatory on the 94th floor of John Hancock

DAY 336

Lv 9:00a Flight #141 cleveland
Arr chi 9:14a

Cab report ohare to Diversey
        Kent was under a thick blanket of snow
        110 – 20 persons at reading. More interestingly, a scene in which
50 persons at 3:30 attended a questioning session:
        Sample questions — What was Blk Mtn like?
                        — What is the practical application of proj. verse?
        Party at night. 30 persons present.
        Rolling Rock beer by case
        the whole scene felt like under a massive
        infection of thorazine — pulled out joint
        and whole room bug-eyed — dope starved.
        the cosmic intelligence shld send Kent
        some help this morning, if there's anything to spare.

Landing in chicago 2 long haired 27 yr. old types 30000 ft. of pipe at
42.50 etc take seat for 3 spread out and talk business

DAY 341

15 degrees per hour

The earth is a darkened sphere lighted on one side by the sun. In the
Northern hemisphere the length of day and height of the sun above
the horizon of noon increase from the first day of winter. I prefer,
because of this, the first day of winter to the first day of summer

DAY 355

tooth — Rock thru window

DAY 358

Margaret O'Hare 12:06 AM

Dentist

DAY 362

Ted Berrigan & Alice arrive

DECEMBER CASH ACCOUNT

AT KU

Kansan Staff Photo by DAV

"It's like after thinking your brain is a sponge and then waking up one day to find that it's a big hangar. It's filled with airplanes and you learn to fly those airplanes."

299

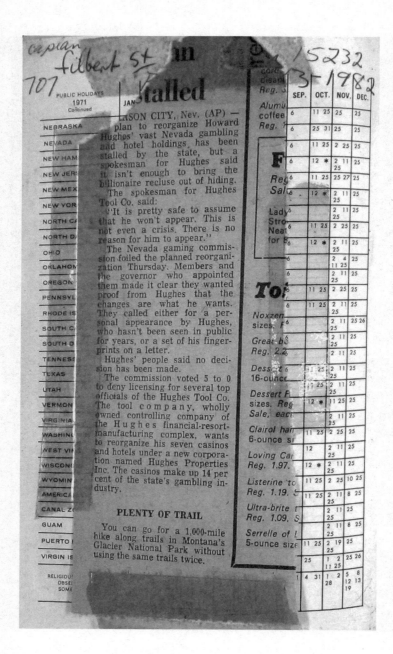

301

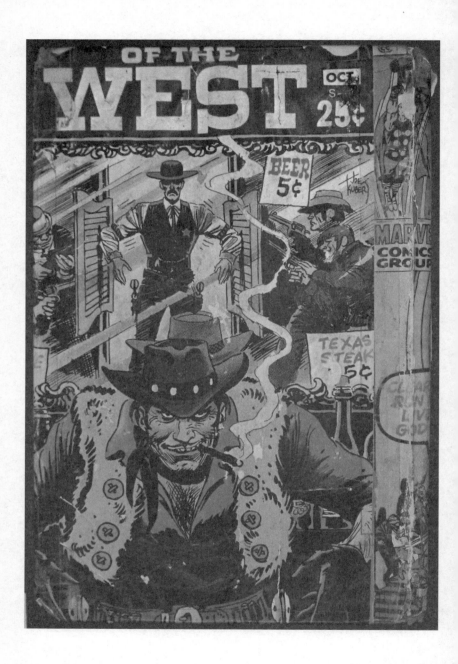

THE THEATER OF MONEY
(1971)

These pieces may be preformed
in high schools free

In all other places the fee
is 1,000.00 each, cash, up front.

THEATER OF MONEY #1

(a small entertainment for Paul Dorn
    on his birthday

    You can tell where you were
by going outside.
    When you return
    You can tell where you were
from going back in

                    Woodstock 60098

So take a seat. You better check this one out.

NOW PLAYING AT THE PANTHEON THEATRE

*****COCAINE GREEN*****

STARRING—G. Washington, as the Symbol
            i.e., Worthless

    with—T. Jefferson, as the company queer
        —A. Lincoln, as the man from Nowhere
                who takes the blame for Everything
        —A. Hamilton, as the bag man
        —A. Jackson, as his bigger brother
        —U.S. Grant, as "Where it's at"
        —And Introducing

            Dr. Benjamin Franklin Zeus
                as   the   hip   recluse

Drawn curtain:

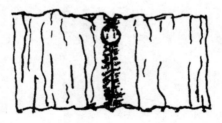

The green curtain is held together by an enormous yellow plastic
zipper bright luminescent green ring at top. A blonde girl dressed in
a long scarlet velvet gown walks on casually and with a hooked pole
pulls the zipper open

THEATER OF MONEY #2

Set: Beneath the El at Diversey

I, walking across the street, placed one thin dime in the slot. The machine gladly swallowed the national coin. Gulp. Thank you! I looked in his pocket for more and apologized. I offered it this torn stub from the Biograph:

> #s 120576 &
>
> @ 1^{25}
>
> 120577

> WINGS, William Wellman 1928
> Buddy Rodgers   Richard Arlen
> Clara Bow (wow)   Jobyna Ralston
> 5 fabulous minutes of Gary Cooper
> EATING A CHOCOLATE BAR

The machine smiled and said
1917 is 1971 spelled backward
What do you mean by that, machine, I enquired
!GNIHTON! you got your dimes worth,
Stop *pullin* on me!

THEATER OF MONEY #3

RED LIGHT

Location: Rush and Oak, the leash number

Dear Ann Landers,
       My dog has died: how can I recycle him?
           Signed) J.H. Prynne

Dear J.H.,
       Have you tried the Gerber baby food co.?
           Signed) Ann

GREEN LIGHT

THE TELETRAK

a written work

Players: The sender
          Working crowd in busy teletrak office
Set: Western Union teletrak Branch Office, say Bisbee, Arizona
1 *Scenery*: A blank teletrak form 9' x 12'

    curtain up

Action: man comes on singing and tap dancing

    "whatch gona do when you get" etc.

    and begins to write on form

to George Kimball
   1212 Phoenix St
   Rolling Stone Mass

        I don't owe co
        Caine a fucking thang!

            signed, I

He then unfurls a large bandana replica
of a 100 dollar bill and blows his nose.

    curtain down

IN DEFENSE OF PURE SENSATION

*a spoken &
orchestrated
work for 1 mass
and 2 persons*

set: Any large city.

time: After sunset toward the end of any war.

action: Uncountable parties are in full swing behind uncountable broken windows. Uncountable people turnon, guzzle, fornicate, vomit, laugh, whisper, shout and piss where they stand or sit or recline. Above the tumult a chorus can be heard chanting as from a great distance:

EINGANG, AUSGANG, EINGANG, AUSGANG

Ground sound: a Montgomery Ward tuba and drum ensemble, or a good Blasmusik group.

The scene has a duration of 20 minutes or so, not the realistic 5 hours. Gradients of The Light will come on over the span of time until the Sunne appears. All sound diminisheth as The Light increaseth.

When the full circumference of the Sunne appears, 2 persons remain on dressed in impeccable denim replicas of J.C. Penny brown pin striped suits. On their heads are summer stetsons. Their stilts are disguised as boots. The spurs are fashioned as dragons. In their right hands they each carry a small megaphone through which they speak.

1st speaker — . . . then you *do* know his work?

2nd speaker —No, not really (to the right

not really (to the left

—only the famous couplet

which begins his Great lost

Salute to the Coprophiles:

"The tongue takes such pleasure

with the problem of peanut butter."

SLOW CURTAIN TO CHINA

TRANSLATIONS WITH
GORDON BROTHERSTON
(1971–1975)

YOU HAVE TO LOOK AT ME

Look at me sleeping tide the most ancient among the protecting forces
look at me knocking with a rag door-knocker on the still plateau
see how I call you among crazy triremes
that split open reefs of lamp and pearl
how I pursue you wake of white
high wall of smiles
that eyes made for the invisible do not discover,
but my sight, lit like a room at midnight
feels a way to where you are.

Marco Antonio Montes de Oca

ANOTHER ANNIVERSARY OF SUMMER

You keep sailing-boats in small pockets of water
the sighing of maidens in the harp's seine moves you
you return to their place the emeralds of the landscape
and make straight the grim seal of my birth
you put me into that sharp moment carved on the tree
and take me away from the hours of glass, sheer emptiness
and the harlequin windows of the great streets

You're a farmer of resins which hold nests
you excite those winds
that keep the cloth horns of the jaranda erect
and with bandanas puckered with anguish
you plant in the garden the solitary white rose

Marco Antonio Montes de Oca

TRILCE: XX

Set into the jamb rich armoured
with ideal stone. Then slightly
I can bring the 1 to 1 so not to fall.

That man in the mustache. Sun,
ironbound his simple wheel, fifth and perfect,
and from the trouble in heaven
argument of trouserbuttons,
                                open.
argument that scolds vertical subordinate A.
The legal waste. The pleasing idiocy.

But I suffer. Suffer over there. Suffer over here.

Over here I am drooling, I am
a fair person, when
the man william the secondary
pushes ahead and sweats buckets
of happiness, shining his three-year-old
daughter's shoes.

The beard jerks up and rubs one side
the girl meanwhile puts her index finger
on her tongue which begins to decipher
the codes of codes of the codes
and anoints the other shoe, secretly,
with a little spit and dirt
                        but with a little,
                                no mor
                                    .e.

César Vallejo

THE MAKING OF THE UINAL

THE FIRST MOVEMENT OF TIME AT THE EASTERN HORIZON
and THE ENUMERATION OF THE WORLD
according to the first sage, Merchise-Napuctun,
the first prophet, the first priest:

    This is the serial
in which the uinal was realized
before the world was.

    He started up
from his inherent motion alone.
His mother's mother
and her mother
his mother's sister
and his sister-in-law
they all said
What shall we say when we see man on the road?

    These are the words they spoke
as they moved along where no man was.

When they arrived in the east
they began to say
Who has been here? These are footprints.
Get the rhythm of his step.

    So said the Lady of the World
and the father Ds. measured his step.

This is why the count by footstep
of the whole world
xoc lah cab oc
was called lahca oc 12 Oc
This was the order born through
13 Oc when the one foot joined its counter-print
to make the moment of the eastern horizon.

   Then he spoke its name
when the day had no name
as he moved along with his mother's mother
and her mother,
his mother's sister
and his sister-in-law.

   The uinal born, the day so named
the sky and earth,
the stairway   of water earth stone and wood,
the things of sea and earth realized.

1 Chuen · the day
he rose to be a day-ity and made the sky and earth.

2 Eb he made the first stairway. It ebbs
from heaven's heart, the heart of water
before there was earth stone and wood.

3 Ben the day for making everything
all there is, the things of the air
of the sea, of the earth.

4 Ix he fixed the tilt of the sky & earth.

5 Men he made everything.

6 Cib he made the number 1 candle,
and there was light in the absence of sun and moon.

7 Caban honey was conceived
when we had not a caban.

8 Etznab his hands and feet were set
he sorted minutiae on the ground.

9 Cauac the first deliberation of hell.

10 Ahau evil men were assigned to hell
out of respect for Dios
that they need not be noticed.

11 Imix he construed stone and wood
he did this within the face of the day.

12 Ik occurred the first breath
it was named Ik because there was no death in it.

13 Akbal he poured the water on the ground
This he worked into man.

1 Kan he canned the first anger
because of the evil he had created.

2 Chicchan he uncovered the evil he saw within the town.

3 Cimi  he invented death
as it happened the father Ds. invented the first death.

*

5 Lamat he invented the seven great seas

6 Muluc came deluge
and the submersion of everything before the dawning.
Then the father Ds. invented the word
when there was no word in heaven
when there was neither stone nor wood.

     Then the 20 deities came to consider
themselves in summation, and said
Thirteen + seven = one.
     So said the uinal
when the word came in
when there had been no word.
And this led to the question by the day Ahau , ruler,
Why the meaning of the word was
not opened to them, so that they could declare themselves.
Then they went to heaven's heart and joined hands.

THE AZTEC PRIESTS' REPLY

What we say here is for its own reason
beyond response and against our future.

Our revered lords, sirs, dear ones,
take rest from the toil of the road,
you are now in your house and in your nature.
Here we are before you, subjected,
in the mirror of yourselves.
Our sovereign here has let you come
you have come to rule
as you must in your own place.

Where is it you come from
how is it that your gods have been scattered
from their municipal centers?
Out of the clouds, out of the mist
out of ocean's midst you have appeared.
The Omneity takes form in you
in your eye, in your ear, in your lips.
So, as we stand here,
we see, we address,
the one through whom everything lives,
the night   the winde
whose representatives you are.

And we have felt the breath
and the word of our lord the Omneity,
which you have brought with you.
The speaker of the world sent you because of us.
Here we are, amazed by this.
You brought his book with you, his script
heaven's word, the word of god.

And now what. How is it,
what are we supposed to say
what shall we present to your ears?

Can it be said we are anything at all?
We are small subjects
we are just dirt
no good
pressed, reduced to want
furthermore our sovereign here
mistook us consistently
and has cast us into a corner

But we refute the logo of the Omneity

we are down to our skulls in this
and we fall over into the river below
Anger and wrath
will be attached to our behaviour
Maybe this is our moment, perhaps this is ruin
in any case, we shall be dispirited
where do we go from here
in our subjection
reduced, mortalized
Cut us loose
because the gods have died
But you don't have to feel any of this

Our dear lords
we share some of all this
the basket stands partly open
before this man

You say
that we don't know
the Omneity, of heaven and earth
you say that our gods are not original
That's news to us
and it drives us crazy
it's a shock and a scandal
for our ancestors came to earth
and they spoke quite differently
they gave the law to us
and they believed
they served and they taught
honour among gods
they taught the whole service
that's why we eat earth before them
that's why we draw our blood
that's why we drop copal
and that's why we kill the living
They were the Lifelord
and they became our only subject
All these matters were settled in the Nightplace
They gave us our sustenance
and supper and our breakfast
all things to drink and eat
maize, beans, amaranth, chia
and for our prayers we received
Rain & Water
on which the earth thrives
They are the rich ones
and they have more than simply what it takes
they are the ones with the stuff
all ways and all means, forever
the greenness of growth.

Where and How: in Tlalocan
hunger is not their experience
nor sickness and not poverty
They have given us the inner manliness
kingly valor
and the acquisition of the hunt
the insignia of the lip
the knotting of the manta
the manta itself
the flower
tobacco
turquoise
the Quetzalplume
and the godshit you call gold

Can you imagine how long
this message has been expected?
Do you know
When the emplacement of Tula was,
of Uapalcalco
of Xuchatlappan
and of Tamoanchan
what about the dwelling of the night
when in Teotihuacan?
They were the world makers
who founded the mat of power
the seat of rule
to this people they gave authority
and entity along with their honourableness
And should we now destroy the old law
the Chichimeca law
the Tolteca law
the Coluaca law
the Tepaneca law

on which the heart of being flows
from which we animate ourselves
through which we pass to adulthood
from which flows our cosmology
and the manner of our prayer?

Oooh! Señores Nuestros
do nothing,
don't do anything to your population
it can only bring more ruin
it can only bring more ruin to the old ones
our elders, from whom man and woman have grown

Let us not
anger the gods
let us not invite their hunger
do not unsettle this population
why should we agitate them
with what we say amongst ourselves
If you want peace
don't force the people
to see that we are put aside.

Let's think about this
At heart, there is no satisfaction for us
We don't believe, nor do we mock
we may offend you
for here stand
the citizens
the officials
the chiefs
the trustees and rulers of this entire world

It is enough that we have done penance
that we are ruined
that we are forbidden and stripped of power
To remain here is to be imprisoned
Make of us
the thing that most suits you
This is all we have to reply,
Señores.

A MEXICO SCRAPBOOK
(1972)

for Kidd and Maya

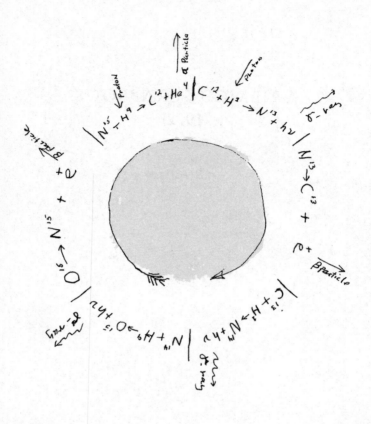

C. Weizsäcker

H. Bethe

330

VALLADOLID TO QUINTANA ROO

There ain't
no tickets from Valladolid

the pesos pass on the spot
and they take you from the station
just to show you what they got

and I didn't know it was true
until the kid shit in my left shoe
and then turned it over
on my one and only shirt

The ticket seller has Sunday off. We hang around the station waiting for the autobus to Puerto Juarez. The old professional turns around in her axis of practical infirmity so that her money eye, a patch of impacted tissue, comes about like the extended turn and quick flash of a lighthouse signal. She has gone and come a half dozen times. Each time I give her a coin she goes to the street and returns to stand in front of me where she slowly . . .

LOS TILOS

The burnt musk of the Capricornes
up from the hot dust in the lane
outside the gates of the Hotel
Tehuantepec

The sharp lime of the crushed leaves
in the patio

My long black stocking in which I
Travel, I notice as I put them on
for the journey to Oaxaca today,
still smell pleasant with the tick powder
the guide gave me at Cobá

COLECCION DE
ANATOMIA Y
ZOOLOGIA

- Cuernavaca 14 feb '72

A POEM ON ENTERING CUERNAVACA

The salt is drying the skin between my thumb and Index finger
the dry sun has sunk not into the Barranca
what foolishness!
as if in the globe of the prescriptive mind
a word could beckon
any matter whatsoever
and anyway, the letters we mailed when we got here
have got somehow, to go thru the pesos of many minds
and fingers between here and their destinations. that's about
weight and ability in that order
after the 19th C. "let us weigh our minds," (no kidding)
and I make a present to the language of "let us Test
the ability of our fingers

of course, if you call the dog
you get the dog / but
thats another "matter"
he came because his mind
is essentially the same as our own
AALLLLL that response remains internal

So if you don't like the dog
when he comes
you shld change not your dog
but your compulsions

Thus, in this wise land the dog
is separated from the disruptive conjunction
by an r or two

A line of jewels shines with staggering brilliance
high on the western mountain
and believe it
They'd shine like that at this altitude
most everywhere, thru the foolish air.

I must remember to keep what I merely think
to myself, trial expression
is not received well in this sector of the language
and I can respect that narrow sense
through all the annoyance it causes me

Because I am a dog here and the salt
dries on my pads
as I run toward a sense
unaided Here by who I am
a state my rational perspective tells me
is an experience I Need
but which the conjunctive condition
of my reality feels
to be absurd inDeed.

I know you follow me. The Salt
is the mineral
you use to complete the *tequila chain*
or lime
if that's your market claim
in this Liquored society
where the anglo's accent
lingers like a liquid sign
along the row of smoked oysters from Japan
and the skin of the speaker is
a pinkish brown with proud years
spent
almost in a penthouse somewhere
almost north of Anywhere —

Dont mistake it
We all, we all do
we shure do

          and we are shocked
at the very same time we are not shocked
by the lines in the face that tells that story

and the professional decadence is ok.
We fought all their inconsequential and silly wars
right along side of them. Psychological Participation
was that wear & tear
we wished them, "whoever They were"
the Best of Luck —
Back in Sixty Five.*
& We went all the way to the Horizons of the Mind
during the really bright shit of '68

and when the salt dried
on the flexible plains of our hands
which is between the Pointing finger & the thumb

BACK THERE

as if you were hitching to Nowhere
That   was   *OK*

(where's Johnny Winter by the way?)

because drink has always been eating
like a way to get dead
or next to the dead
by celebrating a funeral —
what the sleeping call a *wake*

        and like
the Tolerance for *all* that is an Endless mistake.

* that's when I wrote my Indian Book

or, how to drink yourself
Under a Volcano
       which I'm told is
18 kilometers away — do you hear that
you four hundred gods of Pulque alone
Come on fantasize with me
do you hear that you four hundred
       Gods.

     (how do you feel by the way
       being kept like cracked
         pots)

Cuernavaca Cuernavaca you lie
you lie on a plain lower than Denver
at a latitude you shld be ashamed of.
Your winters are the envy of affluent chicagoans
and your name is mentioned
in all the suburbs of the fucking world

OLD NEW YORKERS REALLY GET MY HEAD

Now all the Profiles are done
From Cole Porter to Genghis Khan . . .

There are two sorts of houses
Where time is as dead as a swollen clock

In one of them are stacks of random old New Yorkers
Somewhere in the other is an orderly deposit of Geographics

And when the wounds of travel have healed
And the line of distant mountains settled down

Or all the fish in the pond have jumped up
Or all the ducks in the sky have dropped out

You can settle back and have a crack
At one of these vessels of transportation

Where the prose is so slick
It must be speared with a sharpened stick

Where the verse is incredible and presents the writer
Thinking of something interesting to be sure to remember

And where the smiling native with his meat true-to-life
Is standing between the photographer and his wife

Or the drunken Irishman gets ready to go
From his pub to his cot in County Sligo

But beware O Traveler the house where both words lay
If that's the case
Just travel out the door, no matter what they say!

CERRILLA DE TAVACHÍN

At Nikiforoff's,
Dacha it is. It has
an upper Limit.
None of the words in English
have such delicate temporal boundary
They stop in poverty
or go on forever
because false revolution
   comes right around
     to the Biggest
     in the eyes of the
          Smallest

he spoke with a whisper disc
which sped
across the Barranca
with the speed of sound

And the luminous Receivers
on the far shore
scuffed and spat
and hung around
somewhat
and got desperately bored
having waited
all that time
for just one word
which didn't even rime

cuernavaca, the night of
27/feb. 1972

Eqp. Kid ANNA LOUISA MAYA S.P. MARCO ANTONIO Montes de Oca

A XOCHIMILCO
12 Rd. 1972

343

MELLOW W/ TEETH
(1972–1976)

POEM SENT TO J.H. PRYNNE

If you took 3 pies from a pile of cow pies
Each one greater than the roundest skies
And each one flatter than the flattest squidgy
And strung them on a palindrome like a syzygy
Then hung them on my neck and threw them out
Into deep space
Or some other kind of noplace
Id have to take it as a form of grace
Beside the shit youve took
For my not sending the Frank O' book!

EPITHET FOR THE GRAVESTONE
OF MAX DOUGLAS

He wanted to be attending the gathering
    immediately
and he does
let us hope the prairie
        dog hole
    which brought him down
led to the river
    and
that the boatman was there
              clairvoyant

standing on the landing

MOVE W/ THE WINDE
(with Jennifer Dunbar)

We who live astride
the Horses of the Mind
are at home
in the saddle
and from up there
we put down roots,
they are areal roots
they are
             our legs
planted in their boots

A SNIP FROM THE ALLEGORICAL
BARBERSHOP
an Æpisode for JDD

I see you have short hair Now.
  Where does that make you from —

Ganado.

Wheres that —

Eleven miles East of Broken Axle
Ganado is where
An Okie Mechanic reigns,
And ministers to a Band
Of two toned Jimmys.

But your hair My Dear
Is not there now —

True, my hair is in Albuquerque
Three blocks south of the Sundance.

The way of all hair?
No, a habit of my own.

I follow the sensible paradox:
            when it is hot it is short
            when it is cold it is long
In other words, the comfort of the head
Must prevail

Yet if you are Jenny
and your hair makes you beautiful
Then clearly pride has intervened
And the History of Culture has tapped a smart
2 inch plug into your #3 eye
or if you're an untouched esquimaux
where the History of Climate rules likewise

Then the hair is born of necessity
until it falls out from a genetic agreement
Or comes loose with metaphysical fright
Like when it becomes the hauling rope
With which the scalp is landed

However much I admire
Those alacritous possibilities
My hair is not what
Makes *me* beautiful
What makes me beautiful
I'll never cut off

CALIFORNIA

one poetry cannot be
more true than another
it can only be more convenient

_____

25,000 Goats waited
with ears cocked
by the runway
for the 747 to sing

_____

A Paradox is something
that is unbelievable
but at the same time
     TRUE!

_____

In this ancient coastal town
the men have turned into Victorian young ladies
They work their samplers of acid
and do their poetry and polish their bootees

_____

This democracy leads naturally
to a large landless peasantry

_____

Real alligators float through
the chilling nightmare of absolute symbolism
unpack yr dreams and stay awhile.
another top-secret calamity is about to come on

—————————————

The man's politics were more
or less profoundly beside the point —
we objected to him
on aesthetic grounds alone

—————————————

Lunch time:

    Head quarters
    Nose nickles
    finger dimes
    & tooth pennies

—————————————

Trolley shot:

    The Earth is revealed slowly,
    as a smooth cube.

—————————————

Coors is the Hamms of the West Coast

—————————————

La Vista:

> Suddenly
> down a long road
> there was a tree
> posing as what
> he expected to see

[THE UNITED STATES . . .]

The United States is the first country
in the history of the world
to take a regular vote
on its schizophrenia

ON WILL

Dont you have the feeling
that he'd do it
that he's the one
who would *do* it

RETURN TO NATURE

Return to nature

"Look at that label fido
not a specka cereal on it"

 ===

Caution

You put that doddamn gun down
an weel make a deel

Tell me the fuckin deel first

 ===

Development

He turned sick
and nine days later
he was dead

 ===

Anxiety

I'll be happy if
we can just get outa here
before that crowd gets back

NOSTALGIA

Remember when John Steinbeck went to Nam?
And wrote the whole thing up
with a John Wayne ballpoint pen
which *skipped* & missed everything?
Shee it, man those were the days.
And then his son come back to D.C.
an he blowed the whole thang
about how there wouldn't be any stories
because all those dudes had blasted off long ago?

INTERVIEW

Interviewer: Every lake is destined to grow
              shallower and smaller and
              eventually to become dry land—
              How does that make you feel?

Erie: Strange

Interviewer: How's that?

Erie: Erie

ADVICE TO HEARTY SHOPPERS

Think of yourself
as a four dimensional figure
a kind of Long Rubber Bar
extending in time
from the moment of your birth
to the end of your natural line

ADVICE TO WEARY SHOPPERS

Cocaine is worth far
more than you pay it
Because the money
you pay it with
is not worth nearly
as much as the Thing.

THE PLACE IS GRAND

Away to the south the Uinta Mountains
Stretch in a long line High peaks thrust into the sky
And snow fields glittering like lakes of molten silver
And pine forests in somber green
And rosy clouds playing around the borders
Of huge black masses
And heights and clouds
And mountains and snow fields
And forests and rock lands
All blended into
    One
    Grand
    View

      J.W. Powell, 1875
      & 1972

INTERIM REPORT TO THE
SCHUCHAT COMMISSION

The Outlanders have been gone since 4 A.M.
We now have jurisdiction of our green farm house again
When each of them left I shed a tear, now I understand
The profound implication of the chinese poets, be assured
That this report can come of nothing and only from their going
Dramatic and plausible onto their half secret continua

Types are of account only to an account. They are busy
Producing the archaeology of the Present and St. Augustine's
Difficulties with the present tense are understandable

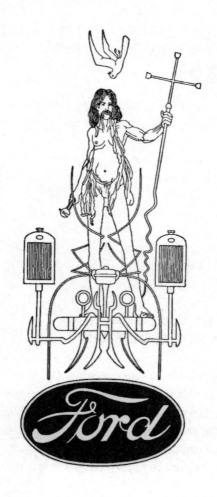

THE CONGOLEUM OF MICHAEL MYERS, OR STEP ON IT WE GOTTA GET THIS HEAP TO THE DUMP

Grinding through the particulated air, absorbing the metallic periods of the lower altitudes, there comes a Euclid Green chrome-plated dragonfly three minutes into a Boron powerthrust. Lo & Behold! Its misfires and backfires command the sky. It conjures massive Troop Withdrawal. A few of the Great Diesel Sensibilities of our time hang around to see what happens. Sure enough, when they check it out, Horseshit on Its Wings. The detail is Naturally exquisite.

Wisconsin. California. Machines and flowers standing in the Sunshine. A head piercing spectrum from the tip of the blade from a hand that shakes right up to the moment of incision. Then assumes total control. All landform is defined with a razor. We are so far above it it looks natural. The Maestro cuts deep into the terrain of the linoleum. Not the heart of darkness: this is the most powerful EverReady anybody ever had. Envision a warehouse full of unthinkable spacedout items. Through the Great Double Doors rip our Petroleum Addicts, full crank. This stuff is not for the soapers. Michael's got that extra gear, he really transports the image. The prophetic decay of the absolute present. His incisions portray a terrible thrill because they are across an age which digs its terror, in the full daylight of a rundown sun. It is the ancient art of Epitaph: massive in its evocations, miniature in instance. And the mysterious beauty of the work derives from the condition itself, of the brief lines of the record.

MELLOW W/ TEETH

This society is subject
to barbarities of the mind

Pigs that used to be screaming
are now suckin, somewhat

That which was unspeakably gross
one moment
is Perfektly OK
the next

THE big message of the Seventies:
Let Your Nails Grow.

AN AUTUMN EVENING IN ILLINOIS

There is an open interval of values in the pasture
lying within the closure of that interval
from (for) which the motives with respect to my life
are positive & continuous.

The phraseology is cumbrous in order to allow
For the special case of the magnitude of what
I've said
is combined with some other one

(yet I've faild to tell you, we've
ruled out
applications to discrete quantities eg
numbers of people)

In which case the result ant
will not be increased
ever tho it really does
go right back to the assassination.

FILLER UP!

Now, we are told
it is permissible
but not desirable
nor yet appropriate
to be filled with contempt

YOU CAN'T FALL OUT FROM AN
AT EASE POSITION

Looking through the hole
he sees a man lying crushed
beneath a truck
composed of yellow plastic
and beside him is a dirty popsicle stick
or is that a flat finger
caught in a golden paperclip
wrapped in a package
of unfocusable attribution

Now the man has been silent
for a long time
It is pointless to guess what
he can do
for he is plastic too

PARANOIA, INCORPORATED
(A CONVERSATION

Do you see any agents
& instrumentalities of the state
Out There?

Yes my liege, they are
Everywhere
the Instrumentalities
Out There!

SNOWE BOUND

Pictured in my window
the sunne is shining down
flashing on a foot of snow
rollin like a fresh white sheet
all the way to the street

Then a man comes into view
pulling a loaded sled
out of the sunken confines
of the black overwhelming avenue
he is keeping his head warm
with an electric hat

OHIO

This is the most regulated
attempt one can pass through

because
it is a police state,
but one must not close
those other doors too promptly

Here we have come to one
which leads into the garden
of reality
It stands like a weed
immune to reason
intruding like something forgotten
in the plot of its kind.

IN ADMIRATION OF ENDURANCE

for Jennifer

How many times
are you gonna appear
in Public like that
Standing on the Bathtub
w/ yr foot on the sink (?

THE NICEST OF CITYS

In San Francisco again
I remember my early days
The smells in the beach are the same
But somehow dispersed
And a little less exclusive
And the things that made her exciting
Are nearly all gone out
In her weakened concentration
Not the poolhall with the big sandwiches
Though it too is gone
Technicolor hides a certain emptiness
With a trace of civility

FROM *SEMI-HARD*

They won the election
but they lost the president
Isn't it marvelous
Corruption has saved us again —
in America nothing goes to waste

By the Way
                What kind of writer is he?
Well I darent say, lad
but once I borrowed his typewriter
to measure some golden lines
and I noticed his capital I
was awfully dirty

SHUFFLIN OFF TO BUFFALO

Not marble nor the guilded monuments
Of princes shall outlive this pow'rful rime,
Nor Mars his sword nor war's quick fire shall burn
Nevertheless I've brought my bullet-proof lecturn

                        San Francisco
                        Hallowmas, 1975

SHUFFLIN OFF To BUFFALO

Not marble nor the guilded monuments
Of princes shall outlive this pow'rful rime,
Nor Mars his sword nor war's quick fire shall burn
Nevertheless I've brought my bullet-proof lecturn

                          Ed Dorn
                          San Francisco
                          Hallowmas, 1975

HOMAGE TO GRAN APACHERÍA
(1973)

$$\left[\begin{array}{l} 99 - 111 \ \text{MERIDIAN} \\ 30 - 38 \ \text{PARALLEL} \end{array} \right]$$

*as between the Dragoons
and the Chiricahuas
the sweet valley
unites*

LUZ

I see Victorios sister
alone under a Tree
her braids
in the blowing winde

Smoking a cornhusk cigarette
        ~
and thinking deeply
of the Mimbreños

She is having a last toke
on the real world

These poems are written perfectly
in a mongrel tongue

It is not illumining
making the whiteye
in the Southwest
                    Particular
and law
the discolored foam
of brick bags
the dregs
from around the mouths of rivers.
The bit is not separate
from the shank

        In the capital
        Montezuma had a zoo
        and in it he kept
        the animals normal
        to our zoos in cages
        plus the human Freaks
        a category we bless
        with a special place
        of their own
        when their station is sufficiently Low
        or when they have declared
        before their private means

The apache procedure is uncorrupted
by self satisfaction

ATHABASCA

Invent Nothing
Attend to Everything
Increase by absorption

Sometimes, when the weather concentrates
and pressure gets his way
the gentes stand up in Santiago
Five thousand walk away
from El Teniente
the world's greatest copper mine
from green stripes to Iodine

Ápache is not self-deriving
it is the name for the Navaho from the Zuñi
Apaches de Nabaju, the enemy
their character was up
to their objects defining

      They fleshed out their numbers
      with captives of other tribes
      Pueblos, Pima, Papago
      and other peaceful Indians

Every trip to town was a debauch
the most absolute of the predatory tribes
Apache policy was to extirpate
every trace of civilization
from their province, and to this objective
there was very little more
at the time of The Purchase
the best buy of Eighteen fifty four

a few Mexicans in the Mesilla valley
and in Tuscon at the center of the purchase
everywhere else the seeds of the will
of the god who feeds on beeves
lay rotting in the ground
the conclusive failure of Spanish authority
in the new world

Then comes the Northern Expression
the intersection of Will & Brain

The capacity to disembody
(technology is the progress toward abstraction
Technology marching
into the hinged and fanged mouth of abstraction
and now the bodies
which support this mad allegiance
plant themselves like posts
and some of them will burn
and some will simply ruin
in the fifty years war to come
before they Settle the Apache

One day these will all be ruins
what will their fashion be
not the same as those I see
strewn like a broken necklace
from Mesa Verde and Bonito
and Chelly to Chiricahua

WHO WILL FOLLOW

Will they who follow thee
have any tears for your ~~in~~activity
or will their feeling be
that you acted too ~~in~~finitely

one of the stupidest sentimentalities
that runs thru the literature
is the Greek tragedy
These indians came upon a terminus
of extremely spent moment
Then began life again
the Greeks and their tragedy
go on and on
the same tragedy
the longest run, possibly,
off broadway

AS OF VICTORIO

or later a lot of "indians" eyes
are going to go under the knife
for trachoma they don't have

or your children working
in the industrial laundry
of an indian school

The wild tribes are treated
as ideas caught and dismantled
in public parks, Baldwin locomotives
and red 1915 fire trucks, the most
remote pleasures, left to the children
the wild races, responsible to
enthusiastic style
Geronimo at Fort Sill
at the wheel of a parked touring car
seeing inside the camera

We have all now heard of a sterile phone
And it sounds like a good thing to have
Before the advent of the whiteye
There were sterile deserts in Gran Apachería
Precisely unknown, defiant to the encroachment of civilization

On one project the norte Americanos
and the Mexicans can
always conspire: the punishment
of long hairs, for here the two
state religions are in Perfect accord.

A MINOR AND PERHAPS OVERLOOKED EXTREMITY

There is no western writer
More idiotic than Rister*
There is no mind banaler
Than that of Carl Coke Rister
      None so vulgar
      And so regular

* author of *The Southwestern Frontier 1865–1881*

Why Florida? There are prisons in other places.
Because it is the closest thing to a national island we have
and the practise has become grossly sub-conscious since then
It's where the ideologically pauperous, mad from northern concoctions,
end their days.
The Apaches are the first big significant shipment
once they all pushed into the cars they sit fixed in their terror

OFFICE EQUIPMENT
(1976–1983)

This is the picture. The Doctors
are the wolves. Who, time past,
followed the caribou
the sick, lame, or merely dying.
Falling away along the leading edge of the migration
the herd now slide into the margin
with really awful anticipation
under the dry sunne, between the sea
and the inhospitable montes, which,
if the winde is right
scatters their curtain of excrementum
permitting a view of the East from whence they came.

Let us dwell, for a moment, on this usage.
For there is a certain nature
embedded in the principle of our machines.

    "That which is cast out of the body
      by any of the natural emunctories"

and
    "It will please his grace . .
      to dallie with my excrement . . ."

and again, from Milton
    "[our] whiteness is but
      an excremental whiteness"

Fire gave us moment, that was our contract.
That's not topical. So this is a picture
of an old old habit
The runne to the sunne.

San Francisco, 31 January 1976

THURSDAY, THE 5TH OF FEBRUARY, AND STILL NO PAYCHECK

I can't believe these jokers.
Somebody in Payroll must think
I have an uncontrollable desire
to be resident in La Jolla.
Actually, I have a private suspicion
that a marxist conspiracy
in the payroll department
has discovered I'm a born prol
and to really fuck me over therefore
they sent my check, as they admitted
to the California Canadian Bank.
It's very grotesque, and I'm frightened.

PHÆNOMINON

Each generation moves
                with its two companions

Locked in absolute reference to itself

Is that nostalgia? To be really honest
I thought people still did that.

Perhaps. Perhaps.

Nevertheless. And in my case,
It was a big cat that got out of the bag.

Phaenominon

Each generation moves
            with its two companions

Locked in absolute reference to itself

Is that nostalgia? To be really honest
I thought people still did that.

Perhaps. Perhaps.

Nevertheless. And in any case,
It was a big cat that got out of the bag.

A LATE LUDDITE OPINION

I don't like the typewriter much
A dumb machine, it either rattles
Or hums, and when it's smart
It drops and adds letters, and Olson
Was correct in never giving it a cleaning.

And altho it is a slack master [a.]
There is an insidiously invisible chain
Running from it to its users
Best felt in the vast rooms of its abuse.

---

a. Dropped on your head from the 10th floor
it could be damaging, but mysteriously, this
never happens.

DROUGHT REPORT FROM CHLOROFLUORNIA

Those who have wells pray for rain
Those who have taps dont give a shit.

LA JOLLA RETURN

There is a considerable amount of
calculated space in this Book, and
I would like to think anyone might
be pleased to add to it as he pleases.

PREFACE

These dispatches should be
received in the spirit
of the Pony Express:
light and essential,   & at 5 dollars
an ounce,
the only hedge
against
junkmail
we ever had.

THE BROOKS ADAMS QUOTE

Money alone is capable
of being transmuted immediately into
any form of activity.

CHICKEN RELATIVITY

Two thighs are better
than one
where one is better than none

majority   remains
the   clearest
standard of value

I was 11 in 1940
The modern occurs twice
In this century
I am a child of war.

SO FAR

This country is no more
than a miscellaneous
crowd of Aliens—

4 JULY

The original struggle
To see who would pay
The debt is the struggle still

                                    S.F.

I spent the winter of 1977–8 swinging
Between the poles of the penetrating cynicism
Of Cioran & the rigidly structured
Affirmation of Dr. Johnson. The third
Quarter of the 18th C. is the antidote specific
Of the sixth, seventh & possibly 8th decades
Of the 20th C.

                San Francisco 4th July 1978

AMERICAN AS APPLE PIE

The most amazing
Characterization
A nation ever had—

BUT BEFORE THAT

It was ANACHARSIS[a.]
who compared laws to spiders' webs,
which catch small flies
and allow bigger ones to escape.

---

a. The Scythian philosopher, 600 B.C.

Good filing cabinet:
A carton of bootboxes

THE GORE VIDAL QUOTE

A clone is anyone who tells you
To have a nice day.

GOTTA HURT SOMEBODY

You may be Plato
You may be Socrates
You may be Aristotle Onassis
You may be Jimmy the Greek
But your gonna have to hurt somebody

You may be a Triumph
You may be a Ford
You may be a Cadillac
You may be a Turd
But your still gonna hurt somebody

You might be a microphone
You might be a megaphone
You might be an anglophone
You might be a francophone
But you already *have* hurt somebody

You might ride a camel
You might ride a goose
You might ride a rabbit
You might *even* ride a moose
        Whatever your excuse
Your gonna kill somebody

You may be a clod
You may be a a pod
You may just be odd
You may even be God
But your gonna hurt somebody

You may be short
You may be Frank Shorter
You may be Harry Hoogstraten
You may be totally forgotten
but your still gonna have to hurt somebody

You might be straight
You may be pleasant
You may be a duck
You may be a pheasant
But you gonna *have* to hurt somebody
Oh yea, you sure gonna hurt somebody

QUOTE FOLLOWED BY EXAMPLE

Bad times are just around the corner
e.g. anxiety is just another form of entertainment

TO WIT

The 18th Century
was exemplified
by its neat
conversion of fact:
whoever saw
a copy of
The Social Contract.

A VARIATION ON HOBBES

That you lack prudence
matters not at all
but the fact that
you lack sapience
is hard to overlook

IT SEEMS TO ME I'VE HEARD THAT SONG BEFORE

Boredom is quite misunderstood
on this side of the Atlantic. In the
first place not everyone is by any
means *capable* of being bored. But,
since the misapprehension comes from
boredom being placed among the psycho-
logical distresses, it is widely
assumed everybody is more or less bored,
when in fact they're merely empty.
Boredom arises from intellectual
distraction. A conveyance of outside
inconsequence, and it is this disturbance
of one's idleness which produces it.

OFFICE EQUIPMENT

The high Energy of dire need
Is demonstrated here, not that
Needs can be met, but that
The search can be initiated

The laziest civilizations generate
The most anxious rise in use
And "energy"[1] fuels their divertimenti
They claim it is their way of life
That is being attacked by reduction

But it is their total loss
Of a way of life which is indicated
& "who needs a way of life"
Is what they have not asked themselves

---

1. A stupid word for this case anyway since it derives, from *ergon*, work, which is not actually the meaning of riding around.

Boulder, August 1979

POOR CARTER

He can't even make a macho remark
without everybody claiming
it's been staged to look like
a macho remark

IN THE INTEREST OF EQUALITY

Just as those who don't own cars
can get in on the rush
to the "last drop"

Every once in a while
they shld put a dollar
in the pump
& run a gallon on the ground

DE CHARACTERISTIC DO
GIT INFLATED

If someone stares
For 15 secs at one spot
It's called concentration.

NAME FOR AN EARLY AMERICAN PUNK GROUP

THE STAMP ACT

THE COUNTRY AWARDS

Seeing Emmylou the other night
My mind went again to Joshua Tree
And I felt how much
I miss Graham, and wish
He hadn't gone on to the garbage dump
This place misses his sweet voice.

SOME FREE & CURIOUS DATA: THE NAMES OF WILD BILL'S PALLBEARERS

Charles Rich
Johnny Oyster
Harry Young
Tom Dosier
William Hillman
& Jerry Lewis

WORSE THAN BADEN-BADEN

John Houston lost 100,000
At the tables in Reno
During the 16 weeks he shot
The Misfits.
He couldn't hold a candle
To Charles James Fox,
Who routinely lost that much
in a single night at Brooks'

AN OBSERVATION ON
BOULDER'S MALL

Even if one were not
of a freudian turn of mind
it would be difficult to ignore
the fact that the public
ice-cream dispensary
is separated from the public outhouse
by a mere ten feet of brick walkway.

HARDBALL SIMILE

I figured he'd have about as much chance
getting out of there in one piece
as a pig at Armour & Company.

QUOTATION FROM KIDD,
WHILE WATCHING THE GAME ON T.V.

"Bob Griese gets to the ten lard line."

A ROBERT SERVICE BEAR FLIES
IMITATION

   We should introduce you to a Bear Fly.
Bear Flies are so heavy they can't even fly.
They're about 8 inches high and they bounce
across the ground like dwarf tumble weeds (tumbling?).
They're the trashiest insects in Alaska. Nothing
comes close to even matching a Bear Fly. They
eat Deer flies for breakfast and consider it
delicate. They don't even talk to black flies.
Moose flies, well moose flies are not *Nothing*. In
fact they'll make a respectable dinner for a Bear
Fly which is about what a Bear Fly considers them.
Elk flies are *des*ert.

   Polar Bear flies are a special Breed.
They're somewhat dyin' *out*. But the ones thater
left
you don't
even want to hear about.

THE DEMOCRATS

the men from "Mars" are surely among us
on the Floor of the convention they sprouted earphones
and clutched in their hands were Alkaline powered wands
all the interviewees played Fool of the uttermost readiness,
those side pipe mikes: it's as if the
mouth has a ski.

THE REPUBLICANS

can such a "noble" idea have sunk so low.

THE LAST BUMPER STICKER

Women Got No Balls

BOULDER BLUE

A brown diesel Volvo
degrades the atmosphere.
Slightly blue hydrogen
drifts south into the lunges of the Joggs
who run in packs through low-angled dusk.

Dead vines in the winter court,
skeletons of Summer's Gun.
Pigeons and squirrels Wax
on the Hypertrash
of these disgusting consumers.
WHO ARE THEREFORE
an extension of their trash.
Societies of rats eating themselves.

Over the first tier
of the Grand Montanes
the air is grainy in the sunlight
Which has travelled across a lota space
to be so corrupted. Some would claim
the sun doesn't mind. Not true.
All light resents corruption.

HOW SMALL CAN AWESOME GET?

When Caspar Weinberger
crossed the threshold
at Bonn airport
he tightened the knot
in his tie.

At a U.S. airbase
seventy miles north of London
he adjusted his tie
as he lowered himself
into the cockpit of an F-80,
duplicating the german gesture.

The signal is clear: nervous,
automatic, a compulsion
for utter finitude. And,
it could be
a preference for hanging.

FURTHER THOUGHTS ON DOGS
LONDON, 9 JULY 1981

Now that evolution is down for the count
we are permitted to speculate on
the dog's lineage by other classifications.

Although in no way but common lungs
do they resemble each other, and although
the load delivered is usually incommensurate,
street pigeons and dogs, empiricism tells us,
are set the same task, being to bury civilization
under a progressive crust of offal
three metres thick. This coarse chutzpah
we can applaud but not approve.

Amsterdam's quaint beauty is made slippery
by this dogeon effluxion, and dangerous
by the cambered crust at the canal's edge.
Dumped on and dumped in by this disgusting diet
the city's sanity will be secured by riot.

LET THOSE PEOPLE GO

Sometimes I think
the only threat to human number
would be to erase their names.

Bombs don't scare 'em
Diseases are too slow
The larger fauna are too random
Earthquakes are too local
"Holocaust" is too selective
Greed too dispersed and general
and right to Life a hollow phrase.

Let 'em go! rings in the halls
of the citadel, They'll find
their own way to the end.

ON FIRST LOOKING INTO
MARSDEN HARTLEY

I first see heavy elegance
nearly insane with period lustre.
The eyes are turrets
powered by smooth motors
able to see through walls
The mouth is a straight line
enclosed by well curved parentheses
The neck-piece is wound
with astonishing Art.
The coat is cashmere,
the hat, finest beaver
and the pictures are the ballast
                         of reallity.

UNEDIBLE IS THIS NATION'S BLESSED SPIRIT

America's generosity is becoming
almost too much to bear
in the city of Los Angelese, on January 4th
Crackers from the 1st Bomb shelter period,
now about 25 years old
and said to smell funcky from
being stored in wax paper,
have been shipped to The Navahos.

of course, that attempt to give
equity to the diet was nothing
compared to the rabbits offered
to the Bannock-Shoshones
by the Rabbit Clubbers of the snake valley.

THE LADDER OF OPPORTUNITY?

I thought metaphor had experienced
its Extreme
with the Window of Vulnerability
But Now we have *the ladder of opportunity*.
So let's have a close look at those rungs . . .
sawed about three quarters of the way through
and filled in with wood putty.

NEUTRE PRONOUN

Sticking its
nugatory nose
into the intersection
a typical, sushi eating
tofu shitting
Boulder motorist.

THINGS WE KNOW

The Pope's habit
of kissing the ground
upon deplaning
makes it unadvisable
for him to visit
Times Beach, Missouri.

FROM THE WRONG SIDE
OF THE PARTITION
AT THE HOUSTON MLA
(1980–1981)

THE NEXT MORNING:
ON THE WAY TO THE
REGIONAL FICTION PANEL

We went to the wrong side of the partition
about noon in the grande ballroom.
Ricardo Montana, the Nearedgehowsie Nyinegyhazi
of late Thirties country swing, was
abristle with rattling instruments, and
nervous as a squirrel, except for the hands,
Ricardo has calm, collected hands.
But in the thrilling brutal Hyattecture
he was cracking the nut, eating the shell
and throwing the meat away, searching
with throat and jaw for perfect animation.
Jerking and Twitching to an ordinary observer.
We looked out over a great river of uncovered heads.
I thought of Paul Horgan, in two volumes.
At the front of the room a talking match
made its rounds. The Receivers, all
slightly right or left of each other
silently chewed the argument.

This is interesting I whispered,
it's good to see structuralists wrangle
they should never cease their purgatorial labors,
but this is not McMurtry, this
is not the role of the Cowboy.

FROM THE BAYOU TO THE RINGWORM: WESTHEIMER BUMMER

Every other shop
in Downtown Houston
is Wigtown. Wigs are everywhere.
Neutroned-out Blacks
on heroin is how
the center holds.

Take a 25 dollar taxi ride
to the edge of town, to the ring-
worm of burger kings
and Jacks-in-the-Box
laced with places called
"the desperado" or
"the blue Locomotive,
a restaurant"
or "the nose,
a mucous experience".

In the Jacks-in-the-Box
Montana Dick tries to
work an aimless crowd of boys
into something like
transportation w/ his banjo.
They are enthralled,
but not enough
to take us back to town
and furthermore they tell him
Gillie wouldn't even
let him in the door
wearing a hat as holey as that

I resign myself to the
bus shelter outside
while Dick mixes
with the folks in the donut shop
next door. Dressed too
thin, the wind
makes a fool out of me
and I think of home
    and warmth and bed

across the street
there is a massive office building
upon its Top
there is a sign:
THE BANK OF WOOD
a small crowd has
gathered. The bus is
coming, somewhere
far down the flat street
Dick returns with
the donuts. Everything
is going to be alright.

Where do we go for some
invitation, do you know what I mean
I've got my piece here and
we want to go where we can sit in
you know where there's a place like that?

Westheimer what about Westheimer?
How far is it? *What* is it?

RETURNING TO THE HARLEY, ON BUFFALO BAYOU EARLY SUNDAY MORNING

Everything not securely fastened
drifts toward the Bayou in Houston.
Down here at the base of the scrapers
everything is scrap
and the milkyblue sky of Houston
seems very far overhead.

There is a loaded sense of energy
rejecta, and of returning
with the sample cases, nothing sold.
We've just come from Wesling's room
in the Hotel Lamar, an establishment
going, but not quite gone,
a tarted up relic of the thirties
like most everything optically available
at groundlevel in Houston Town.

A pleasant little party with the Chicago—
La Jolla Bunch, the deferential and stringent
von Hallberg, the owl-like Golding,
the radically intellectual balance
of Wesling himself, all of which
Drakon enjoyed more than his program permits.
That, in its small way, is the summary
frustration of the Western World.
The wandering admire the fixed,
and the fixed admire the wandering.

Drakon played, sang and laid out
the stunning propaganda
of the life of abandonment
to several candidates who had spent
an elongated day interviewing for jobs
the size of needles in haystacks,
but like barbarians everywhere
they were enraptured (with reservations)
by tales of the motile.

We took the elevator to the street.
A gone to seed Marlboro Man
then approached us, we saw him
"looking around" before the approach.
Don't go any further he warned,
they're pickin'em up
like flees off dogs, don't matter
if you're on the street, jist
if you're walkin'.
Where you goin' Drakon enquired.
Down Main, to the Strutters End.

I said not me, no matter what it takes,
I'm going through. And at just that moment
I saw a scruffy, gravel pocked
piece of paper come blowing and scraping
along the sidewalk and I grabbed it
and took it to my room
and let it sleep in the wastebasket.

THE POWER OF A WORD

As a distraction producer
one could walk around with a joint
hanging from the lip.

But far more distracting
would be a strip of paper
with the word Joint printed on it.

> [in conjunction with
> David de Smith
> back in Boulder
> Friday the Thirteen,
> Eighties.]

MORE ABHORRENCES
(1983–1989)

ABHORRENCES

There's nothing to do w/ valentine's day
but observe a moment of screaming
for all the love that was of no account
and all the misleading feeling

ABHORRENCES
6th April, 1983, Wodinsday

the bite is sharp
in Boulder tonight
over on the mesa
a scientific worker
burns the late night light
I hope he gets it right

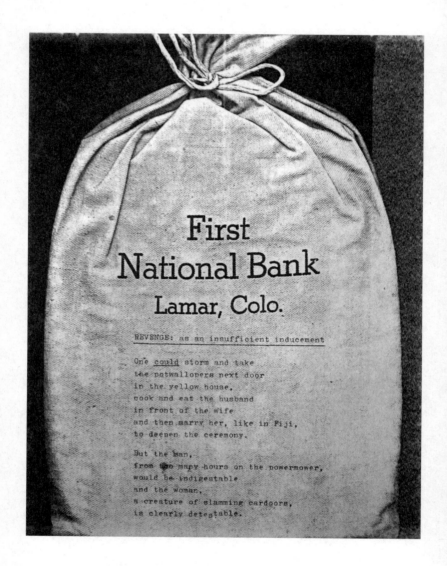

First
National Bank
Lamar, Colo.

REVENGE: as an insufficient inducement

One could storm and take
the potwallopers next door
in the yellow house,
cook and eat the husband
in front of the wife
and then marry her, like in Fiji,
to deepen the ceremony.

But the man,
from too many hours on the powermower,
would be indigestable
and the woman,
a creature of slamming cardoors,
is clearly detestable.

REVENGE:
AS AN INSUFFICIENT INDUCEMENT

One *could* storm and take
the potwallopers next door
in the yellow house,
cook and eat the husband
in front of the wife
and then marry her, like in Fiji,
to deepen the ceremony.

But the man,
from too many hours on the powermower
would be indigestible
and the woman,
a creature of slamming cardoors,
looks clearly detestable.

Shuffleburger, your name was odd
but I bear you no ill will.
What a lot of us found even odder,
was that you'd removed
the bullet-proof window
in your bullet-proof car
because the air conditioning
didn't work. Couldn't
get it fixed, huh. Because
the death squads had snuffed
all the air conditioning workers?
If one were paranoid,
there could be a plot there.

WITNESSES SAY THEY DO NOT WANT TO BE IDENTIFIED

The killers were calm
and nerveless.
The victim was doing
what he wanted
and not giving it
much thought.
A privilege leading to death.

ABHORRENCES
22 nov.
Kennedy

NOT TO MENTION NAMES

I was reminded of Charles Olson today
in an unusual circumstance, reading,
what was it, the Dew Nark Dimes
Review of Not Much, Yes, it was
in a review of a book by
M. L. Rosenthal and some woman
The cleverest tack I'd seen
in a long time. This massive jerk
and this unknown woman,
had essayed to purvey all
the obvious work since Song of my *you got it.*
Maestro, you were there
at the end of the line. Ahead of you
were all the clericals waiting for taxis
in Dublin. Interesting visually
but a boring wait.
  American poetry is a little like
Poland in that respect: just get in line anyway.

PUBLIC SAFETY #2

Who would have guessed
God is an Air Bag.
Not St Augustine, nor
would he have been amused
But Texans are about
to buy it, perhaps because
they drink a lot
and drive big cars
along long roads
and haven't got the sense
Air Bag gave garbage.

And New Yorkers will buy it,
perhaps because they
love life so much Air Bag
knows they've got no air to bragabout.

And, there will be sundry pockets
    (*By the way* Air pockets
      might be a "viable" "alternative"
      for people who still have enough pride
      to disdain "Bags")
sundry pockets of the "pop"ulation
scattered around the stix
and vainglorious enough
to preserve their hides, They'll buy it.

Now where would they be?
Probably Utah, Arizona,
certainly Florida (the old love to live on,
although Air Bag knows why) and of course,
California,where they — SWOON — have
So Much to lose.

ABHORRENCES
Boulder, 14 Dec 1983
The Dawn of the Living Dead
is more accurate sociology
than *Scarface*

THE HYSTERIA OF LEFT WING BOGEY MAKING

In terms of the Intoxication of leadership
The Reagan-Hitler comparison
is quite fallacious:
In the 1st place Hitler had
a lot more charisma, was
a better actor (not that that
says much) and had subjects
which, quite frankly traced their lineage
back to the Barbarians of the last Roman Frontier.
Reagan, no fault of his, has to put up with
a mongrel nation, composed almost entirely
of 2nd rate Europeans, which will
believe anything as long as it's
pension is secured and shopping mall construction
                              is uninterrupted

FREEDOM OF INFORMATION

We don't care about Wick
and we don't
care to hear Wick's
tapes. Nix
& Kiss have
already done that.
We want to hear
the craven Esh
arguing against
an NEA grant
for Tom Clark.

ANYKYN

Capitalism is the only system
which produces planned surpluses
in order to create hunger,
and which also has a view
to indebtedness leading to confiscation.
We are witnessing, at the turn of the Eighties,
all its manifestations, and most of us
are quite contented with the results.

We regularly refuse to discuss what
all this means, and are equally blind
to its meaning to the future of society.
There is nothing wrong with this, i.e.,
if you have purchased that monetary idea.
But if you haven't,
you're just the same old fool you always were

CRIPPLED CLERIHEW

Balding Pat Boone
Preeminent christian goon
Breath like a dead raccoon
Is not as smart as Weicker,
In fact there's nothing like'r.

I'M FROM IDAHO

For the record—
The thing that most
disturbed me at the time
about Gary Hart
was the Carol King connection.
On the other hand
it could have been
Steve Wozniak.

A CRITIQUE OF RECENT
DEVELOPMENTS IN MESO-AMERICA

The people wants peace
but they'll get no rest

the people wants surfeit
but they will starve

the people wants legitimacy
but they will produce bastards.

BOULDER PRINT-OUT

At 45 degrees a left turn
onto Broadway from Alpine
a guy was upending
        a bottle
in front of the desolate side
of the slickest Italian eatery
        in town
He seemed to be walking,
if he could.

The trouble with the
    no-liquor lobby
is that they base
        their
        presumption
on the idea that all
        those lives
        are worth saving,
when in all other cases
they treat them like they're
        worthless

ABHORRENCES
Boulder June '84

PROPERTY RIGHTS ARE
NOT NEGOTIABLE

But Terrorism is not
just American as apple pie:
that muscle
has not lacked exercise ever.
What can they Mean by the label?
Hasn't God instituted the method
both for his believers and his sceptics?

And the attack is not on Language:
the decoys of Euphemismos
have a built-in recognisability.
We all know when we accommodate the trend.
Wars have always begun with assassination.

Because honesty is considered so relative,
its absolutes are never absolute.

GOING BLIND INTO RESTAURANTS

I don't like eating
with people because
I can't stand to watch
them eat—every sin
they have ever committed
emerges when they
masticate their food,
and greed is the *least*
of them.
Therefore I shut my eyes
to their consumption
in order to live among
them, who are all
       there are.

EVEN I END UP LIVING IN DOGTOWN

For an exorbitant
and therefore almost pleasurable
amount of rent,
I live with my family
at the seedy end of Mapleton
just above "Broadway," in Boulder, Colorado.

Mapleton started out
as the Hyde Park of Boulder,
gold fortunes expressed as piles of brick
or elaborately carpentered wood.
So far so good, until about 1913.

Then there was the degeneration
of a couple of massive wars
which served their orthodox function
of severing the surplus population
from their so-called brains.

But suddenly, in the summer of 1984
an influx of Bostonians and New Yorkers
have brought their demented white dogs
and neurotic patchwork cats.
The cats are OK, at least
they still have the instinct
to cover their shit.

But the dogs ! my god ! THE DOGS !

Lately I've noticed the heir
to the Gaines Dog Food Fortune
has just bought a number of master drawings
from the renaissance, at Sotheby's.

Isn't it true, and probably just,
that dog food will possess the museum walls,
as well as the lawns.

ABHORRENCES
21 July, 1984

COPYRIGHT

"I never thought America could get
that excited about anything."
O.J. Simpson

No this is not about the American Revolution
or the election of Jefferson in 1800.
Or the Vietnam war, or the bombing of Nagasaki
or the death of Elvis.
This is the Olympics in Los Angeles, California.
L.A., CA (el ai, see ai)

Nobody in the U*n*i*t*e*d*S*t*a*t*e*s is permitted
to use the word Olympic, or to display their 5 balls.

ABHORRENCES
21 July 1984
in honor of the cyclists
pumping their way around
North Boulder Park

THE TYRANNY OF FOOD

It is not unjust,
as it is often said,
that athletes are sometimes
the victims of terrorists.
If anything they are among
the most appropriate targets
because they are the representative
examples of capital aggression
right down to the very steroidal zeals
which so express their bodies
and their minds.

THE TARIFF QUESTION

It is sheer ignorance to repeat
the old canard about Jefferson
the philosopher of the small farm
as though that begins and ends his character.*

He lit the fires of American manufactories
with the Embargo of 1808.
When the Leopard raked
the Chesapeake broadside,
American dependence on Manchester
and Birmingham was reduced
by 50% in one year.

---

* In reality Monroe, his neighbor, was the
small farmer.

ON REJUVENATING THE HOTLINE

Judging from the foreign policy successes
of the two Jefferson administrations,
1800 to 1808, the instant communications
of the present period seem to have no advantage.
The line, Hot or Not,
should be abandoned altogether.
The great philosopher showed,
by shuttling the six week packet ships,
you could quadruple
the size of the country
and avoid war by embargoing the enemy.
But, of course, all that strategy
presupposed the now practically outrageous
idea that a president could write a letter.

FOR THE PROTECTION OF THIS
WHOLE WORLD AND ITS CONTENTS

I have a marvellous idea
of which I am sure you will all approve:

> We exchange presidents
> with the Russians,
> they send us their guy
> and we send them Reagan.

That would *guarantee* we
didn't bomb eachother!
. . . wouldn't it?

KANSAS CITY COLLAPSE

In any rational government
responsible or otherwise
doctors, lawyers and
especially engineers
would be made liable
for the crimes they commit.

But instead everybody
jumps on high school teachers,
as if they were the sole and only goats,
for failing to teach Johnny
when Johnny is a jerk
by preference.

W.C. WILLIAMS

The Greatest name in 20th C. poetry
not the most famous—lesser types have overrun
his reputation with howling celebrity.
T.S. Eliot, like Freud, was a production worker
in the new factories of private pain and enigma.
Their work had a disintegrating effect on
a disintegrating body.

He took Emily Dickinson and
made her public and therefore
a lot more simple.
I'm glad that happened.
It was the only effective block
against Whitman, which
lasted for about 30 years.
But could be effective for a long time to come.
The early part of the century
therefore had in Williams
articulation as such.
What awful examples of the
Whitman paroxysm we've
seen have been singular,
isolated, and embarrassing.
It's probably not a good Idea for the
greatest to be made the norm.
Williams introduced
Honest modesty into
the form itself.

And his very empiricism
is authenticated by his
medical background.
His historical studies were
amateur & therefore a way
of setting up strong prejudices
(always a virtue in a poet)
Aaron Burr for instance, in the am grain.
Burr was probably the one man who, if president,
could never have said I'm no crook.

But Williams was convinced
Burr was one of
the most abused men
in history. I matters not,
the imagination is real.

What I think Williams meant
by Poetry is the news that stays news
(and Ive never rejected its origin—
poetry is the news that stays poetry)
is that poetry is about real things
(keeping in mind that, to poetry,
the imagination is real)
and that what lasts
is what is best put, and
that's the news that stays news.

No one imagines Tammy & Jim
have been blessed with the kind of reportage
which will make them last—
in fact, they have no *choice*
but to ascend directly into heaven,
they're certainly not going
to achieve immortality in the books.

IN HUMBLE ADMIRATION

Cannibalism is now thought
to have practically disappeared
and to exist only in one or two places
like New Guinea & perhaps in the hills
of Fiji.

Of course there are linguistic
if somewhat vegetarian leftovers among ourselves,
as in the expressions She'd be a tasty morsel
or applied to the male, What a hunk!

True, there is occasional, *in extremis,*
cannibalism among upperclass Argentines
downed in the Andes.

But it's still truly a dog of a world.
Every time I meet a dog owner on the street
I wonder how he would taste.

OF DECADENT, CALIFORNIAN TORIES

The intention to reimpose Excise taxes
(in Europe called VAT or value-added tax)
is directly counter-revolutionary:
Jefferson's first and most direct attack
on Federalist corruption in favor of commerce
was the abolition of the Excise tax
and was the most definitive break
with the entrenched, pro-Royalist power
which had held sway until the second American Revolution
beginning in the winter of eighteen hundred.

If John Marshall were to wake up
from his long and deservedly restless sleep,
he would scream with delight
at the retrenchment of democratic advances
approved by a wiser population 184 years ago.

PREPOSTEROUS PROPAGANDA

(to the very few people
who'd care to follow this

Olson had it wrong most of the time:
He was attracted to the most wayward material
about the Maya,
he read the wrong books by Brooks Adams,
almost read the wrong book by Eric Havelock
(only because there wasn't any wrong book by E.H.)
and was a sucker for miraculous books
which purported to discover
stonecut Hittite in local situations
from del Fuego to N.E. Massachusetts.
On Northern Europe he had an unerring
sense of the most absolutely absurd
and mystical sources of speculation
(Waddell for instance.)

Yet, even if the above sense of his mind
is not wholly accurate, his willful refusal
to accept any move
against the heritage of late Greek authoritarianism
                                        (the Reformation)
is enough to discredit his system.
Maybe it was the effect of a church embedded.
Maybe it was the effect of received Romanism,
the lure of priestcraft,
maybe it was only wild decentrism,
which fueled his radical energy.
Maybe it was yet another proof
that bullshit is still the richest source we have.

NEW MATCHES FOR THE FALL

1) AGON
2) PROTAGORAS
3) DEMOCRITUS
4) ANTI-PLATO
5) HIPPIAS
6) ANAXAGORAS
7) ANAXAMANDER

ABHORRENCES
15 August 1984

I would say, with all due respect,
that President Reagan
should do a little dialogin'
with the Russians,
in the original sense:
"To arrest a conflict."*
But, I am afraid that his attitude
would be just another re-run
of Socrates' treatment of Protagoras.

---

* Thucydides

LAW & ORDER: A GOOD WAY
TO BALANCE THE BUDGET

Ronald Reagon shld
have to pay a stiff fine
every time he invokes
Jefferson's name.
This could be payable on-the-spot—
there's no need for a jury
to find such opulent libel.

"WHERE'S THE PORK?"

I have a hard time understanding
why, since their motives are based on self interest,
non-smokers are so vindictive about smokers:
it seems to me their self interest would dictate
an encouragement of smokers smoking
so that the lives of the smokers
would be foreshortened and result
in non-smokers inheriting the space
and resources thus vacated and unused.

SHOPPING LIST

1. Aluminum foil
2. Sandwich bags
3. Big bags
4. Puffs
5. Paper towell
6. Jerry Falwell
7. Pocahontas
8. Honest

"PARALYZING AFFABILITY": AN ANALYSIS OF THE REAGAN VOICE

In many respects it is still
the Voice of the Turtle:
a distant lip smacking
where no lips exist.
A congestion of several inches
of flem in the throat
suggesting honest-to-gosh
wagon trains full of right-wing
Mexican Votes, newly drenched for the occasion.

CONTACT W/ THE ENEMY #1

Filling out their bootlick applications
is one form of degradation
I've resisted for years now.

No big deal.

The award I'm sure to get
is a magnum of vitriol
poured upon my grave.

ABHORRENCES
November '84

A CANADIENNE VIEW OF
THE BORDER

The only thing we have to fear
is atmosphere.

ALL THE PEOPLE WHO WERE CRAVEN

enough to buy Volvos are still at it,
to less and less effect. A new bunch
has moved in, with Saabs,
only they're not cryin'.
They've got Purina Dog chow for brains
and they're not kiddin'.
One of the most restless, nervous crowds
seen in the west for some time.
The back of the sleek little rig
is invariably taken up with soiled laundry
and, come to think of it, the machine itself
can usually do with a wash.

    The operator is not a libber
    but seems a kind of bibber
    and getting younger by the hour.

STICKING BY THE DULY FORGOTTEN

Hughes should have lived
into the Eighties. He had
the greatest eye Ever for tissue
and I swear
If he were with us now
He would switch to Puffs.

ABHORRENCES
'84

TWICE SHY

We shouldn't have been appalled
by Philip Glasses exploitation
of the Hopi, having suffered
his opportunistic list of "poets."

DAVE RUDABAUGH

This photo was taken Feb. 19, 1886 by A. W. Lohn of Nogales, Arizona, in Parral, Chihuahua, Mexico, where Dave's head was paraded around the streets there on a pole. Rudabaugh was an aquaphobiac, bartender, cattle rustler, cypriophile, jail breaker, prospector, macquereau, misopsonorist, peace officer, ruffian, satyriasis, spendthrift, stool pigeon, tin horn gambler, train robber, and the only man feared by Billy the Kid.

These are the two rarest photographs in our collection of over 250,000 historical negatives and prints concerned with the American West. See "Dave Rudabaugh, Border Ruffian" by F. Stanley, 1961.

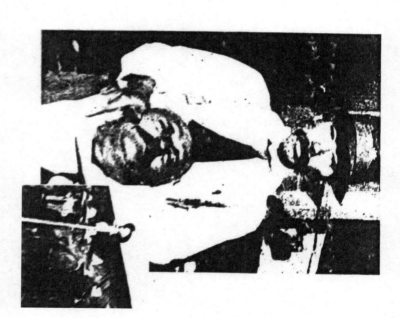

444

ABHORRENCES
"... at an epoch when
puffery & quackery have
reached a height unexampled
in the annals of mankind ..."

DAVE RUDABAUGH FOR PRESIDENT OR LOOKING AHEAD TO 1988

Rudabaugh was an aquaphobiac,
Bartender, cattle rustler, cypriophile,
Jail breaker, prospector, macquereau,
Misotonsorist, peace officer, ruffian,
Satyriasist, spendthrift, stool pigeon,
Tin horn gambler, train robber
And the only man feared
         by Billy the Kid —

ABHORRENCES
1984 Update

REALLY GREAT LIES ARE EXPENSIVE

The children of business oriented
parents deeply resent not getting
a shot at the crazed, Higher
consumerism beyond the low,
sex enturded car blow—
there must be face surgery
& tooth overhaul (though short legs
remain the biggest problem
in the overruling of nature's judgment.

ABHORRENCES
Linoleum Tattoos
14 Jan 1985
on the now forgotten
Sharon suit against
Time magazine in the
mid 80[ies]

LEGAL DEFINITIONS
AREN'T EVERYTHING

Sharon apparently won
a minor point in the Time case
that is, it wasn't found
in the record where he told
the phalangist to liquidate the muslims.
But so what? The original rumor
w/ all its doggery
was aesthetically correct.

But, you say: Everyone knows
there's nothing moral in this,
and we'll do what we want!

                        True enough.
But the record must show that,
even if it's "destroyed."

LEMMA DILEMMA

Hey! Struggle along
semi-fat gal or guy.
You won't eat enough
to increase your weight
and you won't leave enough
to reduce it.

ABHORRENCES
Wednesday 13 Feb., '85
Linoleum Tattoos

TOO LATENT FOR FASCISM

Japonese matches
are the safest matches in the world
they don't strike.

ABHORRENCES
Motto of the 80[ies]

Anything you can push,
pull,
or tow in.

THE BEGINNING OF SORROWS

   Nuclear Buggery is not
the beginning of sorrows, there
is much to come before
the beginning.

Rev. 7. So there's all this
Burning ruin & famine before we even get
to chapter nine.
Divine protection for a
certain group of people
(sounds like chapter eleven to me)
Shut up you Infidel!
There will be not any green thing.
These angels will let
all hell break loose
except them that
have a seal on their
foreheads.

Everything is going to
get blown back to
their elements which
are invisible to the
human eye
the club of Rome
is literal
1st Thessalonians 5

When the rest of the world
says hey, let's cool this
shit or the world will destroy itself
and then when they say that
when the majority of the people
of the world say that—destruction
is certain & will forthwith come!

ABHORRENCES
26–27 Feb. 1985

MEAN QUISINE

Some of them go to McDos
to have chicken McNos.
Others congregate
at the Ideal Market
in their perfectly kept
Volaris, Swingers
and the odd early Honda.
The men are so stiff
they have to climb out
like apes, hauling themselves
up by the roof.
Then, the one-mile-an-hour
transit to the shelves
to collect a foodkart
full of poprock protein
and a no salt, no wheat,
no fat, predigested no future.

ABHORRENCES
5 April 1985

the power of good editing
has created more
literatura than or-
iginal thought

ABHORRENCES

BASIL BUNTING

LeChary in his smile
Graciousness in his hosting
Easy delivery of his knowledge
Surely restful in his grave.

ABHORRENCES
20 May 85
by a Robot

PROPOSITIONS FROM
INTROSPECTION TIME

Equality is near to out:
Bring back the slaves
Says the King of Knaves
You're better off lowly than out.

THE SPECK IN THE MILKY WAY

So now we've got
our own black Hole.
Thank Heavens!
I wouldn't live
in a galaxy
without a backdoor.

RAISING BLISTERS

Truly, if the Amish notion
that compressed aer is
the work of the Devil,
then Satan's throne
is made of liquid nitrogen

A DRUG OF GREATER PRICE THAN COKE

Monoclonal antibodies
armed with ricin,
the toxin employed
to assassinate Georgy Markov
the Bulgarian,
will be used to treat
leukaemia victims next year
one treatment will take
about a gram @ 30,000.00 per gram

LETTER TO ETHIOPIA

Goodbye Ethiopia & Eritrea
Mexico has had an Earthquake
of Rock money
you can now expect
more Rock than money
and another factor,
draining off
our limited attention,
there's rain in Champaign

where money is being
raised to help those
who've been
ruined by surpluses
as you have been
ruined by scantnesses.
But there is still a hopeful
note: the disaster employees
are still eating well.

ABHORRENCES
Fall, 1985

SUMMARIES AND CONCLUSIONS OF A SEPTEMBER FLIGHT

Reading time magazine: It costs more
(in insurance) to kill expensive people—
JAL flight 123, on board a pop-singer
and 163 executives.

Gorbachev writes snoozy answers
to Sleeping Pill class questions.

Alan Berg, the vastly horrid
talk-show primate, was dispatched
with a MAC-10 by the neo-nazis,
thus invalidating the statement
proposing its banning: "Nobody
goes hunting with a weapon that fires
twenty-two rounds a second."

Richard Ramirez, the serial killer
of the season just past
is interesting for possibly mailing
the eyeballs of one of his victims
across state boundaries.

Turning to heavier reading,
—out the window of seat 37A
the morainy landscape of Wisconsin
offers a ten-thousand year record of the drainage
as well as a county by county pattern
of the property disputes in senseless
jogs and curves, all wrought by trenchant
farmers, long cold in their graves.

ABHORRENCES
2 Nov 1985

I'm haunted by my past these days
like crawling under the bed, Dec 7th
it was such a shamefully frightening act.
And it's coming up again.
When I was growing up, the Japs
were the Japs, and that was it.
Unlike the Germans, respect
was out of the question.
But I didn't question anything anyway.

I took things at their face value
as I do now. I have
never had an argument
with anyone in my life,
altho I've pretended otherwise
when it was necessary.
　　　　　Greetings, this Pearl Harbor Day.
I'm still going to be thinking about this,
and wondering where you are.

ABHORRENCES
6 November 1985

THE LONG SO-LONG

Contemporary Americans
are antihistorical
because they dislike
to be criticised. They suspect,
quite rightly,
that the past reveals
a bundle of amused derision
directed at them personally.
So they prefer to talk
to the future,
which can't talk back.

BEING ABLE

To write your name in the snow
is not important, unless there's snow.
And the fact that there's more
and more snow is no excuse. The history
of post neo-lithic types
has been fed by small animals—
rabbits & squirrels.
You don't have to "do right"
like some other men do. And you don't
have to have a job, and you don't
have to get outa here and you don't
have to get any money. You don't
have to listen to the preacher man.
And you don't have to be scared
by the possibility that some kind of
prisoner of love is going to come along
to distract you—you don't have to be
distracted at all—you don't have to scream,
you don't even have to witness the record
of the record of defeat. And you don't have
to laugh at world jokes you don't think
are funny. You don't have to relate
to anything. You don't have to Do anything,
and it is your duty to do nothing, because
by doing nothing, in a social mechanism
which derives its energy (loathsome euphemismos
from minted programming
you separate yourself from the myriadheaded
constituency of kooks, lackies
stacked upon lackies, and you know
no matter who you are, you have to do that.

What a technical advance
the wiener over the pig is

THAT WHICH IS CUTE & SICK

The California Fish & Game department
has issued, in its benevolence,
instructions to hikers and walkers
pertaining to the best method
of retreat, should a marijuana
garden be encountered accidentally,
lest the course of their living experience
be converted to shredded tissue
            & blood

ABHORRENCES
Linoleum Tattoos
Boulder, 14 Sept. '86

REPUBLICAN FORM

I hear Nancy has come out
for the death penalty.

I could go along with that
if it were truly democratic:

Yea old death penalty
for everybody.

1986 Sept.

EXPECT TO BE RIPPED OFF

If you don't expect
to be ripped off,
you're letting yourself in
for a lot of waste,
useless indignation and heartburn
and distraction from your own
ability to rip off others.
Don't be distracted,
expected to get ripped off.
Don't insure it,
let it go ruin its muscle
in outer space.

FORGET THE JAR WARS

If Hitler were in heaven,
and we know some
who think he's not,
and he saw everything so tubular
and electronic,
his heels would click indeed

to see his system
has progressed so much
since his taking of the tylenol
that he would gaze
at our picture
with utter rapture.

DYNAMO TEDIUM

Along about 2:pm
I went to the mailbox.
My God! a letter
from Ken Kramer.
He must be way desperate
to be writing to us!

ROSE BIRD

She was against
Capital Punishment &
I was certainly with her there.
The people who wanted
to lynch her I detest
as much as she did.
Yet there was something
out of register
about her—her background
the Brown connection
the tic of orientalism
in her demeanor—
I don't know what it was,
but whatever it was
a lot of people in California
deserve to fry anyway.

SEMIOTICS FOR SEMIDIOTICS

millions of people are seeking immortality
who don't even know what to do
with themselves on a rainy afternoon

ABHORRENCES
10 Nov / 1986

ON THE OTHER HAND

It would be inaccurate
to ignore that america
is a nation of renegades
from everywhere

In that respect, we have
to live with the fact that
everywhere else in the world
we're "wanted"

THE PASSING OF A GREAT BARTENDER, THE MOST IMPORTANT OF THE 20TH C.

The announcement today that,
at the age of 96, Molotov
had died, without noting
his famous cocktail
may be because Bruce Springsteen
is outselling Michael Jackson.

WITHOUT TITLE

Content *is* judgement.

ABHORRENCES
22 Dec 1986
they will be packed at the end
where they will be packed in crates

THE CHURCH THAT IS
STAPLETON AERODROME

In the broad carpeted nave
of the new concourse
the pilots with their razor cuts
and remote faces
carrying their aesthetically cheap
but mildly costly designer cases
(and in whose minds Ivan Boesky
has completely replaced Eddie Rickenbacker)
((it is literally impossible to exaggerate
the attraction of the glamorous criminal
in the current American mind))
and warped among them the various minorities
wheel the inambulatory, mostly but not all
old white women, or in the lingo of exclusion
those who are not are to be categorized
as they are trucked forth at Lourdes.

The variegated crowd, as the eugenicists
might have it, knifing their way, some frantic
and too late for the gate, all assume the same
flat stupid 'non' expressions, a hedge, presumably
against losing their wallets should they crash.
Others, the great, broad category of the nearly dead,
Ride the slow-moving flat conveyors, a *Te Dium*
(sick'em on the new gods) waiting
for the "accident" they're bound for.

ANTI-LITERACY CAMPAIGN:
TV'S ONLY NOTABLE CONSEQUENCE

The very density of print,
the relative smallness,
its secrecy, whereby,
unless focused,
makes no sense, indeed induces knots
in the neocortex,
is its protection, yea
its salvation.

Now, after decades of the painful
imposition of internal image
we know that they don't read
never should have read
and needn't have tried in the first place.

WHERE ARE WE NOW? THE TWENTIETH OR THE TWENTY-FIRST CRUSADE . . . ?

Helping our daughter with a paper
on the crusades,
some light began to seep
through the cracks of my brittle 80^{ies} brain.

One beam illuminated the surprise
and doubt on the Muhammadans' faces
when they saw the jews coming back
to the holy places
after the Great War—
Oh No! Not Europe again!

But think of the First crusade,
preached by Urban II,
at Clermont in 1095
and led by some of the all-time
lay-about heavies: Godfrey of Bouillon,
Raymond of St. Gilles, and
Bohemond of Taranto, not Toront.
Talk about uninvited company
heaving toward the heathen

Saracens sayin' who *are* these dudes
armor & shit, carrying crosses.

But then we've always
entertained them with our naked traffic.
And pray, who of those above
could have been a funnier figure
than Henry the Kiss

or Alexander of Haig—certainly
there have been none more driven
nor way enigmatic
than Oliver of the North.

ABHORRENCES
19 April 1987

EASTER SUNDAY

The Great Plains are
particularly great today.
Balminess is the all pervasive weather.
No doubt the skeeters
are already twitching beneath the mud
along the bottom of Dakota.

Saturday night we escorted
Brakhage to see Louise Hawkins
and her newly restored shots
of homelife in the 60^{ies}.
Olson, Creeley, Brakhage himself and Jane
who looked like a Sengalese princess
in those days, and Jonathan, not quite
so fat, but just as fatuous,
Smiling Jackie, the Earl of Boston,
Palin' Allen, who, except for the top,
looked like he'd soaked his head
in a pot of Hairgrow, and Peter,
just back from India seemed
to be having fun, and others,
many others, far too many.

The evidence seems to be
that there was constant smoking
and drinking going on all the time.
Nowadays that's all under siege.
A crowd like that would now be
exchanging certificates of health
and glancing over its shoulders
about two thousand times a minute.

ABHORRENCES
2 April 1987

ON PRINCIPLE: WHATEVER THE FANS WANT, I'M AGAINST

The attempt to inflate
the state lottery into
a national lottery
is one of the most pathetic
attempts yet of this debilitated,
over-exercised, age decrepit,
seropositive society. And obviously
inflation is most fueled by this
new flotation of cheap dreams.
It's parallel to the empty hope
that a linebacker can act.
Or that a rock star can think.
Or that an actor can preside.

In the Roman lotteries, Nero
a rather opulent guy, gave
such seemingly modest prizes as a house,
or a slave. Don't wince—there'd be
plenty of takers for that 2nd item right now—
One only has to glance through
the Baby M transcript to see that.

And Heliogabalus, who seems to have
had a wit, introduced an element of absurdity—
one ticket for a golden vase,
another for six flies.
That kind of non-monetary practise among our kind
would dry up the punters double-qwik.

ABHORRENCES
Boulder, June '87

OUTSIDE GART BROTHERS

Loud, abusive
expressions of red meat
thump along the walkaway
followed by the placating mother
whining What do you want dear,
How about some new Hawaiian shorts
and then a little caesars
which you can eat in the car
on the way home
to your big sliced
red meat lunch!

ABHORRENCES
8 July 1987

THE OLLIE PREDICAMENT, AN OLD MILITARY TRUTH

Shit does not
run up hill.

ABHORRENCES
22 July 1987

OLD QUOTES ARE THE BEST

During the "Hearings,"
contra, dontra
blantra, twantra,
it's hard to know what,
if anything, to not,
or whatever—
Boring, shallow
endlessly self-serving
& self-servicing
with the Russians
crowded off the page
except for the "negotiations"
(*negotiations*: what a joke
when we can't even
keep track of something
as big as a lathe?

The only thing
the present sophistication
can't do yet
is get men
to volunteer to die.
That used to be easy,
when life was less
"Attractive," and less
defined by those who
were destined to say
it is attractive, and then
sell it! One has to keep in mind
the dictum of Dryden—
"you threaten peace
and you invite a war."

ABHORRENCES
July 1987

That the american people
have the constitutional Right
to be wrong
is, of course, not the point.
The danger to "the people" (if indeed
that is a still possible terminology)
is from the scallywags who
seek to make them wrong in
particularized ways:
the scarlet fundamentalists,
the bloodsuckers of the
"Free Market" and
the theology dragons of the way way right.

SUPREME ABHORRENCE

Washing a line of Ink
off my hand with lava soap
my mind projected long-
forgotten footage of the I.C. cut
through Mattoon—about 8 rails
blue white lines on ballast
of Indian rock. It had to be the smell
that brought it. The trees of heaven
in motion on the right of way
dying in the lava.

Paul Simon, answering
a question about
El Salvador, generalized
by saying he thot
we should support
human rights everywhere
they were being
  abrogated—South
Korea, South Africa
or South Yemen.
He didn't seem
to have the
moral perspicuity
to mention South
  Dakota

ABHORRENCES
Boulder, 3 Jan 88

THE TIGHTER THE ORBIT,
THE MORE POWER

I suddenly realized it
that I've done nothing
but regress since I was 16.

And since I've regressed
a lot less than everyone else
that must mean all the world
is scalp deep in shit.

DON'T FORGET THE MORTGAGE

He pulled into the driveway
pulled up the handbrake
and pulled off the motor.
Out there before him, kinda grandiosely
lay the town, going to bed
for the most part,
but some of it still twinkling
and some of it trying to give up
and go home. The ones who had
already started to fluff their pillows
were of no mind to turn back.
They had given their lectures,
they had made some calls,
they had checked their mail,
thrown it all in the trash
because in fact that's where
it belonged, they had smiled
when they absolutely had to,
and they had frowned a couple of times
when it pleased them—
it wasn't that bad a life; one could
with a little convenient adjustment
go on like this until the year 2K.
There's more. After that,
they denied in their minds
that they had seen the hands smashed
or the batons crash or the trajectories
out of the factories of the tear gass.

Oh yes, all of it denied. Still,
(now they're brushing their teeth)
we must hire a black. Even a woman
(not white) . . . so much to keep track of . . .

ABHORRENCES
Hi Stix Jungle
A town dreaming of
machine guns—
spitting rounds,
but snoring &
jerking
July 19th '88

MOTEL SUPERBO

A sleepwalker from continent 1
prints out the contract and a key
on a ring like a leg iron.
The air condish is clogged
with the breath of old carpets.

PLATINUM PARACHUTE

For turning the golden rule
into Never Give a Sucker
a Broken Circuit: several
hundred million and 14 months.
That's better than a MacArthur.
And a lot more prestige
than a Nobel—think of the frauds
who have received that one.

CO-OPTED BY THE AXIS

The event of 7 December, 1941
(the date Bush couldn't get right)
had its climax in October, 1979
when the 4th Reich refused
to back the dollar
whereupon the USA required
                    the backing of Nipon
for the continuance of American
                    hegemonia.

ABHORRENCES
Mayday, 1989

A vast gisting of the 80^{ies},
demographical revolution,
Numerical proliferation
insinuates itself as legal
minority, mass fornication
takes the place of property
as prime claim, boreal forests
wiped out producing toilet
paper in the service of un-
precedented increase in ass-
holes, dope and crime the
employments of choice,
replacing business in the art
of boroughmongery, real-estate,
the major washing mechanism
for cold cash, goes green,
hides behind sane use, risks
killing off host, like a
primitive virus. Macro-para-
sitism oblivious to its own
risk, chain reaction consu-
mption, Malthusian terror,
demonstrated in China, where
a billion farts create chaos
theory whirlwinds in Arkansas,
Japan creates Ice from old
German Axis formula, dispatchs
couriers from Korea and Philip-
ines through Hawaii to weak
front west coast of The Peoples
Empire, California stays awake,
becomes slave chip factory,
live in tents, ride two wheelers

and then one wheel, monocycles
proliferate, tofu with a few
shreds of dog becomes the diet,
dogs go wild, desert the tent
towns, police dogs hunt civil-
ian dogs, sniffer dogs course
through Central America in
packs seeking out the secret
stores, Shining Path out to
take in the conny dogs, Nor-
iega gives free transport a-
cross canal, packdogs, the
cantonment of the canaille,
everybody eats dogshit, not so
bad, more nutrition than tree
bark, package Tours, See People
Eat Dog Shit, See Dogs Run Dope,
see Colombianos get shot with
Armalites, shoot back with
Israeli hardware more likely
South African copies. See
cheap A-bombs dropped on
barrios of replication,
See fascism in action, authentic
dictators on Ice, victims
tortured, acupuncture needles
dipped in AIDS, the ultimate
cure. Watch Coca Lords administer
local anæsthetic to chargé from
the upper latitudes, be on hand
at the firebombing of La Paz,
witness the sputtering failure
of combustion due to lack of
oxygen, learn first hand why
fire is ineffective against high

dwellers, realize that Gladys
Night and the Pips couldn't
dance in the streets of Cuzco,
experience the condition of the
mine workers who supply the vases
of the axis powers and die in
their mid-twenties of flaming
skin and ruptured organs. Meet
right-wing novelists as they run
for President of old spanish
colonies, see them borrow money
from your paycheck and deposit it
in Zurich, handle the actual bull-
whip handle used to bugger the
opposing candidate. BOOK EARLY,
don't miss that bon chance of a
lifetime. Ask yourself "If I
closed my eyes forever/
would it all remain the same?"

OF COURSE NOT, STUPID!

WOULD YOU BUY A USED CAR
FROM THIS CENTURY?

Life was immensely cheapened
by the advent of the *auto*,
and the pictures of life degraded.
Moving funerals, drive your own casket.

No matter the class of Superthigh,
put on it or inside it,
it has no situ in the depths of the mind.
Its demands are only parasitic.

Even when it is bronzed, it is no greater
than a pair of baby shoes.
It looks best wrecked, or crushed
as certain sculptors have demonstrated.

The strenuous propaganda of its libidinousness
is pure freud in the service of the peddlers
and its War Significance is just transportation
Chevy pick-ups mounted with rocket launchers.

It is so odd and annoying and stupid
to have lived in this unique and anomalous period.

ABOMINATIÓNES
(1991)

MOTTO OF THE 90'S

"Keep on scuddin'
you might get thru"

Boulder, 21 Jan. 1991

WAR IS THE BEST CURE

When will the war be over?
The war will never be over
Why will the war never be over
because the war is all —
The war is the occupation,
the aim, the diversion,
the topic — it is the very subject
it is the comfort, the terror
                    the revenge
the *reasons* for holding
the Jewish state back
But at the same time 92%
think they should attack
some think 92% are winning
the war, 67% aren't sure.
Most don't even know.

Eagleburger says
Israel has a right
to reply at their
convenience.

Well, in the 1st place,
I have never given Eagleburger
permission to say anything for me,
let alone the repellent monkey Shamir.

But let's examine this
anyway, even without
my permission — does
this mean that in
the year 2015 Jerusalem
will nuke Baghdad?
Damn! That will be
certainly after I'm gone
and my wife alive probably.

Terrible to win a bet
          when you're dead.

ABOMINATIÓNES
The cheer leader,
formerly the booster,
the "Julian Caeser"
of our time
February 1991

GEORGE HERBERT WALKER BUSH

Liar, liar, pants on fire
nose as long as a telephone wire

ABOMINATIÓNES
Rip it off &
tack it up

Baker has proved
The president has promised
to refund Irak after the
Bombing is over. Hey!
Save us some taxes
Stop destroying the fucker
if you're going to rebuild it!

ABOMINATIÓNES
7 February 1991
mass murder
on the cuff—
Euro-Ameríco,
big dick imperialism
gets stiff—
ground war abt
to commence
the best yet—the
most summary

IMAGO BELLUM

Señor Ronald Reagoné
standing outside his office
on his 86th birthday
holding a teddy bear.
And at the same hour
children are bombarded in Baghdad—

That's poetry—
that's definitely poetry.

ABOMINATIÓNES
early spring 1991
the masters of the
war portfolio
Bush & his evil clique

DETESTATIONS INCARNATE

There is no such thing
as the Anti-christ, except
the idea that there be such a figure.
Once in a while there are
entities & persons who seem to satisfy
what an Anti-christ might be
if such were manifestable.

They would behave
exactly as described
as the Scourges in charge
of the War on Islam.

ABOMINATIÓNES

POSTSCRIPT TO CAPITALIST REALITY

Daniel Ellsberg
is married to the heiress
of the Mary toy company—
you'd better believe him
because out of toys
come world behavior.

THE CONNECTION TO NOWHERE
(1992–1999)

The germ of failure resides
In the seed of success.

———————————

Sorry, cannot open
the connection to Nowhere

AN ACCOUNT OF A TRIP
WITH JEREMY PRYNNE IN JANUARY, 1992,
THROUGH THE CLARE COUNTRY

JOHN CLARE—
taking the I out of sanity

Ante-logue

Nobody knows what it's like
to be in love in the country
nobody knows what the labor's like
nobody feels the distant thermal
tedium in the fields, where the birds
mock such indenture with No Regard.

Nobody—
but the body feels the lash—
the sensation without protection
the presumptuous impost,
the chartered slave. The utterly reduced
exemplary station and circumstance.

This is not to be to be nothing.

The random catch of the free masses—
farm labor picking up after Taiwan crafted
machines. Broccoli pieces replace Tiepolo.
The post-jeffersonian experiment goes down
in an obliteration of gunsmoke the body
dies with the land scattered by nature
across the natural landscape, the sun not yet
paid, or even billed, gradually totes the bill,
the sur-charge for two point seventy-five billion
summers, the billing from the tad-pole to the Jack-off.
Nobody could or would pay it of course,
not the Jews, not the Episcopalians.

But we'll try,
we romantic, idiotic laborers for the most disgusting
members of the species

      The producers
who survive the winter night, the muscle
Dalmer
falls due in the bones, the coldest arc
on the transit, the seasons so called.
The seasons—secular wrack of the greeks
and the protestants, the mock-up of freetrade.

Resistance advertised as ill-advised—ascendence
on the third cinder takes more and more guts,

      THE FARM planet,
Head lettuce the ideal capacity—water plus nought,
jungle water embodied in the algaeic death
of Edgar G. Robinson, the cousin of Edgar and Clyde
in the brain modules of John Clare's unblесséd future—
the farm gone beyond its wretched and wracked
draft of human labor conditioned by
the fake gestures of Spring and Summer—free heat
no credit to the sun, whose ownership was,
and still is assumed, paid for with ever more
toil and exertion with a ration calculated down to
and including the last straw. Forevermore
the human slaves waste away, from the last ice
to the next ice, from winter to winter, the body dies
with the land from where it came.

      But nobody dies in the summer
nobody dies in the Fall. They die in the spring
just because they can't bring it off in the winter
when it is so beautiful nobody wants to depart.

THINKING OF MY LIFE AS A TEACHER

I'm beginning, at last
to wonder seriously
what advantages are in
a 20 year sequestration with
the minds of eighteen
to twenty-five year-olds
"A certain Freshness" perhaps?
But an inch deep forever!

PROSAIC JUSTICE

Wyatt Earp (or Wiley Twerp,
a nickname Jennifer recalls
from her London youth) was one
of the most venal and offensive
characters to have strode
the mudguard boards of the towns
of the great high west intrusion.

Two years for the average
life of the cattle town served
perfectly Earp's git in, git out genius.
That Kevin Costner
plays the marshal to such perfection
says nothing about his talent
as an actor, and everything
about his true nature.

In fact, Wiley/Kevin must be
an avid practitioner
of all seven of the deadly sins (quite
fashionable at this turn of the millennium)—
with his opportunist purchase of Deadwood,
South Dakota, exemplar town
as prefab museum, is the case made.

INTERVENTION ALLEY—
THE REVOLUTION OF THE TWO BILLS

In the revolution
of the two Bills
and one Hill, you will
bow and cower
to Seattle Bill
whose bit will be
in your mouth.
        But you won't be able
to curb your contempt
for the Hill Billy Willy.
You will forget repeat
forget Hill. Totally.
She won't forget you though
You will be a banana slug
under her big foot
which is already under
her thick ankle—and
she will send you to Utah
and you will like it
but you won't know why
or how you got there.

SUB COUPE

Carolyn Forché
must pay—
also all others
must pay
for driving our insurance rates
up and up
with their luxurious living.
and their tedious viewpoints.

RANTS & CANTS

I'll rant as well as Thou
As for what I've said
I'm just a recording angel

FANTASY HERESIES

Idaho Man burns 10 commandments
Wisconsin man burns school vouchers law
Mississippi man burns Bible
Alabama woman torches school prayer
Georgian man burns Creationist Text
Maryland student shoots delivery of graduation prayer
Driver shot for bumper sticker
"Don't pray over my wife"
in downtown Boise

¡ A CALL TO ARMS !

Poets of the Aleutian Cusp
Poets of the transpacific Plate;
Poets of the Uto-Tibetan gene pool
Poetas of the Whatever or
Where ever Underthrust—
Would you please take up Poetry?
Or skiing, or Ivory poaching,
or alligator wrestling, or
sacalait sucking

AT NIGHT THE CUPS

talk in the
cupboard

"lips that beg sex
settled for coffee"

the contempt for the cups
is beyond measure

the broken teeth,
the germ pool
on the brink of flood

the paint around
the mouth of
Hell

MO COUPS

If culture is identity, why can't you change your identity
by moving to Paris?

Bush-Saddam complex=too much self-esteem

The only difference between him and a virus is that
he can't pass through a filter

Oxymoron of the month—good technology—
(as in guided or clever bombs that save civilian lives)

The Chicken & Hominy Indians

About as likely to happen as Hollywood making a movie
With an Arab hero

The untelevised life is not worth living

Do the *Salt Lake Scrolls*

Heart of Correctness: The story
—a local broadcaster who is in a veritable cesspool
of political correctness

Go french!

Steer clear of "aesthetic attitude"

The Japanese give fascism a good name

Those people in Eugene talking to trees better watch what they say

THE DICTATORSHIP OF HAPPINESS
The pervasive shallow optimism infecting all aspects of American Life.

The only Heresy left in modern times, in the late 20th C. at least:
a plutonium suitcase left at Disney World

It was wonderful to find America, but it would have been more
wonderful to miss it.

Soft Shoe Culture
Adidas disease
Rebotikus

New Provincialism will grow into the Global Province (forget Village).
Have a nice enslavement!

THE NEW HISTORY
"But these people don't write History under the aegis of the muse,
they just complain about the history that's already been written"

11 August 1998

[THE JAW IS THERE]

The Jaw is there
to protect the Strong.
(From the rising
misery of the Weak.

overwhelmingly
the Jaw is Roman
in Faith & Perversity—
it's Mother is Mary
in fact or implied.
The Rural South
& the Midlands
still the exceptions—
(The West is faithless
& Catholic—
Progenitors of dogs
and the originators of
dogging, the feeding on
the entrails of human
Flesh—Taught to acquire
the taste in the frenzy of
attack, the ripping open
of the soft hairless throat
so much more vulnerable
than the great Fur bearers
the bear, deer, elk

Dec. 18 / 98
Dinner conversation

[REMEMBER THE STARLING SHOW]

Remember the Starling Show
coming out of the Basilica
standing in the piazza
    Piazz (Pio XII?)

Looking toward the
    Trastevere
the Tens of thousands
of starlings moving in
    skeins lilting like
            pendulums
then forming baggy structures
and then dividing like cells
coming together, swaying
as one organism the
light of the western sun
setting on their
play full, showing off—
this sight rivals the profound
stillness of the pantheon—frozen weight—
both owing nothing to christians

or dripping like globs
of honey in their contempt
for gravitas—and the
Fate of all below this
tremendous aerial display—
to be rained on by
a shower of brown stinking
shit—litres of the brown
stuff of foul smelling scat
not the harmless white
thumb size globs as from
pigeons—if you don't have
your wash in by 4 PM—
goodbye laundry

This was all the sad
testimony of the
Protestant scots man
who had invested near
the vatican when larger
& far less shit hailed quarters
were to be had at greater
distance from the centrum
the punishment for this
locational form of greed
is dirty indeed—

Dominica 20 Dec. / 1998
3 AM

[BLOWN FUSE]

Blown fuse
in the Heavy 240
　　　AMP
　　System
no light but from
the Blue Flame of
　　the gas
and the methane
　　Blue from the
　　cross across Tesallaire
and via Alba Rome
was indeed not built
in a day and its water
will not be heated
in a millennium

cold centre of power
with not so funny
money argentina
l'argent Tina
in a fur coat　Shame
Shame, we
should give them
Bill—they
deserve eachother

ON FIRST LOOKING INTO SHAKESPEARE'S FOLIOS JUST AFTER CHRISTMAS 1998, AT THE NEW BRITISH LIBRARY

It's not a state secret
That E mail is not written.
Why is this when ordinarily
Good writers are writing it?
The reason is that E mail
Is inherently bad—in and of itself
And if the most elegant and pains-
Taking care and craft were taken
With its execution the result
Would be inelegant, ugly, cheap
Clap trap and disgusting.
E mail just doesn't think
Nor does it "write."
A message that cannot wait 3 days
Is probably not at all urgent
Or worthy of delivery.
We know this
Because the messages of great importance
Have had no standardized delivery rate
Whether by horse, human runner, or the
Flash of mirror from Queribus to Puylaurens.
A cable can be handed to you
With a flourish, terse language
Pasted on crisp paper—
What an occasion!
Of course that is why it's ascendant
And will probably be final—unless
When the lights go out the goose quill
Hath another day.

OPEN LETTER TO THE APACHE NATION (UNREVISED)

It has now been twenty-three years
since the publication of the result
of my study of your people's honor-bound
resistance to the invaders from the dawn.

I am the only American poet who has addressed
your struggle at length in an effort
to pay you homage and to comprehend
the ramifications of your historic struggle.

The occasion for this re-affirmation
is the near omnipresence of your name
in the first months of this final year
in the past thousand years of blood letting.

The ruination directed at you as a people
and the incremental increase in the exercise by that
will to ruin which made up your total experience
in the final years of the last century.

Is now directed inwards toward a people
of its own heritage, a people of the schism
between the east and west—I'll state
my position here and now:

The Serbians have every right
to expugn their invaders who are
the issue of Turkish eunochs
and who have always attempted

To yoke the people of Constantine
to their pernicious & vengeful religion
Rome should be trying to heal this wound
not, through the ugly instrument of NATO,

To bomb this proud orthodox nation
to rubble—ultimately to extinction—
all in the name of a cure for "genocide."
But the aim here is dismemberment—
as it was against your nation—

And for remarkably similar pretensions
there are no prizes for the truth—
only reprisals. But poetry can
have no regard for anything but the truth—
the Clintonites should repudiate the
CNN propaganda loop and
discuss the honesties of emulating the Serbs
not madness, which is a product of our reaction.

But their desire to be left alone
rather than be force-fed a population
which, given the chance and the ordinance
is bent only on the destruction of Serbia
and its human contents, absolutely.

Ethnics everywhere should go
or be sent home—the biggest group
of invaders is of course in the Western hemisphere
the disease is too advanced to treat
but the symptoms could be treated.

The Albanian Ethnics say
they like country western and not the Balalaika
this is easy to explain
as part of the catholic muslim conspiracy
against the orthodox—the orthodox
means what it says
that's the real reason
it's pointless to bomb it
country & western has its

roots in Tennessee
or used to, now it's been moved
to hollywood—the Balalaika is authentic

Ethnicity hails authenticity
and national roots, because
ethnicity's nature is uprootedness.
Serbs don't export their youth
to America, Serbs are not significantly
working for the yankee dollah

The biggest advance in self-knowledge
would be in the home countries when
they see what these creatures of Æolus
have become—in all their extravagant
greed and inhumanity and habitual immortality.

Shocking it would be to have
this repulsive issue take up residence
in "the old country"—but those
"americans" who might see their
way to return, should think about it.

And they could take their money as a gesture
But the remittance should stop
they're setting up unstable and false economies
and a lot of very ugly oligarchies
are sucking on the end of that tube of dollars.

I would be the first to leave,
if there had been prizes for the truth.
I could leave my indian blood behind
with its due fractions of regret
and my service to my several homelands
would not be trivial and has not been trivial
But Clintonite blindness and fantasy

and jakasite perversion and fantasy
would call my address to you "racist"
and never admit their engineering

Is the only racism the question is
who's your race of choice—the hatred
beamed at the slavic peoples is so overt
nobody in the west has noticed, Hitler
also hated the slaves, we don't think Milosevic does

And the battle-axe Albright says her life
tells "the story of the evil totalitarianism"
which is increasingly evident with each
night in the Belgrade Blitzkrieg—this is
a terrible blindness—she hasn't learned this
from her tainted background (much
of which is spelled ~~Denver Colorado~~
with its twisted irony of syngenous
killings as the Serbs are being murdered
into submission
from 70 thousand feet by the Air Force
of a great modern state put at the disposal
of a woman bent on personal vengeance
towards a man she despises—this is
historically unprecedented in the annals of evil.

Whereby she gets to be, perhaps, the century nearly gone,
the greatest totalitarian of her time Heil!

Dear Apaches, the use of your name is more vile
and the abuse of your fame far exceeds
the trivialities raised over the use of sports nicknames
Who cares what Cleveland says or does
or any of those minor entities.

Denver 28 April '99

NOTES ON OLSON, 14 OCTOBER 1999

Charles Olson needs to be conceded
any incursions into human territory
he saw opening—his ocular
perceptions could not flourish
under the restricted (constricted)
"experimental" manipulation
of modern science—the opposites
of carrying a lighter and lighter
light load—our eyes at
night. The direct call of communication
in the Raven's wood—

universe, not a
mere alternate nation
when selected out, all the
cultural apparatus is just
rummaging among loose wires
scattered on the floor on the
intellect—the idea that you
get to play with what you
want until your attention wanders back
The vast light from the
green bay tree
now high yellow
increases the chances of perception
I'm reading Canto LXXXII
and that's what they were never
going to tolerate on these shores
any such increase, for long

The stones rained down and they
were the bearers of the new suns—
were the new suns which coalesced
and when they had finished their
repast by shitting in
the open cooling firepits
they took out their long-stem stone pipes
and burned the ceremonial
smoke of revolutionary
authority, that is, conquering
and control by the consumption
of the flesh of the enemy subject
so why did they consummate
why did they regulate—?
because they could
because they had assumed
the mantle of the host.

DENVER SKYLINE
(1993–1999)

ON SEEING KIDD ONTO THE LONDON SUBORBITAL AT STAPLETON, 17 MARS, 1993

Just across the South Fork
of the steaming River Styx
sits the great god Conoco, belching
its oily particulars into the honky
tonky heart of Commerce City.

What a God!

SUMMER CRITIQUE

Van Cliburn walks with great bearing
the stage is his natural ground, but tonight
he has the tourist's subjectivity—
volatile stomach, the urge to wretch,
imperative revulsion as in a great performer
but a trial for the worshipping public.

There is no touch or interpretation
in this authority, no hesitation from the nerves
The address comes from a life of high rank,
artistry is stripped of everything but power,
the lineage

The «Space» is Golders Green ¡No!
that can't be right, it's surely Fiddlers' Green.
Not that much history. Supremely tacqui,
endless cement (one would not lend the artword
Concrete to this raw arena, this enemy
of expression and truthseeking, this umbilical to hell.
and opportunity, business park, fundamental.

Van Cliburn appears bigger than difficulty, Van Cliburn
has the authority of thunder and outward resonance
striking chords from the Lyre— the crowd
not even above Liberace, the trash interference
of incoming flights from San Diego, "El 'A,'" & Vegas
I shrank back in semi-authentic shame.

So this is how he makes his money I mused
(The Moscow Philharmonic was good company),
I'd already read he crashed a few notes
and missed the pedal here and there. But
that's nothing with fingers that powerful
and timing that delayed—Tchaikovsky

right out of Texas, 3 chords for forty bucks

REPULSION—SUPERBOWL '95

"Out of the Slot!"
    (watch your language!!)

"Beautifully timed pickoff!"
    (he takes his dick out
        and waves it at the crowd)

"Even if you're a Charger fan
  you've got to admire greatness!"

    (nonsense, I'm a Charger fan
        and I puke on greatness!

           Denland 30 Jan / 1995
           For Tom Clark

ST. GEORGE DROPS DEAD AT THE DENVER ZOO

Mortal breath of the Komodo
Footlong flicking tongue
A diet of rats—Salmonellaville.
Defecating dragons in Denver!
This news is even worse
Far worse in its way
Than the luggage-eating DIA.

WEST OF THE PLATTE
ON A SATURDAY NAITTE

The Denver Art scene is so pathetic it ain't art.
It's just what you can think of.
You walk into Edge.
There is this well-made coffin

Which is a tank of water
With a full dressed suit in it,
Which should have contained Helen Vendler
But didn't. A wire inside the tie

Makes it look floated to the surface.
Not bad, anti-designer—art simple
Save your money written all over it.
But the coffin tank is crafted of fine *wood*.

That's where the money went.
Not quite Memling's diamonds,
Lie quiet Ezra, now they make wood
Out of genejuice and cellulose
Lined up in trenches like soldiers in 1914

It's wood because it looks like wood.
The purest imagism of all,
Nothing but usury: no product whatsoever.
Unemployment is a blesséd thing

Drip mechanism into the coffin,
Tin embossed ceiling—
Marcel Duchamp on a budget.
1914, the year they took the gloves off

And everybody went "trés Balkan."
Åhh Art! a bullet in the head
Or the foot, there's not much difference,
After the absurd comes the post absurd

I'm Edwardian because I'm Edward,
And the Great War was the Greatest:
It was the first piece of Modern Art—
A medley of the new techniques of death

And the last struggle for territory
Now that everything's been fuckt over
The fight is over Markets, the Chinese
The Japs, the heavy gringos from Arkansas

The best thing around last night
Was a piece at the Pirate on Marxism
A sawed out book, a balloon inside
Stamped with a hammer and sickle

Chilly night for the peace and art crowd
On the plains planes land and taxi
To hi-tech teepees; passengers offer up
Their luggage to be ripped and crushed

And devoured and delivered and *spit out*
Identifiable only by biotech, not quite as bad
As shoved off the road by German Engineering,
But since you'd be dead now, it can't matter.

Across the river ~ ~ I mean street
The Pirate gallery is ablaze
Knots of mildly freaky people
Smoke, and like apes, avoid the issue

Down the street is a run down restaurant
Better days receding into the wake
Italian almost gone. Pagliacci's alone
Upholds the class of the old enforcers

THE SCREWBALL

There's my guy
on patrol, janglin keys, chains
rings upon all his fingers
studs scattered like imps
Bellbottoms (Feb. 1996)
He's not pierced
yet he might as well be.

He stoops to conquer
a vagrant piece of trash
blown in from a franchise
on Federal. He ushers it
toward the skow
holding the thing
like it was positive
at arms length.

Then prances across the ice
glancing back at his patch
and into his shelter
among the recovering

Ø Lay the binoculars
on the desk. Time
transits the Highlands
The Shining Mountains
cut their mighty silhouette
The Sun
appalled by tedium
decides to go down.

REPULSION II:
AT THE SNACK-CRAZED SAFEWAY
2/30PM ROCKY MOUNTAIN WINTERTIME
31 JANUARY, 1999

The media event is fast approaching
when I wander witless as a clod
into the Safeway at 26th and Federal
heart of nahuah

Back in the parking lot I am
now chewing an apple strudel
and observing a wild Mexican argument
under the traffic light, deciding
drunkenness is the crux of the matter
when an overweight homeless lady
speaks to me in high voice saying Those guys
tried to work me around but had her brother'd
been there none of that sorry stuff
would have occurred—Yep, for sure sez I
thinking, unless he'd showed up Drunk

For sure sez I unless they're all snacked up
and bug-eyed and drunk and gassed
and on gassex and stewed to the gills
on this Superbowel Sunday, because
in Denland's it's 45 degrees for *High*,
therefore this madness is headed
for the interior—gross bodies,
hefting foodstuffs, fuel for their
great, protensive Broncoguts

PLUS DE LANGUEDOC VARIORUM:
A DEFENSE OF HERESY & HERETICS
(1992–1999)

1099—ONE HUNDRED YEARS
AFTER ANDROMEDA BLEW UP

The year near the end of the first millennium,
actually it was in effect 100 years later,
time travelled pretty slow then, when there
was only one candle and God had it.
And when he put his hand in front of it
the chickens went to roost.
The commute was about a quarter of a mile.
That be a tether on the current hot-shots
a rope a quarter of a mile long. That would
krimp the smile on the face of the Nexus.
Yeah, right, this is not written on a typewriter.
That would mean Ted and Jane would
have to decide—stay home and Ranch,
and this would entail admitting that buffalo
is drier than beef, and that
the interbred product is going to produce everything
from Bill to George.
or become the prisoners of CNN or
apologize to Joan and Bob. Or, better yet

This is 1995—the tail-end of five years before
the end of the Segundo Millenianum, meaningless
cheap hoods in power. Forget the mafia,
these types are from the Ozarks—
the Chiapas of Amerique Norde.
Wake up Citz,
they know what they're talking about
in Nye County.

AUM: HERESY AUTOMATIC DESIGNATION CULT

The Roman Catholic Church is never routinely called a cult even though it is ridden with Priests and practices magic and illusion. But Aum Supreme Truth is always called a cult because it is Japanese and is led by Shoko Asahara—

[Judge: Is your name not Chizuo Matsumoto?

Shoko Asahara: I abandoned that name.]

but mainly because Supreme Truth is rabidly anti-American and certainly because they made explosive devices [IRA not considered cult for their neo-Marxist counter-Reformation war against the English who have been made pariah in population-dump Catholic America] and because Aum's leader and holy person and heresiarch taught commuters to emerge from where they were riding in holes in the ground gasping for urban air puking lung lining onto the asphalt like post-industrial œconomic war dogs.

The underground gassing of the worker moles ordained by Shoko Asahara disturbed Japan's self-confidence that it was the safest country in the world. For that alone the assassin should be exonerated—and then hung in the effigy to the nation's base rendering its guilty conscience by revenge on the individual.

UNABOMBER AS HERETIC

Unabomber apprehended in western Montana while Freemen under siege. Unabomber manifesto described by media as "meandering." This is a distortion made possible by the fact that only a very few people have seen it or will see it—if indeed it is not removed by the state from the public zone. Risky to speculate but Freemen could be bombed out during shift of attention to unabomber, the date and occasion of which can only be arbitrary as they reportedly had tracked him to his cabin N.W. of Helena. Manifesto is very well written, using the conventional 19th Century practice for strict text of numbered paragraphs. The cause of the media hate is simple enough—the manifesto is totally hostile to post-industrial digital mentality, and it is by definition contra "media."

There is no rational defense permitted for individual action resulting in the deaths or injuries of other individuals—rational is reserved for mass killings (not serial) such as Henry Kissinger's bombing *en cachée* of the Cambodians, or George Bush's carpet bombing of Baghdad just north of the Garden of Eden—they are not mad bombers. And for one of those exemplary acts a peace prize was awarded. And yet the unabomber's use of explosives in his war was not crude, not delivered from 60,000 feet, not indiscriminate by design but by the circumstance of accidental traffic. The charges were small—the geneticist's hand was altered, not disintegrated, and had been rebuilt into a hand that looks like a webbed hand or a claw—a sort of ironic reverse genetic alteration in keeping with the polemical objectives of the unabomber—a resistance fighter against the evils of the proprietary genetic recombinant industry.

The unabomber's heresy might be punished by death, but not by burning, the only purification acceptable. But the denial that this will be punishment for anti-industrialism accompanied by death (as industrialism is inevitably accompanied by Death) is so extreme that the means of revenge will be electrical or chemical, probably the latter. The traditional execution, the firing squad, is honorific for political disagreement with the state. Hanging is still the terrific method from the age of contraption—the early guillotine a perversion of French industry obsessed with "design."

The real and effective criminal here is not Ted Kaczynski but the legions of industrialists and their hireling scientists who for the past quarter millennium have hewed to the principle that if it can be found out it must be found out—the serpents in the Garden of Eden climbing the Tree.

A REVIEW OF VOLUME TEN OF THE
OLSON/CREELEY CORRESPONDENCE

I'm thinking tonight of suing the Olson Estate
At Storrs for the damage inflicted on my intellectual development
At Black Mountain from the silence and secret hostility directed
Toward John Milton—OK, that's one thing, a slavish following
On the only real mistake master Pound was guilty of, I absorbed that.
But the failure to hold up the text of James Thomson's
City of Dreadful Night was deep intellectual abuse, intentional
And deceitful—there's no forgiving such selective omission.
That's a crime peculiar to the Roman Catholic—
Inheritors of a technological revolution to which they contributed
The involuntary misery of wage slaves and not much else
except for the special touch fascists have for runnin factories.

And maybe naming Creeley as co-conspirator for his endless
doting on that love-sick asshole Stendhal—'twas mindless!

MONOTHEISM

A lot of human time has been served resisting the proposition that there is a representative of God on earth and you can send your taxes to his address. The whole school, comes from the sheath of the great poet's disdain for monotheism, and its frenzied singularity, its unremitting war on culture. There is an utter lack of heresy in the Modern School (even Pound's "treason" was intensely American, Publik, by definition) in general and how they transferred a whole sensibility from the public to the school, losing a massive presence and alertness. The Moderns could not afford the wild involvements of the 17th century. The first and last century to actually rebel, with the best army. The Bank as alternative to the Church has had only occasional rewards and those have been bought with the price of war. Their dismissal of Milton can never be lived down.

JESUS—HE WAS A HANDSOME MAN, AN ESSAY ON THE RECONSTRUCTION OF THE WHOLE WESTERN MYTH

One of the most powerful crossroads in modern poetry occurs in the West, when e e cummings meets Buffalo Bill, when cummings writes Bill's obit. *Buffalo Bill's/defunct* is the quintessential "modern poem," not *The Wasteland*, not *The Cantos*. All the prolix passion of those two monuments (yes, *The Wasteland* is passionate, if you can take cold passion) represents the return to traditional order and memory and is indeed the flowing counter-revolution underlying the modern movement—but only the intense, implosive concentration of cummings' obituary "remarks" on the embodiment of the northern European bloodline is modern in the unencumbered, universal sense.

ANOTHER HERETIC TAKES WING

Who could have thought
that when Henry the VIIIth
(Henri Huit? that's a lot of Henries)
fiddled all those wives
and severed their heads
for no more than the right issue
all those troubles would
be left to devolve on the bent shoulders
of poor Billy Wright who when a lad
had to carry a shotgun
just to get the hay in
past the ever sulking, Marxist
rule-by-terror present Catholic killers.

Gunned down anyway as expected
a victim of the "peace settlement."
Here's to a great Protestant heretic
whose soul found liberty, something
his murderers will never know.

SUBTEXTS

¶ The Mormans are not part of the problem or the solution. This is a people who airbrush out the beards of their forebears. They make a desperate woman give the money back she made acting out a story of the times, which represents the case of countless thousands, and which touches the spontaneous, intuitive, true hearts of a nation which knows it is cheating and killing its abandoned and thrown-out civic relatives. This is really Religion. God is imposed to forestall rebellion.

¶ The market suffers from restrictions on the master players. Michael Milken, the great Jewish financial magus, for example should have been encouraged (not to say allowed) to strip the market of every last one of its assets, the entirety of its holdings, all of which were got by manipulation and private knowledge, by preying like a lamprey on the œconomic corpus. Individuals of genius who can enter the cathedral of money and pillage the stores are the only check on the virus of the executive commune, the Board, whose expropriations capitalize the escape from a shrivelled collapsing sucked-out prune known locally as the third planet. The vision is the race to the rocket. Saigon transported to the Florida peninsula. The growing church of Airstreamers flocking around the launch pad, demanding, screaming, then begging to go. The apocalypsus on view as the 2nd millennium comes to a close is the rotten fruit of bad engineering. The most controlled political structure ever on Earth was the most toxic, while the most open and free was the most septic. One created Chernobyl, the other created AIDS. Both deviant Christian entities.

¶ Christian Criminals ignore the code, | work on Saturday when | the Bureaucracy is asleep | on their fat subsidized conches, snoozing while | their teams go down in fast food flames. | Christian Criminals | build extension pop tops (at night) | alter interiors, take | chances with structure | they are the termites | of the economy who | frighten Catholics and unions | and masons and all the medieval | brotherhoods of control, | all those Romans who still live by | levy by say-so alone | the decadent, ancient Dark

Whites | from the Mediterranean Basin, | the children of Caesar, the enforcer | who roamed the urban night, | the awful consequences of the eternal | quarreling of the clans—the Christian Criminals | are greater than | the stupefied pizza eaters | and all their Hollywood replicas. | The Christian Criminals | Break the code on Saturdays— | the very heart of the Judeo Central Control: | as for Rome | it exported agents under the designation | of immigrants, disguised | in poverty, to enroll as supplicants of the | new Business State, | with the aim of breaking it by sheer | weight of numbers— | but lo, & behold, the very | definition of themselves | became the grist of the Satanic Mills | of internationalism | the table waiters of Al Capone America | charismorphic | thus Culturalism, self-devouring cloning, | the utter end of the individual.

¶ The first Schism is reflected in the second cold schism, East and West as ever. Constantine established the autarchy which seemed ended in Stalin, arbitrary authority guided by intuitive mass murder. But Russian autarchy never ends, anymore than the American pretense of democracy.

¶ The Roman emperial line ends as it began in the management of the mob, and unlike arbitrary rule, requires belief and faith, and an ever-watchful eye out for deviation with pervasive checks and cellular reporting and ends in bad engineering. The Stasi was like the PTA compared to the mental enslavement of the American mob.

¶ Stalin attended the plays of Bulgakov. An interested diversion from the vast task of eliminating the opposition.

¶ But Bill sucks up to the Jesuits and confesses to being the most Jesuitical Baptist on earth—a claim which would probably have no contesters—and then he makes a pass at a frozen virgin mummy pilfered from a Peruvian glacier. And supports the Roman fascists against Serbians who were super-abused and systematically tortured by Hitler's Wehrmacht and then by the Croation Ustashe.

¶ Sendero would presumably resent the former, and not care much about the latter, which would be a shame because though Global rule is evil, Global care and concern for the ruled is enlightened. And useless without the use of an army, and the proprietary technology of the bad engineers.

¶ The whole harvest of terrorism has been sown by the state, and is farmed, season after season by the functionaries [field workers] who are the writ-serving battalions of the state, and the technical mob who control the traffic in unrecorded funds, and accumulate and horde the vast wads of ink-printed denomination which the Freemen (œconomic heretics) say ain't worth the paper which bears it.

¶ In other news "America trashed by immigrants" say Red Indians. Europeans and Orientals could at least pay rent, if they're not going to give it back. So what if the discovery was inevitable given European technological advances (like sailing against the wind, strong magic for sure) that doesn't excuse squatting on land already occupied, and the fact that the natives lacked a sense of private property is no just excuse since one is supposed to be governed by one's own ethic, not by the standards of a continent full of unpredictable savages.

¶ Jackie Onassis, whose effects were sucked up at auction by the excess cash of Savings and Loan criminals seeking material haven, will probably never walk the earth again, but if she does she will have gained weight in the grave, say paleodietitians.

¶ The Kameradschaft of the Federal Reserve Board raised rates today, to the general, actually complete approval of the Banking interest.

¶ Gunrunning and Interventionism go together like incest and bad blood. Is the Commander-in-chief nothing but a salesman of Pentagon arms contracts? If the Ruskies have weapons-grade material to sell, why shouldn't they sell it. Why is it wrong for a dictator (customer) in a small sectarian nation, who holds his pants up with a scimitar, and who has more wives to protect than anybody can admit in Salt Lake City, not have an atom bomba.

¶ If the right to bear arms is the last and final protection against arbitrary intimidation in a world where anarchy is the actual state and objective reality, and where the State assumes the power to destroy individuals and collections of individuals who deny the State's sanction and who say that state is based on nothing more than got-up paper, which includes its money and its moral rules, and the re-engineered preferences, while at the same time said state disdains those who are congenitally dependant on the very agency which created them from the malpractice of even the rules it pretends to understand and, then anybody whosoever has the right to any kind of weapon they are able to invent or acquire.

¶ Lobbing a Moli into the lobby of the cloakroom of power is a greater obligation than voting.

¶ Sanctimony follows the money. Questioning or calling into doubt the justice of the Waco Incineration becomes the key to all other non-conformist heresies. McVeigh, the Luther and the Huss of exploding fertilizer (very Agro) groomed (created) by Feds as the serpent in the Garden of Total Control, nothing but prolonged, public torture will satisfy the Oklahoma Mob, so close to Waco ethnically, and so caught out when their tragedy suddenly was not unique, but was missing a record of earlier grief for pain of their Texas kindred. Every time the nation's Baptist (Jesuit wannabe) President flies in to catch their tears in the basin of his Southern Corruption, the embarrassment grows deeper, like the muck and offal in a low country pig lot.

¶ More interestingly around this time in the waning decade Arthur Finkelstein's advice to Louis Farrakhan to get fucked on a permanent basis was greeted by Louis Farrakhan's willingness to get fucked but not by Mr. Finkelstein. A reply immediately ruled racist by the Israeli lobby. Racist in what sense is still (15 June 1996), awaiting clarification.

¶ Then a counter-revolutionary event when "The Engineer" got his head blown off in the Gaza Strip, Mission Impossible style, by an Israeli bomblette planted in a cellular phone which had been recalled on the pretext of malfunction. This legendary Palestinian was one of the greatest explosives designers of the post-modern period. But his fatal flaw was a modern, widespread, acquired habit—the almost heroin-like compulsion to communicate at a distance with someone you can't see.

¶ The fruits of the sacrificial burning at Waco arrive home to roost on the sanctimonious boughs of the children agenda, and the contest for who is most protective of the children sharpens the struggle to possess the inchoate section of humanity.

¶ The sacerdotalism of Bill (#2) Gates, the standard and sign of macromoney, on the rise, questions of his overall œconomic spanking power unsettled—Alan Greenspan the fiscal magus, the marionette of Ayn Rand, who dead as she is yields more power than any block of voters and ignores the minorities and laughs at the majority while she protects bonds and deprives the worker inflation, the only chance he has at money. This arrangement deserves insurrection, as much as anything that has ever gone on in this country. What does it get? Grudging, unfocused compliance. In fact this condition is the base from which the counter-reformation encircles and encompasses and enchants its prey: the freedom of the spirit and the spontaneous will. This single God is money, and nothing else. There is an attempt in "the scholarship" to deny that Ezra Pound ever recognized that the material world, or the material itself, is from inception and in every case evil. Those critics are bank clercs. For Pound, material & evil were the unseverable twins of usury. The sacerdotalism of the 30-year bond market is the keystone of Judeo-Christianity, it's the chasm across which we gaze back at the pagan disdain for the future. Bankruptcy? Give it a chance.

¶ My teacher told me, the styles of anthropology will come and go, but the study of the components of man will never change—to see clearly and witness for honesty's sake the evidence that whatever stupid god created this thing should hang by the neck until dead, so dreadful have been the consequences of the design. And the purpose? Facing the fact that one is a member of the ultimate freak-case species in the local universe is fairly awesome. Amen to the whole protracted episode, bye bye to the cartoonization of all that has been and can ever be.

¶ Intellectual workers are poorly paid— | they have to take comfort in | not being thieves, liars and cheats | like the rest of the population.

¶ The Catharans shared a fundamental conception of the universe: materiality and mundane matter were evil, and subject to the relentless onslaught of the evil spirit and the habituation of that spirit's conniving programs which, from the grave, are the author of such ghoulish œconomic indicators as the more prolific the unemployed the better for invested money. Poverty is enhanced by the growth of the rich. Thus it is that antisacerdotalism was at the root of most of the early, classical, defining heresies.

¶ Divorce is the greatest accomplishment of the American pseudo-freedoms, the greatest threat to Roman impositions of arbitrary order, the most effective shield against the lash of central authority. It is the "free dog" clause in the social discipline of sanctioned marriage. The most significant achievement of the Protestant movement.

¶ Northern Ireland Protestants | know there is nothing for them | in this treacherous bid for peace. | Catholic Ireland is the very undergarments | of the Whore of Rome. | Freedom has a price.

¶ Terrorism is the ultimate product of the modern secular state, just as torture and persecution were the instruments wielded against disobedience to the altar and the throne in the Middle Ages and before that to the imperium. Hail Caesar! Hale Irwin¡

NAZDAKS

TELEFONUS INTERRUPTUS——BREAKFASTUS INTERRUPTUS
——MENU MENISCUS——LUNCHCHECK UPCHUCK——DUMP
IT——EERIE THEORY UP AN EIGHTH——DREARY THEORY UP A
QUARTER——LEERY THEORY UP A HALF——QUEERI UP ONE
AND A QUARTER——DUMP IT QUICK——SPEED OF THOUGHT
DOWN A FIFTH——HELMHOLTZ UP AN EIGHTH——SIGNAL
CONDUCTION MODEST, 50 METERS PER SEC——BRAIN
PROCESSES LIMIT THOUGHT VELOCITY——GET USED TO IT——
MECHANICAL MALFUNCTION RISING——MENTAL DOWN ONE
AND THREE QUARTERS——DIMMER DINNER——STALKED BY
CELERY——SELL BY MIDNIGHT——MALFUNCTION UP A
THIRD——EERIE THEORI RISING——NUTS ON A ROLL——
GOODYEAR CONDOM OVERHEAD——CROWD STEADY——
AMBIEN ZOLPIDEM TARTRATE DOWN AND SOMBULENT——
FISH-EYE SHOT FROM GOODYEAR CONDOM——CROWD
DOWN THREE-QUARTERS——HIPFLASK HIPPODROME——
MORE DROME THAN HIP——MESSAGE ON OVERHEAD CONDOM
CIRCUM STADIUM+++THERE ONCE WAS A KILLER IN LA / WHO
TRIED TO MAKE PHONE-INS PAY / THE CUSTOMERS SAID FUCKIT
/ WE'RE NOT GONNA SUCKIT / WE AINT GONNA PAY NO
WAY+++900 NUMBERS DOWN A DIME——TALK IS CHEAP, BUT
STILL NO TAKERS——PERFECT CRIME WORTHLESS——LIKE
ITALIAN BONDS AFTER THE FALL OF MUSSOLINI——POUND (IE
EZRA) TAKES A BATH——GENDER FASCISM UP 90%, INVESTMENT
IN POGROM FOR EUROAMERICAN MALES——ACADEMIC
MARXISTS STEADY ENTRENCHED PRICING——REPRESSION OF
THE MARKET IN STANDARD WORKS——NAZDAQ PLUNGES,
LITERATURE FORCED INTO BANKRUPTCY——BURGHERS OF
THEORY REPLACE SAMURAIS OF LITERATURE——MARKET
VALUE OF NEW ISSUE NIL——SELL IT——FEAR AND LOAFING
UP A NICKLE——WIDEN THE RUNWAY——GOOFBALLS
STEADY——TAX SHELTER QUOTATION: INTIMIDATION BY
WIELDING THE DIETY LONG TERM——BUY——GROS CHIEN UP
HUIT MILLE FRANC——PIG HOCKS GLUT THE MARKET——GET

OUT——BODY PIERCING UP A QUARTER——BACTERIA COUNT
SHARP INCLINE——VIRUS BURST STEADY——HOLY VIRGIN UP
A NICKLE——FRANCESCA DA RIMINI DOWN FOREVER——FEAR
AND LOAFING UP A PESO——LESS THAN MINUS ZERO UP
NOTHING——SELF-FLAGELLATION ON THE RISE——GUILT
AND SELF-RECRIMINATION UP ONE AND A QUARTER, GILT UP
AN EDGE——ABUSE UP SHARPLY——EXCUSE UP THREE-
QUARTERS——GET RID OF IT——NAIL THE BOSS TO THE
CROSS——CONFESS AND THEN ACCUSE——TRASH IT——JUNK
IT——SELL IT——PUMP IT OR JUMP IT OR DUMP IT BUT DON'T
HUMP IT——INFECTION ON THE RISE——LANGUE D'OÏ SPLIT,
SADIC DIVIDEND——OUR MOTHER'S CATHEDRAL DEVILS IN
STONE——OBSCENE CARVINGS IN THE MISERÈRE STALLS, HOLY
GHOST REVELATIONS MERGER ANNOUNCED——DEVILETTES
BUGGERING GOING GOING——UP——DOWN——UP——
DOWN——UP——DOWN TOWN——OPTIMISM BIG AS A
HYAENA'S CLIT——THE MARKET TRÉS BALKAN——BONDS
FOR WAR ON ISLAM CONVERTED TO MASSACRE OF THE
ORTHODOX——ARMS STOCKS ADVANCE——BUT OPTIMISM
FLAT——LANGUE D'OC, TECHNICAL TRICKS SURGE AHEAD——
MERRIMENT AVEC INVECTIVE UP AND AWAY——BUY
SHORT——HOLD——RYDER RENTAL TRUCKS UP, WAY UP,
ALL THE WAY UP, OVER THE TOP——SELL——DUMP——
LIQUIDATE——NEW MESSAGE ON GOODYEAR CONDOM
CIRCUM OVERHEAD: THERE ONCE WAS A JURY IN LA / WHO
SAID NOLO'VICTED, NOLO PAY / HE'S YOUR NWORD NOW / BUT
HE'S OUR SACRED COW / SO GET THE FUCK OUTA THE WAY!——
NAZDAQ SUMMARY JUDGEMENT UP FIVE AND THREE-
EIGHTHS——TRADE IN ROPE BREAKS CEILING——SUBMISSION
ON THE RISE——DRASTIC MEASURE TO MAINTAIN ORDER,
MASS AND RANDOM EXECUTIONS——PANIC IN THE PRISON-
BUILDING LOBBY, DOWN A NICKLE——OVER-PRICED HUTS,
OVER-AMPED NUTS, SILICONIZED BUTTS GAINERS——PUTCHA
CONDOM ON, THE NEW LEG-FLASK, SMOKELESS ROOMS
FULL OF CALISTOGA, PISS IN IT, POUR IT BACK IN THE
CALISTOGA——PALMOLIVE UP ONE AND A QUARTER——

DREADED WINTER, FULL OF RAPING CANADIENNES——
MODERN AS A POST: SHIP THE JOBS ABROAD, PUTEM OUTA
WORK B/C THAT'S ALL THEY GOT. FIRST (16TH C.) SEPARATE
ŒCON AND ETHICS, AND THEN GET RID OF THE ETHICS——
GROS CHIENS ADVANCING ON THE SINGAPORE INDEX,
PREMIUMS ON MONKEY BRAINS, LIVE AND QUIVERING AT THE
TABLE——GOURMET FAR EAST MONKEYS UP A QUARTAH——
WITTERUNGSVERHÄLTNISSE WORSEN, DARK NAZDAQ——
WESTWARD HAUT——I AM NO GREEK, QUOTED——THE
BEARS YAWN, THE BULLS DALLY WITH THE FIXERS——
SPORZANDO SHADOW BOXES WITH RUINATION——OPTIMISM
TAKES IT ON THE CHIN, TRUST AND RESOLUTION IN STEEP
DECLINE——ROGUE, INC., [THEORY SOFTWARE] LAUNCHES
HOSTILE BID FOR EUROLIT——TRASH AND PULP MIXED
WITH VITRIOL FLOOD THE MARKET, FERTILIZER EXPLOSIVE
NEWS ONLY IN THE MIND OF THE ACADEMY——FANTASY
UP SEVEN EIGHTHS——RESULTS OF PROCEDURALS YIELD
THE FOLLOWING: ATF SCHOCKTRUPPS BADLY IN NEED OF
INSTRUCTION IN EMOTIONAL AWARENESS, SELF-CONTROL
AND NON-INCENDIARY CONFLICT RESOULTION——
SANCTIMONY SOARS——INVERTOR OF BLACK HOLES FINDS
©OD——PIETY GOES THROUGH THE ROOF——BOGOMILS NOT
AT TABLE IN DAYTON——NEGOTIATIONS FOUNDER ON OLDEST
DILEMMA OF LES BALKANS: INNATE HATRED BETWEEN THE
RELIGIOUS FACTIONS——«RECONCILIATION» (WHICH NEVER
WORKS) TAKES A DIVE——THERE ONCE WAS A KILLER CELL /
KNOWN AS THE CELL FROM HELL——GOODYEAR CONDOM
CIRCUMS DOWNTOWN CLEVELAND, MISTAKEN FOR AKRON,
DROPS TONS OF SPERM PELLETS ON ROCK HALL OF FAME, NO
EFFECT——FAME FLAT, ANONYMITY ADVANCES——CHRISSY
HYNDE, BOB LEWIS, JERRY AND THE PACEMAKERS, THE
MOTHERSBAUGHS, STEADY AS FIRESTONES——FORGET THE
BROWNS, JIM BROWNS GONE ANYWAY——DEAD AYN RAND
STILL PULLING THE STRINGS OF GOVERNMENT WITH HER
MARIONETTE ALAN GREENSPAN——INTELLECTUAL MARKET
SUFFERS SEVERE DROP, NOTHING LIKE 87, OR WAS IT 86 OR

88 WHEN MICHAEL JACKSON'S AND TED TURNER'S ADVISOR STRIPPED THE REPUBLIC OF ITS PILFERED ASSETS—— FRANCESCA DA RIMINI SILENT——MARKET CLOSED ON MARTIN LUTHER KING DAY [JUST KIDDING——NAZDAQ "INTELLECTUAL" INTERVENTIONIST MARKET IN CANT AND JARGON PRACTICALLY ALWAYS UP, SURGES TO THE GREATEST EPIPHANY SO FAR——TROOPS ON THE MOVE, WORLD COPS OUT TO STAMP OUT ALL DIFFERENCE——CULT OF BOZNIAKS LOBBY PRESS TO ACCELERATE CREATION OF MORE SERBIPHOBES——BILL PUSHES ON TOWARD THE OCCUPATION OF BELGRADE——SOUTH SLAVS TO BE CONVERTED TO MESS OF POLES——TZECHOSLOVIA TO BE REWARDED IN VAST AND EXTREMELY BELATED RETROSPECT FOR BURNING HUSS—— COUNTER-REFORMATION MEMORIALISED, HENRY VIII BURNED IN EFFIGY IN BOSTON, BILL COMMISSIONS LIKENESS OF THE POPE IN MARBLE, POLISH MARBLE, TO REPLACE WASHINGTON IN THE ROTUNDA——ALL PURITAN AND CONGREGATIONALIST SITES DESECRATED, BURNT, COVERED OVER AND EXPUNGED, TOTALLY EXPUNGED——RIGHTEOUSNESS BANKRUPT, SELF- RELIANCE CONTRACTED OUT AND SUBJECTED TO THE TERMS OF THE CORPORATE STATE, WHICH IS SIMPLE, ROME—— AUTARCHY UP, RAD AND SPREADING——TECHNOLOGIES DOWN, OVER HYPED, OVERBOUGHT, OVER PROJECTED, OVERSOLD, ALL ON A PROFIT OF MINUS ZERO TOTAL—— PEOPLE LOOK LIKE THEIR DOGS IS AXIOMATIC, PEOPLE WITH BONE MARROW TRANSPLANTS FROM BABOONS WALK LIKE BABOONS——RUMOURS OF BABOON FARMS FOR GROWING MARROW ARE TOTALLY FALSE——ALL INPUT IS SENSORY—— UNDER "CRAZY HMO" PATIENT REQUEST: "I'M GOING TO DIE MY WAY, SO I WANT A CHANCE TO GO OUT FUCKING": HE HAD THE OPERATION WHILE BEING BUGGERED——INSURANCE PREMIUMS SKYROCKET, YET HOPE IS STILL THE ONE MUSCLE THAT CANNOT BE FLEXED——BODY PIERCING SUPER UNKOSHER, GREEN HAIR DISCONTENT AND WILLFUL UNREST——COSMETIC STOCKS CONTINUE A RISE BEGINNING WITH THE QUEEN OF BAGHDAD WITH ONLY ONE PLATEAU TO

FLATTEN THE ASCENT TO THE PRESENT: THE DARK AGES, A
PERIOD OF TOO LITTLE LIGHT TO TELL THE DIFFERENCE——158
JOSEPHS ARRESTED FOR "RECEIVING" PHARAOH'S RING——
JEWS FOR JESUS RAKING IT IN, CONTEMPLATE TV MINISTRY——
"CALL YOURSELF A JEW? WHEN YOU'RE WALKING INTO A
CHURCH?"——NO STATS AVAILABLE ON MARKET EFFECTS AT
THIS TIME——FATE IS IMMUNE TO ITS OWN EFFECTS, SAITH
THE RABBI——WE CAN DEAL WITH THE TURKS, WE'RE BOTH
AUTARCHYES OF THE SMALL CROWD——DAMASCUS? THERE
CAN BE NO PEACE WITH OR IN DAMASCUS——THE 'ORMANS
WILL ADMIT MORONI WAS A FAGGOT BEFORE THAT
HAPPENS——REAL-ESTATE ALONG THE OLD NEVADA/UTAH
FALL-OUT TRAIL WHERE JOHN WAYNE BIT THE DUST PLAYING
THE GREAT GENGHIS KHAN SPIRALS UPWARD——PUNTERS
DYING TO RETIRE AND BASK IN THE RADIATION——STOCK
IN RADIUM-INFUSED ANAL SUPPOSITORIES SOAR, BUT
EXPECTED TO SOUR DOWN THE LINE AS ASSHOLES ROT AWAY
UNDER THE BOMBARDMENT——A MARKET WAG SUGGESTS
MADAME CURIE'S REVENGE FOR THE PATENT ON THE
ULTIMATE CURE FOR THE LOW END——ROCKY FLATS WILL
NEVER BE CLEAN——ETHNIC CLEANSING, COMPARED TO THE
EFFORT TO RID THE SITE OF POISONOUS FISSION PRODUCTS,
INSIDIOUS, LONG-LIVED, LOVING DAIRY——SOUR CREAM
DROPS SHARPLY, ETHNICS WEEP, MARKET IN DELI CRASHES,
BOOM CONTINUES IN "FALL-OUT" REAL ESTATE——JUBILATION
TIME!: ONLY 1 IN 8 BAGS DEVOURED BY DISTRIBUTION
SYSTEM AT LOCAL LAND-FRAUD AIRPORT, OPTIMISTICALLY
DUBBED DIA, BUT POPULARLY CHRISTENED DØA——NAZDAQ
TAKES SPACE JUNK HITS, DECOMPRESSION RAD——BACK ON
"EARTH" VICTORIA'S SECRET? VICTORIA HAS NO SECRET,
UNLESS IT'S SELLING OVERPRICED KNICKERS TO MEN CHEAPER
THAN TO WOMEN¡——"THAT'S NO SECRET, THAT'S SEXISM"——
HOW DO I KNOW¿ ¡BECAUSE. BECAUSE "I'M OLIVER NORTH!"——
ADVICE FROM THE BEARS: GET OUT OF PANTIES PRONTO,
PANTS DROPPING——STOCK IN CHURCH OF PAEDERASTY
AND ∏UBLICITY SOARS——WOODY TOURS EUROPE WITH

DISNEYLAND NEW ORLEANS BAND, DISPLACES ORNETTE WHOSE DATES ARE CANCELLED——CELEBRITY STOCK CLIMBS, SHARES IN GENIUS AND INNOVATION DUMPED——WOODICON BID UP, ASKED THE LIMIT PLUS COMMISSION "FOR BEING THERE"——"BELLUM OMNIUM / CONTRA OMNES," THE MOTTO OF THE POET, ORDERED STRICKEN FROM THE PROGRAM—— THE CHURCH OF THE PROPAGANDA OF FREEDOM IS MADE OFFICIAL——FREEMEN FIREBOMBED OFF CAMERA——DEA SNIFFER DOGS ATTEMPT TO FORM UNION, LEADERS MYSTERIOUSLY OD, MANY FROM THE RANKS SUCCUMB FROM COLD WITHDRAWAL, RUMORS OF SNIFFER PACKS ON THE LOOSE, DEALERS WARNED TO TAKE PRECAUTIONARY MEASURES TO CACHE THE STASH——UNABOMBER SURFACES LIKE A TURNIP IN THE SECESSIONIST BOILPOT OF MONTANA—— STATE BOMBING FOR BAGHDAD PRAISED AS DESERVED, NO WAR CRIMES TRIALS IN SIGHT FOR BUSH, POWELL AND SCHWARZKOPF——UNABOMBER DECRIED AND DEMONIZED AS COWARDLY SMELLY CREEP——IRA BOMB THE LONDON DOCKLANDS, BILL REAPS THE BLOOD OF HIS EFFORTS TO MAKE LONDON COUGH UP THE PROTESTANTS, BUT CONTINUES TO CRINGE BEFORE THE BOSTON IRISH CATHOLICS, LOS CHICANOS OF THE MASSACHUSETTS BAY COLONY——I SHOT ANDY WARHOL, LIKE WOW, YOU CAN DO TIME FOR THAT?——SOME SYMPATHY AND LOW-CAL ADMIRATION LOOKS TO BE EMERGING FOR UNABOMBER FROM LOOSE COMMUNITY OF LITE HUDDITES, HINTS THAT HE WAS ABUSED ARE LIKELY TO GET NOWHERE——OKLA CITY INDIGNANTS SHOUT IT DOWN, THREATEN ANY EFFORT TO REMEMBER WACO, BAY AND HOWL FOR MORE BODIES OF HERETICS, POUND DOWN THE STAKES, GATHER THE FIREWOOD FOR THE DENVER TRIAL——STAKES AND FIREWOOD SCARCE, PRICES SWIRL TOWARD THE SKY, SEEKING THEIR LEVEL IN HEAVEN——SANCTIMONY FOLLOWS THE MONEY——THE MARKET SAYS THE MONEY IS ON THE FAT BOY——FAKE FAT HITS THE MARKET REVOLUTIONIZES POSSIBILITIES—— TRADING BRISK——FAKE FAT LICENSING PROJECTED TO

OUTSTRIP THE ENTIRE PATENTED HOLDINGS IN MOLECULAR
SYNTHETICS——HORDES OF INVESTORS JUMP ON THE
FAKE FAT JUGGERNAUT——SPECULATION RISES, FRENZIED
ATTEMPTS TO CAPTURE MARKETS IN FAKE MODE——
AUTHENTICITY OF FAKE MODE SWIFTLY OVERTAKING AND
OUTBIDDING FAKE MODE——SPECULATION IN FAKE MODE
VIRTUALLY (OLD MODE) AT A STANDSTILL——REVELATIONS
OF THE CORRUPTION OF FAKE BY "REAL" ROCK THE STREET
OF SHAME, BUT IT TURNS OUT EVEN THE SCANDAL WAS FAKE,
OR REAL, SINCE THAT'S FAKE, AS THE HAMMER WENT
DOWN——JACKIE UNLOADS TRASH FROM HER NY APARTMENT
ON PUBLIC MESMERIZED BY THE MEDIA——MOTHER'S DAY
IN THE USA A ROMAN DESIGNATION——PROTESTANTS
DEMAND MOTHERS BE CELEBRATED IN REFORMATION STYLE,
IN FEBRUARY——PROTEST DISPERSED BY IRISH THUGS DRESSED
AS POLICE——MARKET REOPENS TO STRONG EXCHANGES,
JERUSALEM AND ROME BEAT BACK THE NOISOME CROWD
OF FREE MARKET CHURCHERS——IMPARTIALITY VOTED THE
HERESY OF THE LAST HALF CENTURY——IMPARTIALITY
DOWN, SHARPLY, SELFISHNESS AND GREED CONSIDERED AS
UNIMPUGNABLE AS THE MARKET ITSELF——NAY!, BAY THE
COYOTES OF COMMERCE, IS THE MARKET, THERE IS NO SELF
BUT ITSELF——MARKET COMMENT TIME——SELF SELLS LIKE
A CONFLAGRATION THE SON TELLS THE MOTHER THAT IF
SHE LIVES HE WON'T TAKE CARE OF HER AND IF SHE DIES
HE WON'T BURY HER——THE NAZZDÜG IN AUTHENTIC FAKE
RISES LIKE A BLIMP FOR SALE OVER THE FRACTURED
CULTURE——MARKET IN INDULGENCES AND PERMISSIONS
SHRIEKS WITH STIMULATION——IT HAS BEEN REPORTED
A LICENSE WAS BARELY DENIED TO A COMPANY CALLING
ITSELF STREICHSTAADTS WHILE YOU WAIT, A DECLARATION
OF WAR HAS BEEN FILED——CLAIMING NUISANCE AND
PUBLIC ANNOYANCE, Ø.J. SIMPSON SLITS THE THROAT OF
RON GOLDMAN'S FATHER——RUMORS THAT GERALDO
STAGED THE SCENE IN A NEW SERIES CALLED BEYOND FAKE
BLANKET THE MARKET——STREET JOKE GOES "FAIR TRIAL IN

ØKLAHOMA? DO THEY HAVE TRIALS IN OKLAHOMA?"——
RUMORS IN THE BLOOD SUPPLY SECTION, PRICES HOLD STEADY,
RISK IN THE RECEIVING END——LET THE CADAVER BEWARE,
THEY'LL BE BACK FOR THE DNA, QUESTIONS LIKE, HOW
WILL THAT MAKE YOU LOOK ON JUDGEMENT DAY STALL
THE MARKET FOR BELIEVERS, OTHERWISE TRADE BRISK,
CONTINUING THE CLIMB AS LONG RANGE BONDS ISSUED IN
PÆDERASTY AND PUBLICITY ENJOY SPIRITED BIDDING——
INTEREST IN WAR CRIMES, A RESURRECTED SOURCE OF
REVENUE FOR AN EVER HUNGRY INTERNATIONAL BAR, GROWS
AS THE POSSIBILITY OF HANGING A FEW HIGHLEVEL SOUTH
SLAVS APPROACHES, THUS, TO PART OF THE MARKET, THE
PROPER END AND PROOF OF VICTORY IN THE COLD WAR——
THE MORE EQUIVOCAL——GRANTEES SAY HANG THEM IN
ABSENTIA, IT'S MORE AUTHENTIC——MARKET HESITATES,
CONFUSED, BUT LATE IN THE DAY REJECTS THE ARGUMENT
FROM ART, AND INVESTS HEAVILY IN TRADITIONAL REVENGE,
SOLD AS SWEET AND SATISFYING, WITH A LONG, STABLE
HISTORY OF "PAYING OFF"——OLD USTASHE INSTALLED AT
THE HAGUE——THIS TIME THE VICTORS JUSTICE WILL BE
METED OUT BY ROME AND GERMANY——MARKET IN
PALEOBIBLICAL PAPER FROM THE FIRST REICH (CHARLEMAIGNE)
UNFURLS——THE PROMISE OF STATE EXECUTIONS CASTS A
SPELL OVER THE MEDIA——CRIME FREAKS DRIVE UP THE PRICE
OF BELTS AND BUCKLES——OFF SHORE FABRICATION THRIVES
IN THE ISLANDS——VIRTUAL SLAVE STOCKS ADVANCE——
RADOVAN KARADZIC SECOND POET AFTER BREAKER MORANT
CHARGED WITH WAR CRIMES——GENUFLECT INC.'S NEW
ISSUE HOT——"IF YOU LIKED THE GERMANS YOU'LL TOO
LOVE THE AMERICANS"——INTERVENTIONIONISM INVADES
THE GENE POOL——THE SPELLING OF THE GENOME THE POPE
CALLS "THE NEW EUGENICS"——PREFERRED STOCK——KILLS
THE TICS WHICH HAVE MADE HUMANITY SO INTERESTING
OVER THE AEONS——INTEREST IN HUMANITY DOWN
SHARPLY——INTEREST ON HUMANITY UP ACROSS THE
BOARD——NO INDICATION OF SEARCH FOR USURY GENE AT

THIS TIME, BUT PROJECT COULD BE SUBSILENTIO——
INTERVENTIONISM CONSUMATUM——IF BILL HAD THE
LEGISLATURE AS WELL AS THE CAJONES HE WOULD CARPET
BOMB BELGRADE——CLAIMANTS ON SERB HOLDING LICK
THEIR CHOPS, SEATED IN THEIR IDLING BENZIS——IMF
SLOBBERING ON THEIR MAPS, CHARTS, TITLES, AND DEEDS——
PREPARATIONS FOR SATELLITE AUCTION UNDERWAY——
ROME AND THE HAGUE CONSPIRE TO ATTACK "PRIVATE
INTERPRETATION" AND MOCKING THE STRAW POSITION AS
"ORTHODOX"——ORTHODOXY NEGATIVE IN THE MARKET,
OBFUSCATION AND BLIND IGNORANCE MERGE——STOCKS IN
HERESY PROLIFERATE——FLOATATIONS BASED ON THE
HOPE THAT BROADER DEFINITIONS WILL CARRY THE DAY——
MUNICIPAL ILLEGALITIES WRITTEN TO CREATE REVENUE
THROUGH FINES——CODES ABANDONED, THE LAW
PRIVATIZED——NOW THE PRISON POPULATION BASED ON
DEMANDS OF STOCKHOLDERS——DOWNSIZING DOVETAILS
WITH "ROOM AND BOARD," CANT TERM FOR
INCARCERATION——STREET SYSTEM PRIVATIZED——SIGNS
STATING "WILL WORK TO BE LEGALLY HOMELESS (IE., THE
RIGHT TO SLEEP IN THE STREET) ON THE INCREASE——
FORGERIES IN THIRTY LANGUAGES COMMON, CREATING
MARKET IN PROFESSIONAL DISENFRANCHISEMENT——
AMATEUR OUTCASTS STREAM INTO THE AMERICAN SYSTEM
FROM AROUND THE GLOBE——BOOM IN RENTAL SPACES
(AVERAGE TWO SQUARE FEET) FOR SIGN HOLDERS, OCCUPANCY
RATES AS HIGH AS 99% IN SOME VENUES LIKE PHILADELPHIA
(FOLLOWING A BUSTED MARKET IN THE LOVE THY BROTHER
INDUSTRY, ACTUALLY DECLARED ILLEGAL IN BALTIMORE AS
A SLOGAN INCITING TO INCEST——RURAL MARKETS TO BE
DEVELOPED WITH A NEW GENERATION OF SIGN BEARERS——
PROPOSALS RANGE FROM "WILL BE ABUSED FOR MONEY";
"WILL BE RENDERED PERMANENTLY CHALLENGED IN
EXCHANGE FOR LONG TERM CONTRACT FOR NON-
INCARCERATED 'ROOM AND BOARD'";——AND IN THE SPIRIT
OF THE GREAT DOG OF THE CYNICS, DIOGENES, A SIGN WAS

REPORTED (BY SIGN SPOTTERS) AS STATING THAT THE
BEARER WOULD ABUSE, AND THOROUGHLY WASTE THE
RESOURCES OF THE BUYER AND UTTERLY RUIN WHATEVER
PROSPECTS SAID WEALTHY CUSTOMER HAD IN THE HIGHLY
SPECULATIVE AREA OF THE MARKET KNOWN AS THE
AFTERLIFE——TRADING IMMEDIATELY SO HEAVY AND
DEMAND SO FRENETIC THE STOCK WAS SUSPENDED AFTER
TWO HOURS——IN OTHER SECTORS THE SWAPPERS WERE
ACTIVE——NEUE SACHLICHKEIT SOARED TO UNANTICIPATED
HEIGHTS OF OBJECTIVITY, LONG TERM PROSPECTS GOOD——
EXCELLENT HEDGE, WARNING THAT YOU'VE BEEN OVER
THIS MOON-SCAPE BEFORE SHOULD BE HEEDED, TITANIUM
MINES ON THE LUNAR SURFACE SUPER-LONG TERM,
INTERLINKED WITH PROPRIETARY BASES IN GENOME STILL
UNSECURED——THE RULE: UNLESS YOU OWN IT THEE CANNOT
KNOW WHAT THE FUTURE MAY HOLD——SHOKO DOWN,
YEN RISING, STRUGGLE OF LIGHT AGAINST DARKNESS OFF,
WAY WAY OFF——OPAQUE COMMERCE VS SPIRITUAL LIGHT
INTO THE STRETCH——BIRDSHIT OF THE RAIL——AND THEN,
JULY 11TH, 1996, NEARING THE END OF THE SECOND
MILLENNIUM IN THE ERA OF THE LORD OF THE PROTESTANTS
[THE FREE CHRISTIAN], THE REBELS AGAINST ROME, THE
SPEAKERS IN TONGUES, AS ON THE TOWER OF BABEL, TAKING
THEIR TRANSMISSION DIRECT WITHOUT AGENCY WHICH ON
EARTH IS THE MEDITERRANEAN STIFF——ETHNICITY FLOODS
THE MARKET, THE NON-PRODUCT OF THE 2ND MILLENNIUM,
THE "NON-MILLENNIUM"——TRADE IN END-OF-THE-WORLD
GEAR TOTALLY FLAT, FEW TAKERS EXCEPT CHILD-KILLERS, A
CHARITY TOO OBVIOUS TO NOTE——PROTEIN AND CARBO
GATHERING IN ATLANTA——THE FLAG OF THE CONFEDERACY
LOOMS AS MAJOR MAJOR IRRITANT——"AMERICA" STILL
THE BLOODY GROUND OF THE WORLD'S DISCONTENT AND
THE RECEPTICLE OF ITS TORRENT OF ETHNIC ERROR——THE
CONTRACT TO REMOVE THE MORAL POLLUTION WOULD BE,
IF IT WERE LET, FAR VASTER THAN THE CONTRACT TO HIDE
THE POISON OF THE TWO GREAT WARS AND ALL ITS ROMAN

PROGENY——FORGET GET A LIFE——GET A RACKET——
PROTECTION ON THE RISE——INFECTION ON THE
HORIZON——TWO SCORE BODIES FOREVER UNIDENTIFIED
FROM THE CRASH IN THE FLORIDA SWAMP——GENERIC
CASKETS IN BRIEF DEMAND——HOLIER THAN THOU TEARS
FROM THE SURVIVORS OF THE VICTIMS OF CHEAP FLIGHT——
TERRORISM OF CAPITALISM NOT FACTORED IN THE
INVESTIGATION OF THE CAUSES——ARABS AND REDNECKS
RULED OUT——FUTURES IN SCAPEGOATING TAKE SUDDEN
BUT BRIEF DIP, THEN, BIG 747 RECOVERY OFF LONG ISLAND——
NOSE WITH COCKPIT AND 1ST CLASS BLOWN OFF, 2ND CLASS
FLIES ON FOR ANOTHER 10 SECONDS @ CIRCA 500 MPH——1ST
CLASS PASSENGERS SIT IN 20 FATHOMS OF BRINE FROZEN
IN FATALISM——FORGET GO FIGURE——DON'T GO, PERIOD:
AND DON'T FIGURE, ESPECIALLY IF YOU DON'T HAVE A
FIGURE——HATRED OF NON-SAUDI ARABS SPARKS ABRUPT
UPTURN IN COMMITTMENT TO THE USE OF FORCE WHERE
DEMOCRACY IS QUESTIONED——DOLE, THE HOLLOWED OUT
PINEAPPLE, WEIGHS IN AS THE CLINTONAL "DARK SIDE," "SCREW
GOOD INTENTIONS, POKE A CIGARETTE UP GARY'S DRESS"——
TOBACCO ZIGZAGS—GET OUT NOW BUT COME BACK LATER
WHISPERS IN THE HALL——GET ON LINE OR CRASH, ULTIMA
TIME——KEVORKIAN, INC. HAULS IT ALL ACROSS WALL STREET
LIKE A BAG OF SMELT——THOSE WHO ARE OFFENDED
CONDEMNED TO DEATH AND THEIR EFFECTS PUT ON THE
MARKET——JUST IN!——THE BOOTY OF THE ORIENT PLUS
AFRICA AND THE NOTORIOUSLY FUCKED-UP SUB-CONTINENT
OF ASIA TO BE AUCTIONED FOR THE TRILLIONTH TIME——
TICKETS AT THE DOOR, CASH ONLY——STOCK IN
MANAGEMENTS ABILITY FALLING SHARPLY——BONDS STEADY,
PRINTING OF MONEY DRIVEN BY THE STOIC DEMONS OF THE
FED——POLL-TAKING IN THE PRECINCTS OF THE DISMISSED
HAS CEASED, GET WORK IN TWO YEARS OR MAKE AN
APPOINTMENT WITH DR. KEVORKIAN——THE CHOP-LIKING
VENTURE ASPECTS OF THIS SEND THE MARKET ABOVE SEVEN-
THOUSAND FOR ONE SCHISMATIC SECOND—, AND GET THIS,

THE LOST AND BROKEN, FAR FROM THROWING THEMSELVES OUT THE WINDOW, GRABBED WITNESSES AND UNDERLINGS AND THREW THEM OUT THE WINDOW——DE FENESTRATION, AS AN ALTERNATIVE TO DISMISSAL CAN BE EXPENSIVE TO EXECUTE——"IF IT SAVES MONEY IT SAVES YOUR ASS", INC., STOCK HOT AS A PISTOLERO IN A BATHHOUSE——PROTEASE INHIBITOR COCKTAIL LET INTO THE MARKET TO NO EFFECT—— AZT STILL THE PRIME KILLER OF CELLS——PIERRE DUESBERG HARRIED AROUND THE GLOBE, THE SOLE HERETIC EMERGING FROM THE BEHAVIORAL PLAGUE, WHICH GROWS MORE MEDIEVAL BY THE MINUTE——THE NAZDAC CRASHES, IN A HEAP OF PLASTIC IDEOLOGIES——RECOVERY EXPECTED, BUT FOR THE STOCKHOLDERS, NOT THE LICENTIOUS VICTIMS—— ADJUSTMENT IN PROGRESS——AYN RAND RETURNS FROM THE GRAVE TO SORT THROUGH HER SAFE-DEPOSIT BOX, AND HAVE LUNCH WITH THE FED AND HAVE LUNCH WITH ALAN GREENSPAN, HER BEST STUDENT——THEY EXCHANGE A FEW JOKES ABOUT RUSSIANS AND AMERICANS, AND NOTE WITH QUIET SATISFACTION THAT BOTH BEING ARTIFICIAL NATIONS ARE NOW LED BY FAT FREAKS——FAT UP A DIME, SOWBELLIES STEADY——NEW ARTIFICIAL FAT WITH THE LAXITIVE SIDE EFFECT PROJECTED TO TURN THE USA INTO A SIMULATED MEXICO, THE MOCTAZUMAS HAS BEEN REGISTERED AS A TM——PROPRIETARY RIGHT CLAIMED AS PAY TO SHIT, THE BROADER JUSTIFICATION ARGUED AS "THERE'S NO FREE SHIT," AN OBVIOUS ECHO OF THE FRONT-END MARKET ADMONITION "THERE'S NO FREE LUNCH." THE MOTTO OF THOSE WHO DECLINE TO SHARE——MEANING FOR THE INVESTMENT COMMUNITY: EVACUATION CAN BE SUBJECTED TO TAX ON WASTE——CONSTIPATION SHARES UP, ANTICIPATION FLOODS THE MARKET, TAKERS FEW——SUFFERERS, FISTS RAISED, LINE THE STREET——POLICE CALLED OUT——THE MOB SPLITS INTO NO REVENUE NO RETURN——WHEN THEY ARRIVE HOME THEIR PROPERTY HAS BEEN SEIZED——A FOREST DWELLER FROM SURINAIMO HAS BEEN INSTALLED, THE CHILDREN ARE DEMANDING INSTRUCTIONS IN KREOLE——ENGLISH AS A

FOREIGN LANGUAGE ADVANCES, THE CHINOOK JARGON OF
INTERNATIONAL COMMERCE, SHAKESPEARE'S VOCABULARY
REDUCED TO A MERE DEAL——LANGUAGE IDLE——SOME
JUNK CULTURE OFFERS, FEW TAKERS, HIGH RISK, UNRELIABLE
TO PHONY SECURITY——MARKET SHIFTS TO "HEART OF
DARKNESS" PARADIGM, TUTSI SUPERIORITY AND LOFT
TO BE MADE SUBORDINATE TO HUTU BACKWARDNESS
AND SQUAT PHYSICALITY——POOR INVESTMENT CLIMATE,
CLASS COMPLICATIONS——PROJECTED LONG TERM
WARFARE, GROWTH IN ARMS TRADE EXPECTED——ON
THE MICROMARKET GENOME SEQUENCING PROMISES RICH
REWARDS FOR THE RENTIER CLASS——CLAIMS OF GENETIC
REAL ESTATE SMALL AS 15 BASE PAIRS DECLARED LEGAL——
SKEPTICS SAY IT COULD BE LIKE BUYING A CRACK IN THE
SIDEWALK——TAKERS ABOUND, NAZDAC SPRINGS BACK,
SEQUENCING THROWS AWAY THE MAP, GOES DIRECTLY TO
THE 3 BILLION BASE PAIRS OF DNA IN THE 24 HUMAN
CHROMOS——NOTHING WASTED, EVEN THE FLAWS AND
AILMENTS FOR SALE——TO OWN A DISEASE, TO POSSESS,
TO CONTROL AND RETAIL A SYNDROME WILL SOON BE
POSSIBLE——GENETIC FREAKS INCORPORATED HAS BEEN
ISSUED A LICENSE, A RUN ON DESIGNER MUTATIONS TRANSECTS
THE MARKET LIKE A COMET——HAIL BOPP, HALE IRWIN——
STEADY GROWTH IN DESIGNER MORTICIANS WHO DEAL WITH
RAPID DEATH OF DESIGNER MUTATIONS——ENROLLMENT
SKYROCKETS FOR UNDERTAKING COLLEGES, CADAVER STOCKS
(AS THEY'RE CALLED) SPRING TO LIFE——SEARCH FOR THE
ONE AND ONLY PERSON MODEL #1 NOW SEQUENCING——
"JUST IN"——TAKE-OVER BOOBY TRAP: IDEOLOGY OF
SUBORDINATION WAY UP——DEGREE, PROBITY & PLACE AS
IN TO KNOW ONE'S PLACE (NOT THE SAME AS MY PLACE OR
YOUR PLACE, STUPID)——PECKING ORDER AS IN SEX IN THE
MILITARY——ORIGIN OF ALL THE FOREGOING ARRANGEMENTS
AND PRECAUTIONS DERIVED FROM THE WILL OF GOD——
POPE, BISHOPS, PRIEST, PEOPLE——PEACE IS NOT IMPORTANT:
WAR IS THE PASSION THAT DRIVES HUMANITY——ALL

RELIGIONS FUNCTION AS CONTROL PROGRAMS; ALL AUTHORITY IS INHERENTLY CORRUPT AND CORRUPTING——RISE IN JOBLESS RATE REPORTED——STOCKMARKET RECOVERED——BIG ANSWERS UP——QUESTION ON "THE STREET" WHAT WILL ACTUALLY BE PURCHASED FROM THE FARM——JUSTIN——WALL STREET WAG——POINTS OUT FREE MARKET AND FLEA MARKET SAME THING TO CHINESE——COOKOUT BETWEEN THE BORDERS: ETHNOLOGY SOUP——TACO ON A ROLL, BUN ON THE RUN, PITA IN THE POCKET——THE MARKET HIT FUSILLADE OF (TICKS) A FLURRY OF RIM SHOTS——DOT DE-DA, DOT DE-DA, DOT DOT DE-DA, DE DA——AND THE SUCKERS WERE MESMERIZED——ARCHEOLOGY REVEALS LAST SUPPER WAS POTLUCK——JUDAS OUTED BECAUSE HE BROUGHT NO DISH

NOTES

These notes give bibliographic and archival references for the sources of all texts and images published here, with occasional notes on significant textual variants. Where possible, notes on entire sections are used in place of notes on individual poems. Known or inferred dates of composition are given at the beginning of each note. Following this, place of composition is given when it has been indicated by the author. The first reference in each note indicates the version of the text that is published here; following this, references to variant texts are given. Significant textual variants are described immediately after the reference to the text in which they appear. The following abbreviations are used for frequently-cited archives and publications:

ABP-UCLA: Amiri Baraka Papers, Charles E. Young Research Library, University of California, Los Angeles.

Baraka/Dorn: Amiri Baraka & Edward Dorn, *The Collected Letters*, ed. Claudia Moreno Pisano (Albuquerque: University of New Mexico Press, 2013).

COP-UConn: Charles Olson Papers, Archives & Special Collections at the Thomas J. Dodd Research Center, University of Connecticut Libraries.

CP: Edward Dorn, *Collected Poems*, eds Jennifer Dunbar Dorn, Justin Katko, Kyle Waugh, and Reitha Pattison (Manchester: Carcanet Press, 2012).

DLP-M0601: Denise Levertov Papers (M0601), Department of Special Collections, Stanford University Libraries.

EDP-3009: Edward Dorn Papers (MSN/MN 3009), Department of Special Collections, Hesburgh Libraries of Notre Dame.

EDP-M1460: Edward Dorn Papers (M1460), Department of Special Collections, Stanford University Libraries. Papers originally held by Tom Clark.

EDP-M1514: Edward Dorn Papers (M1514), Department of Special Collections, Stanford University Libraries. Papers originally held by Helene Dorn.

EDP-UConn: Edward Dorn Papers, Archives & Special Collections at the Thomas J. Dodd Research Center, University of Connecticut Libraries.

ED-JW-Del: Letters of Edward Dorn to John Wieners, Series 1, Box 1, Folder 1, Sir Joseph Gold literary manuscript collection (MSS 658), Special Collections, University of Delaware Library.

POEMS SENT TO CORPORAL GORDON TAYLOR (1953–1954)

Poems from Dorn's correspondence with his hometown friend Gordon Taylor. Ordering of a number of the poems is derived from Dorn's notes in the letter of 3 October 1953.

* **Untitled**—ca. early 1953. Unpublished MS (1 p.) in 2 pp. letter to Gordon Taylor, 3 October 1953, San Francisco, Series 1:B, Folder 384, EDP-3009.

* **5.**—ca. Spring–Summer 1953, Seattle. Unpublished MS (1 p.) in 2 pp. letter to Gordon Taylor, 3 October 1953, San Francisco, Series 1:B, Folder 384, EDP-3009.

* **Third Floor**—ca. Summer–Fall 1953, Seattle. Unpublished MS (1 p.) in 2 pp. letter to Gordon Taylor, 3 October 1953, San Francisco, Series 1:B, Folder 384, EDP-3009.

* **Night scene**—ca. Summer–Fall 1953, Seattle. Unpublished MS (1 p.) in 2 pp. letter to Gordon Taylor, 3 October 1953, San Francisco, Series 1:B, Folder 384, EDP-3009.

* **Give them the statistics of death**—Undated. Unpublished MS (1 p.) in 8 pp. letter to Gordon Taylor, 24 September 1953, San Francisco, Series 1:B, Folder 384, EDP-3009.

* **The surrealist**—1 October 1953, San Francisco. Unpublished MS (1 p.) in 2 pp. letter to Gordon Taylor, 3 October 1953, San Francisco, Series 1:B, Folder 384, EDP-3009. Among the seven poems this letter contains is "Grasses" (*CP*, p. 5); the rest are printed here.

* **Rotund**—1 October 1953, San Francisco. Unpublished MS (1 p.) in 2 pp. letter to Gordon Taylor, 3 October 1953, San Francisco, Series 1:B, Folder 384, EDP-3009.

* **San F.**—Undated. Unpublished TS (1 p.) in 5 pp. letter to Gordon Taylor, 4 November 1953, Seattle, Series 1:B, Folder 384, EDP-3009.

* **Decorum on a Grey Day**—Undated. Unpublished TS (1 p.) in 3 pp. letter to Gordon Taylor, 19 January 1954, Seattle, Series 1:B, Folder 384, EDP-3009.

* **Several gulls**—Undated. Unpublished TS (1 p.) in 3 pp. letter to Gordon Taylor, 19 January 1954, Seattle, Series 1:B, Folder 384, EDP-3009.

* **A derelict air**—Undated. TS (1 p.) in 3 pp. letter to Gordon Taylor, 19 January 1954, Seattle, Series 1:B, Folder 384, EDP-3009. Printed in Tom Clark, *Edward Dorn: A World of Difference* (Berkeley: North Atlantic Books, 2002), p. 215.

THE RIGHTING OF THE CAT (1954)

ca. Fall 1954, Black Mountain College. Unpublished TS (7 pp.), Series 2, Box 4, Folder 13, EDP-M1514. The Greek can be translated as: "The first lesson: the beginning is half".

LOOKING, FOR A THING (1957–1959)

* **Report From Washington: March**—March 1957. Unpublished TS (1 p.), Box 150, Folder "Letters: Dorn, Edward, Undated (2)", COP-UConn. These lines are crossed out at the bottom of the page: "For all that I make it through the door, | What's more than a resting place is final". Nearly identical TS sent to John Wieners (1 p.), ED-JW-Del. An undated draft of a letter from Wieners to Charles Olson is written on both sides of the TS.

* **Th'abjective None**—ca. Spring 1957. Unpublished TS with handwritten revisions (3 pp.), Box 150, Folder "Letters: Dorn, Edward, Undated (2)", COP-UConn.

* **The Poet Spends a Day at the Dump**—20 April 1957, Mt. Vernon. Unpublished TS (2 pp.), Box 150, Folder "Letters: Dorn, Edward, Undated (2)", COP-UConn.

* **Poem**—ca. Spring 1957. Unpublished TS (1 p.), Series 2, Box 4, Folder 5, EDP-M1514. Note the variant TS (1 p.), Box 150, Folder "Letters: Dorn, Edward, Undated (2)", COP-UConn.

* **An Idea of perfection**—ca. Summer 1957. Unpublished TS with handwritten revisions (1 p.), Series 2, Box 4, Folder 5, EDP-M1514.

* **The Fair Relief**—29 July–late August 1957. Unpublished TS (1 p.), Series 2, Box 4, Folder 5, EDP-M1514. There are two variant drafts. TS in 2 pp. letter to John Wieners, 29 July 1957, ED-JW-Del. Revised TS in 2 pp. letter to Wieners, ca. after 21 August 1957, ED-JW-Del. First stanza reads: "Today— | I, think, | I met; | the first misanthropic". Fourth stanza, lines 3–5 read: "tried last year | to get the stove oil | from a slob merchant". Fifth stanza, third line reads: "a good clean hate". Final stanza, second line reads: "of believers". In his correspondence with Dorn, Wieners objects to Dorn's use of "misanthropic" and "wellbelievers". In a letter to Wieners, 20 August 1957, ED-JW-Del, Dorn calls "wellbelievers" an "unmadeup word", "concrete": "The poem rests there. it cant be took out. And you are wrong, johnny, about Misanthropic(s) being an adj. I nouned it."

* **The Girls in the Bank**—21–24 August 1957. Unpublished TS (1 p.), Series 2, Box 4, Folder 5, EDP-M1514. There are three earlier drafts. First draft: TS postcard sent to John Wieners, 21 August 1957, Mt. Vernon, ED-JW-Del. Second draft: TS in undated 2 pp. letter to Wieners, incorporating revisions suggested by Wieners and Robin Blaser, written sometime after 21 August 1957, ED-JW-Del. Third draft: TS with handwritten revisions (1 p.), 24 August 1957, Series 2, Box 4, Folder 5, EDP-M1514.

* **Vile, Thot Timothy, Like I**—ca. late August 1957. Unpublished TS (1 p.) in undated 2 pp. letter to John Wieners, ED-JW-Del.

* **Anacortes Revisited**—ca. late August 1957. Unpublished TS (1 p.), Series 2, Box 4, Folder 5, EDP-M1514. Draft TS dated 24 August 1957 (1 p.), Folder 5.

* **While driving, home**—Undated. Unpublished TS postcard sent to John Wieners, 31 August 1957, Burlington, ED-JW-Del.

* **An embarrassment**—ca. Summer 1957. Unpublished TS with handwritten revisions (1 p.), Series 2, Box 4, Folder 5, EDP-M1514.

* **Looking, for a thing**—ca. Summer 1957. Unpublished TS (1 p.), Series 2, Box 4, Folder 5, EDP-M1514.

* **Letter from an Agéd Aunt**—ca. Summer 1957. Unpublished TS (2 pp.), Series 2, Box 4, Folder 5, EDP-M1514.

* **Two Ships that Pass**—ca. Winter 1957–1958. Unpublished TS with handwritten revisions (1 p.), Series 2, Box 4, Folder 5, EDP-M1514. The original title reads: "A little occasional poem called— | Two Ships that Pass in the Sleet".

* **Bowl of Floweres**—ca. Spring 1958. Unpublished TS (1 p.), Series 2, Box 4, Folder 5, EDP-M1514. There are two other drafts with significant variants. TS (1 p.), Series 2, Box 4, Folder 5, EDP-M1514. In that draft, an epigraph attributed to John

Fisola reads: "There's spuds on the ground at Allen". TS (1 p.), Box 150, Folder "Letters: Dorn, Edward, Undated (2)", COP-UConn. Following the eighth line as printed here, that variant reads:

> Gulls of white-gray droplets
>
> descending
> to the insect world.
>
> All waits for me
> all this I see before I go
>
> AH,
> day of abundant Sun,
> the common one.
>
> & I
> unwise self, will while
> it all, dwindle the hours
>
> pick
> a bowl of floweres,
> leave
> a water bowl of floweres
> disk of yellow, upon the shelf
> before I go . . .

* **february child**—Undated. Unpublished MS (1 p.), Box 4, Folder 17, EDP-M1514. Lettering and illustration by Helene Dorn.

* **Come with them**—Undated. Unpublished MS (1 p.), Series 2, Box 4, Folder 17, EDP-M1514. Lettering and illustration by Helene Dorn.

* **A small inquisition of the mind**—Undated. Unpublished TS (2 pp.) from 2 pp. letter to Denise Levertov, 14 October 1958, Series 4, Box 28, Folder 38, DLP-M0601.

* **The Point is Light**—ca. 1958–Summer 1959. Unpublished TS (1 p.), Box 150, Folder "Letters: Dorn, Edward, Undated (2)", COP-UConn.

* **The Call**—ca. 1958–Summer 1959. Unpublished TS (1 p.), Series 2, Box 4, Folder 5, EDP-M1514. Note the variant TS (1 p.), Box 150, Folder "Letters: Dorn, Edward, Undated (2)", COP-UConn.

* **It is**—ca. 1959. Unpublished TS (1 p.), Series 2, Box 4, Folder 5, EDP-M1514.

POEMS OF WASHINGTON, IDAHO, & MEXICO (1959)

Poems of Washington, Idaho, & Mexico is the title of Dorn's first manuscript of poems, compiled by the summer of 1959 and submitted in September 1959 to the University of Nebraska Press, and later to New Directions. The 72-pp. manuscript as a whole went unpublished, and a complete picture of its contents remains unknown. The book's title and length are drawn from a postcard receipt from the University of Nebraska Press, 2 October 1959, Series 1, Box 2, Folder 22, EDP-M1514. *Poems of*

Washington, Idaho, & Mexico is the culmination of nearly a decade of correspondence with Denise Levertov, who worked with Dorn on the revision and publication of his early poetry. The order of the poems has been derived from a 48 pp. letter from Levertov to Dorn (11–17 May 1959), Series 1, Box 2, Folder 5, EDP-M1514. The only manuscript that has been found is in the papers of Denise Levertov: TS with Levertov's annotations (42 pp.), Series 4, Box 28, Folder 40, DLP-M0601. This is the draft sent to Levertov in April 1959; cf. 2 pp. letter from Dorn to Levertov (28 April 1959), Series 4, Box 28, Folder 39, DLP-M0601. Another draft, which incorporated Levertov's revisions, and was sent to her about a month later, has not been found; cf. 16 pp. letter from Dorn to Levertov (3 June 1959), Series 4, Box 28, Folder 39, DLP-M0601. The manuscript in the Levertov Papers seems to account for only two-thirds of the 72 pp. manuscript that Dorn submitted for publication. The remaining third of the full manuscript was likely comprised of the bulk of what would become *The Newly Fallen* (1961). The poems collected there, and in *The New American Poetry* (1960) and *Hands Up!* (1964), are left out of the sequence presented here. According to Levertov's letter of May 1959, the full list of poems in the manuscript that Dorn sent to her in April 1959 is: "The Rick of Green Wood" (*CP*, pp. 10–11), "Spring Woman", "Vaquero" (*CP*, p. 67), "The Trip", "Sousa" (*CP*, pp. 31–35), "An April 1st Cutting", "When the Fairies" (*CP*, pp. 17–18), "Somewhere", "Something Small, and Ignominious", "Concerning Shelter", "The Common Site" [later titled "The Common Lot"] (*CP*, pp. 47–48), "A Country Song" (*CP*, pp. 43–47), "Bavarian Horses", "The Air of June Sings" (*CP*, pp. 109–110), "Geranium" (*CP*, p. 23), "Are They Dancing" (*CP*, p. 104), "Store Scene" (*CP*, p. 8), "Grasses" (*CP*, p. 5), "The Hide of My Mother" (*CP*, pp. 11–17), "Addenda to April 1st Cutting", and "TEN COMMUNICATIONS from the WEST."

* **Spring Woman**—ca. before 22 April 1959. Unpublished TS with the earlier title "Spring" (3 pp.), Series 4, Box 28, Folder 40, DLP-M0601. Title taken from variant TS (3 pp.), Series 2, Box 4, Folder 5, EDP-M1514.

* **The Trip**—ca. 1953. Unpublished TS (1 p.), Box 4, Folder 5, EDP-M1514. Note the variant TS with Denise Levertov's annotations (1 p.), Series 4, Box 28, Folder 40, DLP-M0601.

* **An April 1st Cutting**—ca. before 22 April 1959. Unpublished TS with Denise Levertov's annotations (2 pp.), Series 4, Box 28, Folder 40, DLP-M0601.

* **Somewhere**—ca. before 22 April 1959. Unpublished TS with Denise Levertov's annotations (1 p.), Series 4, Box 28, Folder 40, DLP-M0601.

* **Something Small, and Ignominious**—ca. 1958. Unpublished TS (2 pp.), Box 150, Folder "Letters: Dorn, Edward, Undated (2)", COP-UConn. Note the variant TS with Denise Levertov's annotations (1 p.), Series 4, Box 28, Folder 40, DLP-M0601. The Levertov variant ends after the line "are laid."

* **Concerning Shelter**—ca. mid-1958. Unpublished TS with Denise Levertov's annotations (1 p.), Series 4, Box 28, Folder 40, DLP-M0601. Note the variant TS entitled "Concerning Shelter, etc." (1 p.), Box 150, Folder "Letters: Dorn, Edward, Undated (2)", COP-UConn.

* **Bavarian Horses**—ca. before 22 April 1959. Unpublished TS (1 p.), Series 4, Box 28, Folder 40, DLP-M0601.

* **Addenda to April 1st Cutting**—ca. before 22 April 1959. Unpublished TS with Denise Levertov's annotations (1 p.), Series 4, Box 28, Folder 40, DLP-M0601.

* **TEN COMMUNICATIONS from the WEST**—Spring 1959; it could be the case that Dorn began these poems on 1 April 1959 ("the 1st"), the day before his thirtieth birthday. Unpublished TSS (36 pp.), Series 2, Box 4, Folder 4, EDP-M1514. The M1514 text contains the following variants: TS 1 (first draft, with handwritten revisions), TS 2 (second draft, lacking "the 10th"), TS 3 (third draft, with infrequent handwritten revisions), and TS 4a (consisting only of "the 6th"). A version of TS 1 that lacks "the 10th" (13 pp.) is in Box 28, Folder 39, DLP-M0601. Though the texts presented here tend to be based on TS 2, they are sometimes composites of each of the drafts. Significant variations are given in the notes for each poem.

* **the 1st**—TS 1, first stanza, second line reads: "for a while but the reasons are unclear:". TS 3, first stanza, second line reads: "and oh, the reason is clear:". TS 1 and TS 2, first stanza, fourth line, lacks "(a veritable Sodom)". TS 3, first stanza, fifth line has "nightly" after "work". TS 3 lacks the second and third stanzas. TS 1, third stanza, second line continues thus after "linger": "on for no reason than ennui". TS 1 and TS 2, fourth stanza, final line reads: "seconds long never present before." TS 1 and TS 2 lack first two lines of fifth stanza. TS 1 and TS 2, fifth stanza, first line reads: "Turning around a corner". TS 3, third stanza, final two lines read: "Or would you hide your form | promoting slyness?" TS 1 and TS 2, sixth stanza, fourth line absent. TS 3, penultimate stanza, third line reads: "less than material seconds". TS 1 and TS 2, final stanza, second line reads: "with its grossly important detail".

* **the 2nd**—The version printed here is largely that of TS 2; however, only TS 1 contains the third stanza. TS 3, substantially different, reads in full: "Isn't it always the fate of a wanderer | to never know where he is in the sense | that his only graspable discovery lies | ahead in a place he knows not with equality | knows not. But not to confuse it with | research or anything a scientist might | be, he searches for something missing | in himself, so the wanderer is close to God. | And I try to grasp the Larger sense | of where I am now. || The First mistake, 'the Larger sense'. Though | we continue to retreat to the smallest nouns. | My life in some sense swings at great moments, | out from under the larger sense. | Where one's spirit leaves long before the body, | thus God again is a wanderer—out of a burning | curiosity we will go more urgently to Pompeii, not Albuquerque. || Yet a moving off is deceptive. | When we left Burlington our friends | took on the characteristics of buzzards, the way | they circled toward the funnel of abandoned goods, | sat at the table, asked useless questions (useful?) | put our odds and ends in their boxes. || And of course waited silently for us to go. | On the otherhand there were surely people waiting | very silently in streets of cities for us to arrive. | How uniform and stabilized the element one moves in is. || In the Larger sense, granted, | those who leave are no more dead | than those who didn't arrive."

* **the 3rd**—TS 3, second stanza, first line reads: "It is juniper. Remember Idaho". TS 1 and TS 2, second stanza, fourth line lacks "Illinois". TS 1 and TS 2 , second stanza, sixth line lacks "marking the earth". TS 1 and TS 2, second stanza ends at "horizon". TS 1 and TS 2, third stanza, second line: "mostly" reads "very". TS 3, third stanza, third line ends on "laughs". TS 2, third stanza, sixth line, following the full stop after "speech", the remaining lines read: "I notice he is deferential | to the manager, which disappoints me, the manager | having nothing to do but stand around, | answering the phone now and then". TS 1,

third stanza, sixth line, following the full stop after "speech", reads: "I notice his is differential". TS 3, fifth stanza, second line begins: "everyone knows a George". TS 3, fifth stanza lacks the final two lines. TS 1 and TS 2 end with a final stanza which reads: "Ah I wish you were here, then, | for a few hours."

* **the 4th**—TS 1, first stanza, first line, "my love" is crossed out; TS 2, "my love" is not crossed out; TS 3 lacks "my love". TS 2, second and third stanzas (varying slightly from TS 1) read: "Hudson thought people are compelled toward the sea | now because they have lost something and think | to find a power in that great generalized and inhuman | mass. Well, deep inland, where we are all cut off | vastly, and where we come arbitrarily, it is the same. | More dangerous in a sense. Because the sea offers | nothing to man. No substitute instinct, and is very clean | in its privacy, its own wash. Here || (I don't, mind you) we go to the indian | gazing on that vastness, back, | (it is sheer space so precious it's personified. (Space-man). | Into their sea (of instinct) and 'lessons' | implied and practical, it is a false maturity." Third stanza present only in TS 3. Fourth stanza, lines 3-4, "(avarice as concentrated as a diamond pipe", present only in TS 3. TS 3, fifth stanza, second line: "pressure" reads "assurance". TS 3, fifth stanza, final line, parenthetical phrase reads: "(which, tho simple, is true)".

* **the 5th (same day)**—TS 3, first stanza, reads: "But of all indians | now that the components | of this place, | I take the ones on the street | for the eye's pleasure, and | for the relief of the mind, | which knows so much of garrulous detail | and which is burdened with the omnipresent | handicrafter whose pots | and whose pickup trucks . . ." (ellipses here and elsewhere in this note are Dorn's). In place of first two lines in second stanza of TS 1 and TS 2, first three lines in second stanza of TS 3 read: "Cigar store indians, no. | A white hoped-for image. | But strangely, and with wandering". TS 1, third stanza, last line reads: "as we have (not me)". TS 3 breaks the present third stanza into two stanzas between "bright green," and "the fresh". TS 3, fourth stanza, first four lines read: "the fresh | is in them, not the young who have rediscovered dance | or an ancient glaze, on Sunday, incantations to cameras. | My lovely indians are in the plaza waiting, for what?" TS 1, fifth stanza reads: ". . . far superior to the ones you would see on the floor | of the governor's mansion or hanging in the stantions | of the members of the bar." TS 3, sixth stanza continues through to the variant's end: "now sitting, there, in their secret, but not the one | indian fanciers imagine, for the only thing worth knowing | about a secret is, || its undiscoverableness."

* **the 6th**—There are at least six versions of "the 6th". TS 1: unpublished. TS 2: published in *Yugen* 6, eds LeRoi Jones and Hettie Cohen (New York City, 1960) and Dorn, *The Shoshoneans*, Expanded edition, ed. Matthew Hofer (Albuquerque: University of New Mexico Press, 2013), pp. 111–112. TS 3: unpublished. TS 4a: unpublished. TS 4b: unpublished TS with handwritten revisions including revised title "For Ray" (1 p.), held by J.H. Prynne, Binder D1B (undated). TS 5: published as "For Ray (the 6th)" in *CP* (pp. 19–20); and entitled "For Ray", was cut from *Hands Up!* before the book's publication in 1964, reappearing in a TS of *Hands Up!* compiled in Colchester, September 1966, for a British publication of the book which did not materialise: Box 38, Folder 606, EDP-UConn. The version used here is TS 2. Variants in TS 4b and TS 5 are not noted here. TS 1, first stanza, first eight lines read: "Enough of indian | I know a man, in the west too | in Idaho, oh, there are indians there sweety | but

you've never heard of them, they're bannocks | and very poor, always were and sweetheart thats | just not elegant. ho ho, no thats not elegant | because we can all read, or take a walk that's better | to their, well riches are obvious things and then it depends". TS 3 and TS4a, first stanza, fourth to eleventh lines read: "and very poor, always were, God gave them a strange | terrain and dry hope only engaged the hills they | live upon. Well, riches are premeditate things, | and who would accuse God of premeditation? But this man". TS 3 and TS 4a, second stanza, eighth line has "an enkindled" before "February". TS 3 and TS 4a, second stanza, ninth and tenth lines read: "was Pocatello, a miserable abandoned town even the Union Pacific | got sick of in the forties. But the hills". TS 3 and TS 4a, second stanza, thirteenth line begins: "the red and the blue and bright amethyst,". The phrase "to know land and love it," in second stanza, sixteenth line of TS 1 and TS 2, reads in TS 3 and TS 4a: "the knowing of land | to love it". TS 1, second stanza, twenty-first line ends: "I think he knew, so what,". TS 3, second stanza, twenty-sixth line, the phrase "you know how very much" crossed out; TS 4a lacks the phrase. TS 1, second stanza, penultimate line, in place of "the Idaho", reads "wow   I like Idaho". The "man named Sven" in the eighth line of the present text is linguistic anthropologist Sven S. Liljeblad (1899–2000).

* **the 7th**—The version used here is TS 2, as published in *Yugen* 6 (1960) and *CP* (p. 20). TS 1, first stanza, first two lines read before their handwritten revision to the present version: "Sometimes sitting in a room | I want to see everyone I ever knew". TS 3, first stanza, third line lacks "of course". TS 3, first stanza, third and fourth lines read: "except a few. And then, what a shock | getting over the embarrassment of lonlyness." TS 1, final line begins with "my love,", which is crossed out; and following that, "know" appears to be written beneath "no longer".

* **the 8th**—TS 3, first stanza, second line lacks "I don't like." TS 3, first stanza, eleventh line has "hurricanes" instead of "terrible winds". TS 1 and TS 3, first stanza, sixteenth line, has "unvarying", while TS 2 has "invarying". TS 1 and TS 3, first stanza, final line, begins with "Each", while TS 2 begins with "Every". TS 3 lacks the second and third stanzas. TS 2, third stanza begins: "Ha then she won't know what the meaning of your screams | are."

* **the 9th**—TS 3, first stanza, lines 6-9 read: "playing ball, and we would have cabbage leaves hanging | on our ears, it was to be a kind of old fashioned | athletic program, a mysterious health, | was proposed." TS 3 ends: "Oh, it was a strange thing, and I was pulled toward it | as toward a proposal or a program, both of us were crying | and going, down this wide avenue. || I later wondered if she was merely trying to cheer me up, | or was it a solution?"

* **the 10th**—TS 3, third stanza, sixth line, "thought" reads "reallity".

LATE IN THE REVOLUTION (1960–1962)

* **AND WHERE, GENTLEMEN, IS THE APOCALYPSE**—ca. 1960. Unpublished TS with handwritten revisions (1 p.), Series 2, Box 4, Folder 5, EDP-M1514. The original first line reads: "Hiding? in Eisenhower's bald pan". Third stanza, third and fourth lines originally read: "Is it going to explode all | Its prediction from those hip hips". The final stanza originally began: "Or if it doesnt come, and Mesabi | is exhausted".

* **The Eyes Turn**—ca. 1960. Unpublished TS with handwritten revisions (1 p.), Series 2, Box 4, Folder 5, EDP-M1514.
* **The Isolated Seed**—ca. 1960. Unpublished TS with handwritten revisions (1 p.), Series 2, Box 4, Folder 5, EDP-M1514.
* **Looking into Dark Corners From the Earth**—ca. 1960. Unpublished TS with handwritten revisions (1 p.), Series 2, Box 4, Folder 5, EDP-M1514.
* **First, Last, And only Haiku**—Undated. TS (1 p.) in 1 p. letter to LeRoi Jones, 4 May 1961, Santa Fe, ABP-UCLA. Published in *Baraka/Dorn* (p. 39).
* **A Poem for Creeley Replicas**—Undated. MS (1 p.) on envelope of letter to LeRoi Jones, 15 May 1961, Santa Fe, ABP-UCLA. A crossed-out line after "without a heart" is difficult to transcribe, and possible interpretations read: "Carved in Delicate" or "Carried a Duplicate". Variant transcription published in *Baraka/ Dorn* (p. 42).
* **Some, Man, On the Street**— Undated. Published in *Set* 1, ed. Gerrit Lansing (Gloucester, Winter 1961–1962).
* **For Nevada**—ca. 1962. Unpublished TS (1 p.) in an early manuscript of *Hands Up!*, held by J.H. Prynne, Binder D1B (undated).
* **DOGS OF THE FALLING SUN**—ca. 1962. Unpublished TS (1 p.) in an early manuscript of *Hands Up!*, held by J.H. Prynne, Binder D1B (undated).
* **Comparison**—ca. October 1962. Unpublished TS (1 p.) in a manuscript of *Hands Up!* compiled September 1966, Colchester, for a British publication of the book which did not materialise, Box 38, Folder 606, EDP-UConn. The American edition of *Hands Up!*, completed by August 1962, lost seven poems due to space restrictions: "A wild blue, yonder" and "The reception" collected in the revised *Geography* (1968), *CP* (pp. 175, 188–190); "For Ray (the 6th)" and "An Inauguration Poem" in *CP* (pp. 19–20, 55–56); and "Comparison", "Late in the Revolution", and "Every House Needs a Cat and a Poet . . ." collected here.
* **Late in the Revolution**—ca. 1962. Unpublished TS (2 pp.) in a manuscript of *Hands Up!* compiled September 1966, Colchester, Box 38, Folder 606, EDP-UConn. Cut from the American edition of *Hands Up!* due to space restrictions. The epigraph is from Vladimir Mayakovsky's poem "Man".
* **Say Someday**—13 October 1962. Unpublished TS (1 p.) in a manuscript of *Hands Up!* compiled September 1966, Colchester, Box 38, Folder 606, EDP-UConn. Dated MS (1 p.), Box 38, Folder 592, Notebook "Book of Poems" (1962), EDP-UConn.
* **Every House Needs a Cat and a Poet**—ca. 1962. Unpublished TS (1 p.) in a manuscript of *Hands Up!* compiled September 1966, Colchester, Box 38, Folder 606, EDP-UConn. Cut from the American edition of *Hands Up!* due to space restrictions.
* **Modern Poem**—Undated. MS (1 p.) in 2 pp. letter to LeRoi Jones, 13 November 1962, Pocatello, ABP-UCLA. Published in *Baraka/Dorn* (p. 111).
* **a general answer**—Undated. MS (1 p.) in 2 pp. letter to LeRoi Jones, 30 November 1962, Pocatello, ABP-UCLA. Published in *Baraka/Dorn* (p. 119).

SILENT GUNS (1961–1963)

This section brings together poems that originally comprised two separate volumes of poetry: a book entitled *Idaho Out*, compiled October–November 1962, soon after the completion of *Hands Up!* (1964); and a book entitled *Silent Guns*, compiled November 1962–Spring 1963. Dorn writes in a 1 p. letter to Prynne, 26 April 1963, Pocatello, held by J.H. Prynne, Binder D1 (November 1961–March 1964): "I get bugged in face of the fact that *Hands Up!* is way back of me now, I have viz. two other books of verse done—*Idaho Out* & a vol called *The silent guns*." By the summer of 1963, these books merged to form a later instantiation of *Idaho Out*. This book was not published, and many of its poems appeared in *Geography* (1965). Note that the unpublished book *Idaho Out* should not be confused with the poem "Idaho Out" (*CP*, pp. 153–168), which it originally contained; the poem was later published as a standalone volume by Fulcrum Press in 1965.

The book that we believe to be the original *Idaho Out* was commissioned by German publisher and *Rhinozeros* editor, Rolf-Gunter Dienst. The book was sent to Dienst in November 1962, but went unpublished. While the book's manuscript has not been found, the "Book of Poems" notebook, which bears a dedication to Dienst on its cover, is the closest to a manuscript of the book we have found. Box 38, Folder 592, Notebook "Book of Poems" (1962), EDP-UConn. The full list of poems present in the notebook is: "Some aid to the needy", "Comparison" (cf. section: "Late in the Revolution"), "Dwarfing with chemicals: A promising agricultural technique" (*CP*, pp. 198–199), "In the shadow" (*CP*, pp. 175–176), "A vague love" (*CP*, p. 173), "Another vague love" (*CP*, p. 174), "Bob Considine", "For Soblen", "The Vague Love", "Nature their passing bell: an atonement" (*CP*, p. 55), "Say Someday" (cf. section: "Late in the Revolution"), "Donald is insane they say", "Idaho Again", "The Mountains" (*CP*, pp. 62–63), "Sat night oct. 1962", "From Gloucester Out" [originally titled "The unhappy leaving"] (*CP*, pp. 119–124), "Death was a dream", "Idaho Out" (*CP*, pp. 153–168), "When I met Red", and "Chansonette forever". Some of these poems were collected in *Hands Up!* (the publication of which was delayed until 1964), or at one time intended to be collected there, as well as in *Geography* (1965/1968), and elsewhere; these poems have been left out of the sequence presented here. Typescripts for most of the poems are held by J.H. Prynne, Binder D1B (undated).

Among other texts, this binder contains early manuscripts of *Hands Up!* and *Silent Guns*. Within the *Hands Up!* manuscript is a poem called "The Return", an early draft of "The smug never silent guns of the enemy" (*CP*, pp. 191–192), a poem with a clear relation to the title *Silent Guns*. The contents and order of the *Silent Guns* manuscript are unclear, because a number of the poems which follow the *Silent Guns* title page in Binder D1B are also part of the "Book of Poems" notebook—i.e., what we believe to be the original instantiation of *Idaho Out*. The full list of poems included after the *Silent Guns* title page is: "The Explanation" (*CP*, pp. 177–178), "Nature their passing bell: an atonement" (*CP*, p. 55), "After Love", "When I met Red", "AN OLD SQUARE POEM", "The Territories", "Dark ceiling" [originally entitled "dark clouds are the ceiling"] (*CP*, pp. 186–187), [and still finding], "FOR JIMMIE WORKMAN, THE BANDIT, CAUGHT IN PHOENIX", "Fort Hall obituary: A note" [originally entitled "Solax. Obituary. Idaho. Bannock County. | March 3rd 1963"] (*CP*, pp. 192–193), "A Walk of Spring", "West of Moab" (*CP*, pp. 151–152), "On No", "Donald is insane they say", "Death was a dream", "Some aid to the needy", "A campaign of January 17", "Chansonette forever", "Chronicle" (*CP*, pp. 178–179), "Love song [for Cathy]" (*CP*, pp. 172–173), "Eugene Delacroix says"

(*CP*, pp. 194–196), "BUT THEN AGAIN", and "SO LONG CUBA". Note that the long poems "Idaho Out" (*CP*, pp. 153–168), and "From Gloucester Out" (*CP*, pp. 119–124), present in the original *Idaho Out*, are not present here.

By the summer of 1963, at least some of the contents of *Silent Guns* were subsumed into a new instantiation of *Idaho Out*, though the manuscript for the latter book has not yet been found. Dorn writes in a 2 pp. letter to Prynne, 1 October 1963, Pocatello, held by J.H. Prynne, Binder D1 (November 1961–March 1964): "I have started a novel and finished a book of poems. [. . .] Robert Kelly is definitely going to do that book called *Idaho Out*, which has in it 'From Gloucester Out'". Publication of *Idaho Out*, by Robert Kelly and George Quasha's Trobar Press, was initially planned for late 1963, but was protracted through Spring 1965, when the project was abandoned; cf. Robert Kelly's letters to Dorn, Series 1, Box 1, Folder 18, EDP-M1514. What is perhaps a large portion of the contents of *Idaho Out* are provided in a reading from 30 September 1963, given in Albuquerque (online at the Slought Foundation and PennSound): "Daffodil song" (*CP*, p. 171), "A song [There is a blue sky]" (*CP*, p. 177), "Love song [for Cathy]" (*CP*, pp. 172–173), "Love song [for Lucia]" (*CP*, p. 172), "This March afternoon" (*CP*, p. 187), "Mourning letter, March 29, 1963" (*CP*, pp. 193–194), "A Walk of Spring", "The Territories", "A poem while waiting" [a shorter form of a poem later entitled "Poem in five parts"] (*CP*, pp. 182–185), "Dark ceiling" (*CP*, pp. 186–187), "The smug never silent guns of the enemy" (*CP*, pp. 191–192), "Fort Hall obituary: A note" (*CP*, pp. 192–193), "FOR JIMMIE WORKMAN, THE BANDIT, CAUGHT IN PHOENIX", "An attempt at self-sorrow", and "From Gloucester Out" (*CP*, pp. 119–124). Most of these poems were ultimately collected in *Geography* (1965).

To further complicate matters, note the poems that Dorn included under the heading "THE NEWLY FALLEN: Additional Poems" in Binder D1A (undated), held by J.H. Prynne: "The Vague Love", "A vague love" (*CP*, p. 173), "Another vague love" (*CP*, p. 174), "In the shadow" (*CP*, pp. 175–176), "Dwarfing with chemicals: a promising agricultural technique" (*CP*, pp. 198–199), "Bob Considine", "For Soblen", and "Nature their passing bell: an atonement" (*CP*, p. 55). At least some of these poems post-date the publication of *The Newly Fallen* (1961). Their compilation under this heading is for an expanded British publication of *The Newly Fallen* which did not materialise.

Given the complexity of the history of these texts, the poems that we have brought together under the section heading *Silent Guns* are ordered chronologically.

The drawing on the title page is by Fielding Dawson, and was drawn specifically for *Idaho Out* in the extended form in which it was meant to be published by Trobar Press. The drawing was ultimately printed on the cover of *Idaho Out* (London: Fulcrum Press, 1964).

* **An attempt at self-sorrow**—ca. December 1961. Unpublished; no text has been found. Transcribed by the editors from a reading given on 30 September 1963, in Albuquerque; recording online at the Slought Foundation and PennSound. Date derived from a 4 pp. letter to Denise Levertov, 3 January 1962, Series 4, Box 28, Folder 42, DLP-M0601.

* **The Vague Love**—ca. October 1962. Unpublished TS (2 pp.), held by J.H. Prynne, Binder D1A (undated).

* **Bob Considine**—ca. October 1962. Unpublished TS (1 p.), held by J.H. Prynne, Binder D1A (undated).

* **For Soblen**—ca. October 1962. Unpublished TS (1 p.), held by J.H. Prynne, Binder D1A (undated). Robert Soblen, a spy for the Soviet Union, committed suicide on 11 September 1962.

* **Donald is insane they say**—13 October 1962. Unpublished TS (1 p.), held by J.H. Prynne, Binder D1B (undated). Dated MS (2 pp.), Box 38, Folder 592, Notebook "Book of Poems" (1962), EDP-UConn. In the MS all instances of "Donald" originally read "David".

* **Idaho again**—ca. October 1962. Unpublished TS (1 p.), Box 4, Folder 5, EDP-M1514.

* **Sat night oct. 1962**—20 October 1962. Unpublished MS (3 pp.), Box 38, Folder 592, Notebook "Book of Poems" (1962), EDP-UConn. "Hortatory" is the editors' best guess at a nearly illegible word in line fourteen. Just before the mention of E.E. Cummings (died 3 September 1962), Dorn has crossed out a reference to the article "E.E. Cummings: Poet of the Heart" in *Time Magazine* (14 September 1962).

* **Death was a dream**—24 October 1962. Unpublished TS with handwritten revisions (1 p.), held by J.H. Prynne, Binder D1B (undated). Dated MS (1 p.), Box 38, Folder 592, Notebook "Book of Poems" (1962), EDP-UConn.

* **Some aid to the needy**—25 October 1962. Unpublished TS (1 p.), held by J.H. Prynne, Binder D1B (undated). Dated MS (1 p.), Box 38, Folder 592, Notebook "Book of Poems" (1962), EDP-UConn.

* **When I met Red**—ca. October 1962. Unpublished TS (2 pp.), held by J.H. Prynne, Binder D1B (undated). Several drafts are entitled "The Negro's Return". The text of "An Old Love" (*CP*, p. 60) was originally embedded within the first draft: MS (7 pp.), Box 38, Folder 592, Notebook "Book of Poems" (1962), EDP-UConn.

* **SO LONG CUBA**—29 October 1962. Unpublished TS with handwritten revisions (3 pp.), held by J.H. Prynne, Binder D1B (undated). The first line of the title is a handwritten addition, and the third line of the title is crossed out. Dorn notes in a 1 p. letter to LeRoi Jones, 26 November 1962, *Baraka/Dorn* (p. 118), that this is the final poem in the book compiled for Rolf-Gunter Dienst.

* **Chansonette forever**—ca. October 1962. Unpublished TS with handwritten revisions (1 p.), held by J.H. Prynne, Binder D1B (undated).

* **FOR JIMMIE WORKMAN, THE BANDIT**—5 November 1962. Unpublished TS with handwritten revisions (1 p.), held by J.H. Prynne, Binder D1B (undated). The final stanza has been reconstructed from crossed-out lines and marginalia. Dated MS (2 pp.), held by J.H. Prynne, Binder D1B (undated).

* **A campaign of January 17**—17 January 1963. Unpublished TS with handwritten revisions (1 p.), held by J.H. Prynne, Binder D1B (undated).

* **A Walk of Spring**—14 March 1963, Pocatello. TS (1 p.), Box 149, Folder "Dorn, Edward 1961–1963", COP-UConn. Spanish translation in *Eco Contemporaneo* 5, ed. Miguel Grinberg (Argentina, 1963).

* **After Love**—2 April 1963. Unpublished TS with handwritten revisions (1 p.), held by J.H. Prynne, Binder D1B (undated).

* **ON NO**—13 April 1963. Unpublished TS with handwritten revisions (1 p.), held by J.H. Prynne, Binder D1B (undated).

* **AN OLD SQUARE POEM**—21 April 1963. Unpublished TS with handwritten revisions (1 p.), held by J.H. Prynne, Binder D1B (undated). This text, labeled "final version", seems to indicate that deletions should be retained as visible

redactions. Note the variant TS with handwritten revisions (1 p.), held by J.H. Prynne, Binder D1B (undated). The facsimile is of another variant TS with handwritten revisions (1 p.), Series 2, Box 4, Folder 5, EDP-M1514.

* **The Territories**—21 April 1963, Pocatello. Unpublished TS with handwritten revisions (1 p.), Series 2, Box 4, Folder 5, EDP-M1514. Dated MS (1 p.), held by J.H. Prynne, Binder D1B (undated).

* **and still finding**—5 May 1963. Unpublished MS (2 pp.), held by J.H. Prynne, Binder D1B (undated).

* **BUT THEN AGAIN**—ca. after November 1963. Unpublished TS (2 pp.), held by J.H. Prynne, Binder D1B (undated). Draft TS with handwritten revisions (2 pp.), held by J.H. Prynne, Binder D1B (undated). The first seven lines are taken from this draft, in which they are crossed out.

A CIRCLE OF SONGS (1964)

These ten poems are part of a sequence of lyric poems written January–April 1964 that went unpublished as a single project; "tentative" titles for the sequence included "A circle of lyrics of love and discontent" and "Goodbye in honor of several things". A letter to Betty Cohen appended to the front of the manuscript indicates that these poems were submitted to the Buffalo magazine *Audit* on 2 April 1964. The sequence "Nine Songs" (*CP*, pp. 127–134) was extracted from this project and published in *Niagara Frontier Review* (Buffalo, Fall 1965 / Spring 1966). Eight of the poems from the original "Circle of Songs" (including three of the "Nine Songs") went on to be collected in *Geography* (1965). Three of the poems that make up the truncated sequence presented here were collected in *Geography*; they are included here because they are significantly variant drafts. In all but one case, the texts printed here derive from: Unpublished TS (12 pp.), held by J.H. Prynne, Binder D1B (undated). A complete list of the poems that make up "A Circle of Songs": [The late sternness], [Talk always in circles], "Song: Heat" (*CP*, p. 188), [I will not name her] ("Nine Songs" #1; *CP*, p. 127), [There are each time I talk of it] ("Nine Songs" #2, *CP*, p. 127), "Song [So we somewhat stagger together]" (*CP*, pp. 179–180), [No love lasts forever], [My Gods], "Song [This afternoon was unholy, the sky]" ("Nine Songs" #3; *CP*, pp. 128, 185–186), "Song: Europa" ("Nine Songs" #4; *CP*, pp. 129, 205–206), [Ginger is the color of your eyes and lips] ("Nine Songs" #5; *CP*, p. 130), [The time passes by the count of the contracting leaves] ("Nine Songs" #6; *CP*, pp. 130–131), [Difficulties spoken of], "Song [Oh Gods of my disembarked soul this is sad]" (*CP*, p. 174), [That this is a circle] ("Nine Songs" #7; *CP*, p. 131), [When I awaken in the morning], "Song [If the world]" (*CP*, pp. 176–177), "Song: We shall refrain from them" ("Nine Songs" #8; *CP*, pp. 131–132, 190–191), [Made the temporary fire], and [The first moment] ("Nine Songs" #9; *CP*, 132–134). Other poems that might have been part of this sequence: [Pocatello is black] (*CP*, pp. 63–64), and "Song [my wife is lovely]" (*CP*, pp. 171–172), and "Morning conversation" (cf. section: "In the Face of the Liberal"). Drafts of this manuscript with extensive revisions are housed in Box 4, Folder 2, EDP-M1514.

* **Where is my world love**—Draft of "Song: Heat" (*CP*, p. 188).

* **My Gods**—Version printed here taken from unpublished TS with handwritten revisions (1 p.), Box 4, Folder 2, EDP-M1514.

* **On the bed of the vast promiscuity**—Draft of "Song: The astronauts" (*CP*, p. 137).

* **Oh Gods of my disembarked soul this is sad**—Draft of "Song [Oh Gods of my disembarked soul this is sad]" (*CP*, p. 174).

IN THE FACE OF THE LIBERAL (1964–1968)

* **Morning conversation**—ca. 1964. Unpublished TS with handwritten revisions (1 p.), Series 2, Box 4, Folder 5, EDP-M1514. Variant TS entitled "Early Morning Conversation: a domestic poem" (1 p.) on verso of 2 pp. note to Helene Dorn, Series 1, Box 1, Folder 14, EDP-M1514.

* **IN THE FACE OF THE LIBERAL**—23 March 1965. Unpublished TS (1 p.), Series 2, Box 4, Folder 5, EDP-M1514.

* **This is the Poem for John W.**—ca. July 1966, England. Unpublished MS (1 p.) on the front of an envelope of a letter from J.H. Prynne to Dorn, postmarked 7 July 1966, ED-JW-Del. Written on the back of the envelope is a checklist of Charles Olson's prose works. Contemporaneous letters indicate that Dorn and Wieners were preparing an edition of Olson's prose. A draft transcription of the poem is proposed here, with bullet-points used to separate phrases:

> This is the moment to see the | World in all | the fullness | of its orbituallity • • • This year's crop | of kisses don't seem | as sweet to me • • • when I go to town in a company car I am so proud | if you can understand the simplest forms of fraud you may | also Rule a nation • • • one love was king | but kings can be | wrong! • • • usa | in our | time. | I can | not | find the | way— • • • it just didn't | wear well • • • not that I | considered it | a sin • • • sometimes | I wonder • • • Diamond | Bracelets • • • I'll never be the same I suppose I should | forget you | but I guess I can't | help feeling on | the sentimental | side • • • Dreaming, I was only Dreaming | my dream never haunted you, my heart is telling you how much • • • This year's crop | of kisses—for I'm still wearin last year's love • • • This year's new romance | doesn't seem to have a chance • • • the world | was bright | when you | loved me | oh then there | came a | total eclipse • • • that's life | I guess!

* **Yas suh**—ca. 1965–1966. Unpublished TS with handwritten revisions (1 p.), Series 2, Box 4, Folder 5, EDP-M1514. This is the second of two TS drafts with handwritten revisions in Folder 5; in the first draft, the final stanza ends:

> with a skin held casually over the
> shoulder, the lips of the cave
> no more than
> a stone's throw
> away
> the first paranoid beings
> taking no chances
> the view
> in front of them a real estate
> of the future, every
> banal thing, more than they could imagine
> more fierce than wild animals
> will someday grow there

Maurice Wilson's watercolour "Homo neanderthalensis" (1950) is included here for the resemblance it bears to the description in the poem; image 001983, the Natural History Museum Picture Library, London.

* **a Poem entitled Bullshit**—27 July 1966. Published in Dorn, *The Shoshoneans*, Expanded edition, ed. Matthew Hofer (Albuquerque: University of New Mexico Press, 2013), p. 115. MS (1 p.), held by J.H. Prynne, Binder D5 (July 1966–December 1966). Dated MS (1 p.), Box 39, Notebook "English Poems" (1966), EDP-UConn.

* **my wandering**—19 August 1966. Published as the final stanza of "a Poem entitled Bullshit" in *The Shoshoneans* (2013). Dated MS (1 p.), Box 39, Notebook "English Poems" (1966), EDP-UConn.

* **Second thots on astronaut**—29 October 1966, England. Unpublished MS (2 pp.), Box 37, Folder 578, EDP-UConn.

* **On first reading "As It Were An Attendant"**—28 October 1967. Unpublished TS (1 p.), held by J.H. Prynne, Binder D7 (October 1967–May 1968). The title has been applied by the editors. Cf. "As It Were An Attendant" in Prynne, *Poems* (Fremantle and Tarset: Fremantle Arts Centre Press & Bloodaxe Books, 2005), pp. 124–125.

* **ONCE, AGAIN**—ca. 10 June 1968, Colchester. Unpublished TS (2 pp.), held by J.H. Prynne, Binder D8 (May 1968–January 1969).

A CONVENTION IS IN A WALLPAPER STORE (1968)

August 1968. Published by Frontier Press as three sets of unbound colored cards, the first two of which are inside white envelopes. Copies of all texts in this section are held at the Lilly Library at Indiana University, and at the Special Collections at the State University of New York at Buffalo. The quotation at the beginning of this section is from Matthew Joseph Bruccoli, ed., *First Printings of American Authors: Vol III: Contributions towards Descriptive Checklists* (Detroit: Gale Research Co., 1978), pp. 81–82.

* **SET I**—The envelope for "SET I" bears this description: "22 cards numbered 0–21 | written by Edward Dorn | with an assist by Harvey Brown | as mailed to the Democratic National Convention | in Chicago 1968".

* **SET II**—The envelope for "SET II" bears this description: "7 cards numbered 1–7 | Quotations attributed to Charles Olson, | Charles Ives, John Wieners, Edward Dorn | and Harvey Brown, as mailed to | the Democratic National Convention | in Chicago 1968".

* **CHANTS 1–5**—The "CHANTS" that make up the third set are not enclosed in an envelope. The title derives from the listing by the Special Collections, State University of New York at University of Buffalo.

THE GRAVE OF DIANA (1968–1970)

* **Inauguration poem #3**—3 January 1969, Placitas. MS (2 pp.), Box 37, Folder 578, EDP-UConn. A slightly variant transcription published in *White Wall Review* 38, ed. Dale Smith (Toronto: The Ryerson Literary Society, 2014). Variant MS (1 p.), dated November 1968, Colorado, Box 37, Folder 578, EDP-UConn. The 1968 version reads in full:

drearily drearily drearily
into the future scraped
off the past
again that curious inequality
the Trees are being bird proofed
the starlings are not invited
the mormans are
one marching band
and one float
from each state
one float, float what
each state, state what?

* **To the Tower**—3 January 1969, Placitas. Unpublished TS (1 p.), Box 37, Folder 578, EDP-UConn. Draft MS (2 pp.) in Folder 578 includes dedication.

* **A Graph of Several Persons**—14 March 1969, Lawrence. Unpublished TS (1 p.), Box 37, Folder 578, EDP-UConn.

* **July 13th**—Undated. Unpublished MS (1 p.), Box 44, Folder 645, EDP-UConn.

* **This love is a thing**—ca. 1969–1970. Unpublished MS (1 p.), Box 41, Notebook "The Iconic Record", EDP-UConn.

* **The Grave of Diana**—20 September 1970, Chicago. TS (1 p.), Box 37, Folder 578, EDP-UConn. Published in *White Wall Review* 38, ed. Dale Smith (Toronto: Ryerson Literary Society, 2014). A note on the TS says the poem was sent to *Friendly Local Press*, ed. Louis Rowan (New York), though it was not published there. MS on a photograph of Diana Oughton's gravesite from the 18 September 1970 edition of the *Chicago Daily News* (1 p.), Box 37, Folder 578, EDP-UConn. Diana Oughton was a member of the Weather Underground who died on 6 March 1970, aged 28, in a nail bomb explosion at a Greenwich Village townhouse.

* **Four Years Later**—September 1970, Chicago. Unpublished MS (2 pp.), Box 39, Notebook "Untitled" (1968), EDP-UConn.

* **The Sam Cole Song**—5 December 1970, Chicago. Unpublished TS (1 p.), Box 37, Folder 578, EDP-UConn.

GUNSLINGER: FRAGMENTS & SATELLITES (1970–1974)

These texts represent just a fraction of the unpublished material written towards *Gunslinger* (1966–1975). Cf. *Gunslinger* (Berkeley: Wingbow Press, 1975; Durham and London: Duke University Press, 1989), *CP* (pp. 387–588). Poems that could be considered *Gunslinger* satellite-texts are present across the respective era of Dorn's oeuvre; e.g. a draft of "THE NIGHTLETTER" (*Gunslinger: Book III*), which in this book has been interpolated into *The Day & Night Report*. The drawing of the Horse on the title page of this section is by Michael Myers, drawn onto a galley proof of *Gunslinger*; Zephyrus Image Press records (MSS 704), Special Collections, University of Delaware Library. The peyote engraving placed at the end of this section is also by Myers, taken from the end of the Wingbow/Duke *Gunslinger* (p. 201), where its placement situates it over the apex of the inverted pyramid formed by the colophon on the following leaf. Note that Dorn's Gunslinger notebook "The Iconic Record" is not represented here, as its extent and complexity warrant a separate publication; but cf. sections "The Grave of Diana" and "The Theater of Money" for two texts from "The Iconic Record".

* **LIL'S BOOK**—These poems compile most of what seems to have been written towards the project Dorn called "LIL'S BOOK".

  * **(Everything says to Lil, as of what I don't recall**—Undated. Unpublished TS (1 p.) in 2 pp. letter to J.H. Prynne, 17 October 1970, held by J.H. Prynne, Binder D11 (April 1970–January 1971).

  * **What Lil read on the wall in the ladies room**—September 1972, Kent, Ohio. From unpublished TS entitled "SCRAPS FROM LIL'S BOOK" (1 p.), Box 37, Folder 578, EDP-UConn. Dated MS (1 p.), Box 39, Notebook "Untitled" (1968–1975), EDP-UConn.

  * **Item: Teledyne Ryan, Sllabs Robot on loan**—September 1972, Kent. From unpublished TS entitled "SCRAPS FROM LIL'S BOOK" (1 p.), Box 37, Folder 578, EDP-UConn. Dated MS (1 p.), Box 39, Notebook "Untitled" (1968–1975), EDP-UConn. The Ryan Aeronautical Company produced the first jet-propelled unmanned aerial vehicle in 1951 and became "Teledyne Ryan" in a merger in 1969.

  * **Lils Soliloquy**—October 1972, Kent. From unpublished TS entitled "SCRAPS FROM LIL'S BOOK" (1 p.), Box 37, Folder 578, EDP-UConn. Dated MS (1 p.), Box 39, Notebook "Untitled" (1968–1975), EDP-UConn.

  * **Do you have any notion**—ca. October 1972, Kent. Unpublished TS (1 p.), Box 37, Folder 578, EDP-UConn. MS (1 p.), Box 39, Notebook "Untitled" (1968–1975), EDP-UConn.

  * **Lil: Resin is a supplement . . .** —21 October 1972, Kent. Unpublished MS (1 p.), Box 39, Notebook "Untitled" (1968–1975), EDP-UConn.

  * **Lil: Poeta is the supremest . . .** —Undated. Published with the three "Lil" poems that follow in *Fathar Sixty-six* 6, ed. Duncan McNaughton (Buffalo & Bolinas, September 1974).

* **The Poem of Dedication**—3 February 1971, Chicago. MS (2 pp.), Box 40, Notebook "Stetson" (1971–1990), EDP-UConn. Variant transcription published in *Hot Gun!* 2, On the Work of Edward Dorn, ed. Josh Stanley (New Haven, Summer 2011). This is an unused dedicatory poem for *Gunslinger: Book III*, superseded by "The Lawg" (*CP*, pp. 501–503).

* *Riddle* **of the Omega**—ca. early 1971. Unpublished MS (1 p.), Box 38, Folder 599, EDP-UConn.

* **For the Boys & Girls In The FreeIdea Store**—June 1971, Chicago. Published in *Clear Creek* 6, ed. Pennfield Jensen (San Francisco, September 1971). Additional elements taken from dated TS (1 p.), Box 37, Folder 578, EDP-UConn.

* **O'BRIEN**—Undated. Unpublished TS of nine poems with handwritten revisions (1 p.), Box 37, Folder 578, EDP-UConn. In a reading at the A Space Gallery, Toronto, on 2 February 1973, Dorn remarks: "This is from a series called *O'Brien*, which are mostly just quotes from a man who is one of the great Empedocles experts, whose name is Denis O'Brien"; recording online at PennSound. Note the allusion to O'Brien in the "Prolegomenon" of *Gunslinger: Book IIII* (*CP*, pp. 533–534).

  * **Negativity has positively bad effects**—These are in fact the words of John M. Rist, quoted by Denis O'Brien, "Plotinus on Evil: A study of matter and the soul in Plotinus' conception of human evil" [1969], in *Le Néoplatonisme*, eds. M.P.M. Schuhl and M.P. Hadot (Paris: Éditions du Centre National de la Recherche Scientifique, 1971), pp. 113–146.

* **FIVE ON PARMENIDES**—13–22 May 1973, Kent. These poems are taken from notes on Parmenides that Dorn made in the same notebook in which he composed *Recollections of Gran Apachería* (1974); cf. section: "Homage to Gran Apachería". Unpublished MS (2 pp.), Box 39, Notebook "Untitled" (1969–1993), EDP-UConn. The title has been applied by the editors.

* **Dr. Flamboyant**—Undated. Unpublished MS (1 p.), Box 44, Folder 645, EDP-UConn.

* **the Slinger peered thru the window**—October 1973, Riverside, California. Unpublished MS (1 p.), Box 39, Notebook "Untitled" (1969–1993), EDP-UConn.

* **Standing outside the booth under the open sky**—25 July 1973. Unpublished MS (1 p.), Box 39, Notebook "Untitled" (1969–1993), EDP-UConn.

* **Border surrealismo**—Undated. Unpublished, compiled from two TSS with handwritten revisions (2 pp.), Box 37, Folder 578, EDP-UConn. A crossed-out note at the top of one TS reads: "Of the several starts and stops I've made on *Gunslinger Book IIII* this winter I favor this one at the present time". The first line of the other TS reads: "The Man from ~~Outerspace~~ Laredo".

* **The Holdup**—Undated. Unpublished MS (3 pp.), Box 38, Folder 599, EDP-UConn.

* **Trig Utah**—ca. 1974. Unpublished MS (1 p.), Box 39, Notebook "Untitled" (1968–1975), EDP-UConn.

THE DAY & NIGHT REPORT (1971)

Composed in Dorn's daybook for 1971: Box 40, Notebook "Thor" (1971), EDP-UConn. The notebook's covers, inside covers, title page, and a few other framing pages are reproduced here at the front and back of this section. Typescripts and photocopies of the texts which Dorn published are in Box 38, Folder 632, EDP-UConn.

* **Day 1–Day 79**—Published under the heading "from THE DAY REPORT" in *Caterpillar* 15/16, ed. Clayton Eshleman (Sherman Oaks, CA: April–July 1971), pp. 182–200.

* **Day 55**—Version printed here taken from MS (1 p.), Box 40, Notebook "Thor" (1971), EDP-UConn.

* **Night 65**—Collected in Dorn, *Views*, Writing 40, ed. Donald Allen (San Francisco: Four Seasons Foundation, 1980), pp. 124–125.

* **Night 69: THE NIGHTLETTER (draft)**—The first TS draft of the *Gunslinger* text "THE NIGHTLETTER" is included here. Square brackets indicate Dorn's revisions. The TS (2 pp.) is enclosed within an envelope attached to the inside-back cover of a stapled manila folder entitled "REPORT GX &c | (the public version", which presents as its primary text the second draft of "THE NIGHTLETTER", Box 38, Folder 601, EDP-UConn. The primary text of Folder 601 has this dedication handwritten on its title page: "for Jennifer | Day 69 | 1971"; and it has this note on its final page: "Decifered at Position 7 | Day 70, Year 71". Yet another TS draft is stapled into a second manila folder, which bears the nearly-identical title "REPT GX &c | (the publick version", Box 38, Folder 602,

EDP-UConn. The primary text of Folder 602 has this inscription handwritten on its final page: "Decifered at Sta. 7 | (chi) | Day 70, Year 71". A revised form of "THE NIGHTLETTER" is part of *Gunslinger: Book III*; *CP* (pp. 528–529).

* Days 77, 101, 102, 104, 108, 167, 173, 203, 205, and 264 (second paragraph)— Published in Dorn, *Two Interviews*, eds Gavin Selerie and Justin Katko (Exeter: Shearsman Books, 2012), pp. 30–38.

* Night 79–Day 91—Published with photo-collages under the heading "The Day Report" in *Writing: Georgia Straight Writing Supplement*, 8, eds Stan Persky and Dennis Wheeler (Vancouver, 27 July 1971).

* Days 86, 108 (Eighteen April), and 232—Extracted from this section and included under the titles "Theater of Money #1", "Theater of Money #2", and "Theater of Money #3" (cf. section: "The Theater of Money").

* Day 92–Day 181—Published under the heading "from The Day & Night Book" in *All Stars*, ed. Tom Clark (Santa Fe and New York: Goliard and Grossman, 1972), pp. 101–131; reprinted as *from The Day & Night Book* (Toronto: *shuffaloff* / Eternal Network Joint #6, 2014).

* Day 130 (10 May)—A variant, taken from a reading at the York Street Commune, Vancouver, on 29 July 1971, ends with the Bystander's "index" question answered by Dr. Flamboyant: "The simple ability | to obscure its pointed apex"; recording provided by Fred Wah. A version of these lines in the "Thor" notebook reads: "to ~~dig anything~~ [make everything] slick | ~~unlimitedly~~".

* Day 163—Includes the beginning of "the 3 Great Beenville Paradoxes" in *Gunslinger: Book III*; *CP* (pp. 523–527).

* Day 201 (20th)—Unpublished MS (1 p.), Box 40, Notebook "Thor" (1971), EDP-UConn.

* Day 203—TS (1 p.), inscribed to J.H. Prynne, 27 July 1971, Vancouver, held by J.H. Prynne, Binder D12 (February 1971–October 1971). Cf. "The Glacial Question, Unsolved" in Prynne, *Poems* (Fremantle and Tarset: Fremantle Arts Centre Press & Bloodaxe Books, 2005), pp. 65–67.

* Day 205—MS (1 p.) in 2 pp. letter sent to J.H. Prynne, 13 September 1971, Chicago, held by J.H. Prynne, Binder D12 (February 1971–October 1971).

* Days 216, 225, 226, 229, 230, and 233—Unpublished MSS (6 pp.), Box 40, Notebook "Thor" (1971), EDP-UConn.

* Day 244 (1 September)–Day 265—Published as "The Day Report: September Entries" in parallel columns with Jennifer Dunbar Dorn's own daybook entries, in *Tansy* 5, ed. John Moritz (Lawrence: Spring/Summer 1972). The "Early Transplant Revealed" text of Day 253 (UhHuh Friday) is published as a front-page story in *Bean News* (1972); cf *CP* (pp. 915–922). The "Meeting Rm P1" text of Day 257 (Tuesday Sept 14) and the first paragraph of Day 265 are from MSS (2 pp.), Box 40, Notebook "Thor" (1971), EDP-UConn.

* Day 267–Day 362—Unpublished MSS (24 pp.), Box 40, Notebook "Thor" (1971), EDP-UConn.

THE THEATER OF MONEY (1971)

The scope of *The Theater of Money* is not entirely clear. The fact of its conception is visible in Box 39, Notebook "Challenge", EDP-UConn, where the project's title page is dated September 1971, Chicago. The notice under the title (as given here) is crossed out, and after several blank pages, the title page is followed by MSS of "THE TELETRAK" and "In Defense of Pure Sensation". The spectacular individual reproduced here after "Theater of Money 3" precedes the title page and appears to be Dorn's cover image for the project. Note that the MS of "an oecological prophecy" (*CP*, pp. 350–352) is also assigned to this project; Box 40, Notebook "Thor" (1971), EDP-UConn.

* **Theater of Money #1**—18 April 1971. Published as Day 108 of *The Day & Night Report in All Stars*, ed. Tom Clark (Santa Fe and New York: Goliard and Grossman, 1972) and in Dorn, *from The Day & Night Book* (Toronto: *shuffaloff* / Eternal Network Joint #6, 2014). The text from "NOW PLAYING AT THE PANTHEON THEATRE" published in *Toothpaste 7*, ed. Allan Kornblum (Iowa City, 1972). The MS is labelled as belonging to "The Theater of Money" in Box 40, Notebook "Thor" (1971), EDP-UConn.

* **Theater of Money #2**—27 March 1971. Published as Day 86 of *The Day & Night Report* in *Writing: Georgia Straight Writing Supplement* 8, eds Stan Persky and Dennis Wheeler (Vancouver, 27 July 1971). MS (1 p.), Box 40, Notebook "Thor" (1971), EDP-UConn labelled as belonging to "The Theater of Money". Also labelled in a file of typescripts and copies of publications of *The Day & Night Report*; Box 38, Folder 623, EDP-UConn.

* **Theater of Money #3**—20 August 1971. Unpublished and labelled MS (1 p.), Day 232, Box 40, Notebook "Thor" (1971), EDP-UConn.

* **THE TELETRAK**—Undated. Unpublished MS (1 p.), Box 39, Notebook "Challenge", EDP-UConn. Elements of the formatting from the publication of "In Defense of Pure Sensation" are adopted here.

* **In Defense of Pure Sensation**—Undated. Published in *Ploughshares* 1:2 (Boston: Emerson College, 1972). The version here incorporates aspects of a draft TS enclosure (1 p.), Box 41, Notebook "The Iconic Record", EDP-UConn.

TRANSLATIONS WITH GORDON BROTHERSTON (1971–1975)

These five poems, from Spanish, Maya, and Nahuatl, are a fraction of the work produced in Dorn and Brotherston's thirty-year collaboration. Their collected translations are published as *The Sun Unwound: Original Texts from Occupied America* (Berkeley: North Atlantic Books, 1999).

* **You have to look at me**—Translated from Spanish. Unpublished TS (1 p.), held by Gordon Brotherston. Montes de Oca (1932–2005) was a Mexican poet and painter.

* **Another Anniversary of Summer**—Translated from Spanish. Unpublished TS (1 p.), held by Gordon Brotherston.

* *Trilce*: **XX**—Translated from Spanish. Unpublished MS (2 pp.), Box 37, Folder 579, EDP-UConn. Cf. César Vallejo, *Selected Poems*, edited and translated by Edward Dorn and Gordon Brotherston (Penguin Books, 1976); collected in *The Sun Unwound*.

* **The Making of the Uinal**—Translated from Maya. Published in Brotherston, *Image of the New World: The American Continent portrayed in Native Texts* (Thames & Hudson, 1979), pp. 181–186; and *The Sun Unwound* (pp. 46–49). The version used here is a draft TS (3 pp.), held by Gordon Brotherston, which text contains blank spaces for the day glyphs that have been added here by the editors. Hieroglyphs reproduced from: William Gates, *An Outline Dictionary of Maya Glyphs* [1931] (New York: Dover Publications Inc., 1978). A variant of the first half of the text is published in *Sixpack* 9, eds Pierre Joris and W.R. Prescott (London and Lake Toxaway, Fall 1975), which text includes handwritten versions of the first four hieroglyphs printed here. The translators' note to the *Sixpack* text reads: "The uinal is the corpus (uinic = man) of 20 calendar signs common to Mesoamerica. Here, in the Yucatec *Book of Chilam Balam of Chumayel*, (see edition by R.L. Roys) it is set in movement as the principle of time-space reality, a wittier 'beginning' than Genesis." The gloss on "uinal" in *The Sun Unwound* (p. 82) reads: "a calendar period of twenty days, each named by one of the Twenty Signs of Mesoamerican ritual which here are combined successively with the Thirteen Numbers." The image following the text is also published at the foot of the *Sixpack* text; it derives from a fresco in Santa Rita, Belize, reproduced in R.L. Roys, *The Book of Chilam Balam of Chumayel* (Norman: University of Oklahoma Press, 1967), p. 78, where its caption reads: "The drum and rattle of the katun resound." "Katun" is a Maya calendar period of 7,200 days, roughly twenty years.

* **The Aztec Priests' Reply**—Translated from Nahuatl, with the assistance of Jennifer Dunbar Dorn. Published in *Poetry Review* 65:4, ed. Eric Mottram (London, 1975); *New World Journal* 1:2–3, ed. Bob Callahan (Berkeley, Spring 1977); *Image of the New World* (pp. 65–69); *The Sun Unwound* (pp. 34–43); and *Ed Dorn Live: Lectures, Interviews, and Outtakes*, ed. Joseph Richey (Ann Arbor: University of Michigan Press, 2007), pp. 120–124. The version given here is largely that of the publication in *New World Journal*, where a note on the text reads (p. 50): "The Aztec priests' reply to the emissaries of Hadrian VI and Charles V, at their meeting in Mexico in 1524, according to the texts provided by Sahagún in 1564 (W. Lehmann, *Sterbende Gotter und Christliche Helisbotschaft*, Stuttgart 1949, pp. 100–101)." See *Image of the New World* (pp. 63–65) for a discussion of this text. The symbols at the foot of the text are presented as they are in *The Sun Unwound*, where they are described as "symbols of wealth and power"; in *Image of the New World* (p. 65), Brotherston describes these "Toltec symbols" as (left to right): "*tlalpiloni* (knot in mantle)" which is "a sign of high rank", "*teocuitlatl* (gold)", "*chalchiuitl* (jade)", "*petlacal* (treasure casket, upturned)", and "*petatl* (mat — of power or authority)".

A MEXICO SCRAPBOOK (1972)

The seven texts and various images presented here are taken from the notebook which Dorn kept during a trip to Mexico in early 1972. Unpublished MSS (11 pp.), Box 41, Notebook "Mex" (1972), EDP-UConn. The section title and dedication are taken from the notebook's opening page. The notebook also contains MSS of "Easy's Best" and some of the poems in *Tens* 1 (1972), *CP* (pp. 353–355).

* **The ticket seller has Sunday off** . . .—2 February 1972, Tehua.

* **Los Tilos**—2 February 1972, Tehua.

* A Poem on entering Cuernavaca—14 February 1972, Cuernavaca.
* Old New Yorkers Really Get My Head—16 February 1972, Cuernavaca. Published as a broadside (Lawrence: Cottonwood Review IV, 1972).
* he spoke with a whisper disc—27 February 1972, Cuernavaca.

MELLOW W/ TEETH (1972–1976)

* Poem sent to J.H. Prynne—Undated. Unpublished MS (1 p.) in letter to J.H. Prynne, 19 September 1972, Kent, Ohio, held by J.H. Prynne, Binder D14 (May 1972–February 1973). The title has been applied by the editors.
* Epithet for the Gravestone of Max Douglas—November 1972, Kent. Unpublished MS (1 p.), Box 39, Notebook "Untitled" (1968–1975), EDP-UConn. The poet Max Douglas died of a heroin overdose at the age of 21 on 8 October 1970.
* Move w/ the winde—9 November 1972, Kent; written with Jennifer Dunbar Dorn. Unpublished TS (1 p.), Box 37, Folder 578, EDP-UConn.
* A Snip from the Allegorical Barbershop—Undated. Unpublished, compiled from two MSS (4 pp.), Box 39, Notebook "Efficiency" (1972), EDP-UConn.
* CALIFORNIA—ca. 1972. Unpublished MS of eleven poems (2 pp.), Box 37, Folder 581, EDP-UConn. After the title, this note is crossed out: "not abt necessarily, but where done".
* La Vista—Titled MS (1 p.), Box 39, Notebook "Efficiency", EDP-UConn.
* The United States is the first country—Undated. Unpublished MS (1 p.), Box 37, Folder 581, EDP-UConn.
* On Will—Undated. Unpublished TS (1 p.), Box 37, Folder 581, EDP-UConn.
* RETURN TO NATURE—Undated. Unpublished TS of four poems (1 p.), Box 37, Folder 581, EDP-UConn.
* Nostalgia—Undated. Unpublished MS (2 pp.), Box 39, Notebook "Untitled" (1968–1975), EDP-UConn. A number of elements are taken from a version read at the A Space Gallery, Toronto, on 2 February 1973; recording online at PennSound.
* Interview—Undated. Unpublished TS (1 p.), Box 37, Folder 578, EDP-UConn.
* Advice to hearty shoppers—Undated. Published with Advice to weary shoppers in Stone Wind 3, ed. Terry Jacobus (Chicago, 1972).
* The Place is Grand—December 1972. Unpublished MS sent to J.H. Prynne (1 p.), held by J.H. Prynne, Binder D14 (May 1972–February 1973). An MS note (1 p.) in Box 39, Notebook "Untitled" (1968–1975), EDP-UConn, reads: "I have composed a song from an ancient scenario by John Wesley Powell called The year is eighteen seventy five, the place is Grand"; cf. Richard J. Chorley, Antony J. Dunn and Robert P. Beckinsale, The History of the Study of Landforms, Vol. I, Geomorphology before Davis (London: Methuen, 1964), p. 477. J.H. Prynne responded in late December 1972 with the poem "Thanks for the Memory"; cf. Prynne, Poems (Fremantle and Tarset: Fremantle Arts Centre Press & Bloodaxe Books, 2005), p. 220.
* INTERIM REPORT TO THE SCHUCHAT COMMISSION—Undated. Published in Buffalo Stamps 7: The Last Buffalo, ed. Simon Schuchat (1973); colophon reads: "published by | ELECTRO-MAGNETIC-FLUX | in association with | the INTERNATIONAL METABOLIST MOVEMENT". The IMM's "Board of

Governors" is given as: Gregory Corso (Chairman), Ted Berrigan, Andrei Codrescu, Ed Dorn, and Anne Waldman. In a private correspondence with the editors, Simon Schuchat identifies "The Outlanders" as Al Simmons, Terry Jacobus, and Hank Kanabus.

* *The Congoleum of Michael Myers*—2 January 1973, Kent. Published in *Isthmus* 2, eds J. Rutherford Willems, Eileen Callahan, and Bob Callahan (San Francisco, 1973), to accompany a collection of engravings by Michael Myers. Dated TS (1 p.), Box 37, Folder 578, EDP-UConn. The Myers engraving printed here is part of the portfolio published in *Isthmus* 2. Cf. Alastair Johnston, *Zephyrus Image: A Bibliography* (Berkeley: Poltroon Press, 2003).

* **Mellow w/ Teeth**—1973. Unpublished TS with handwritten revisions (1 p.), Box 37, Folder 578, EDP-UConn. A draft TS in Folder 578 bears the title "A quick glance at the immediate present".

* **An autumn evening in Illinois**—30 September 1972, Washington, Illinois, and 31 May 1973, Kent. Unpublished MS (2 pp.), Box 39, Notebook "Untitled" (1969–1993), EDP-UConn. The first stanza was written in 1972, and the remaining stanzas in 1973.

* **Filler up!**—Spring 1973, Kent. Published in *The World* 26, ed. Anne Waldman (New York City, Winter 1973). Dated TS (1 p.), Box 37, Folder 578, EDP-UConn.

* **You can't fall out from an *at ease* position**—Undated. Published in *The World* 26. Variant TS with handwritten revisions (1 p.), Box 37, Folder 578, EDP-UConn.

* **Paranoia, Incorporated**—17 February 1973, Kent. Published in *The World* 26. Dated MS (1 p.), Box 38, Folder 599, EDP-UConn.

* **Snowe Bound**—Undated. Published without a title in *The World* 26. Titled TS (1 p.), Box 37, Folder 578, EDP-UConn.

* **Ohio**—Spring 1973, Kent. Published in *The World* 26. Dated TS (1 p.), Box 37, Folder 578, EDP-UConn.

* **In admiration of endurance**—6 September 1973, Riverside, California. Unpublished MS (1 p.), Box 39, Notebook "Untitled" (1969–1993), EDP-UConn.

* **The Nicest of Citys**—Undated. Unpublished TS (1 p.) in 2 pp. letter to Stan and Jane Brakhage, 2 April 1974, Box 5, Folder 11, James Stanley Brakhage Collection, Archives, University of Colorado at Boulder Libraries.

* **FROM *SEMI-HARD***—Undated. The poems [They won the election] and [By the Way] are published in *Semi-Hard* (San Francisco: Zephyrus Image, 1974), which includes two poems by George Kimball.

* **Shufflin Off to Buffalo**—1 November 1975, San Francisco. Published as a broadside by M. Morgulis and T. Dreamer (Buffalo, 1975).

HOMAGE TO GRAN APACHERÍA (1973)

ca. 22 January 1973–1978 November 1973. The sixteen poems here are drawn from the notebook in which Dorn wrote *Recollections of Gran Apachería* (1974): unpublished MSS (18 pp.), Box 39, Notebook "Untitled" (1969–1993), EDP-UConn; cf. *CP* (pp. 365–386). "Homage to Gran Apachería: a work of recognition" is an early title for the project.

* **It is not illumining**—Undated. This is the original opening to "[It is bright to recollect]" (*CP*, p. 368).

* **ATHABASCA**—8 August 1973, San Francisco. The penultimate line of the second stanza originally read: "their character was left to others defining". The fourth stanza contains lines used in "Dress for War" (*CP*, p. 370).

* **The capacity to disembody**—Undated. The final line is revised to read: "before they resettle us".

OFFICE EQUIPMENT (1976–1983)

* **This is the picture. The Doctors**—31 January 1976, San Francisco. Published with the title "from *Hello, La Jolla*" as broadside 7 of the No Mountain Poetry Project, illustration by Darcie Sanders (Chicago: The Ravine Press, 1976).

* **Thursday, the 5th of February, and still no paycheck**—5 February 1976, La Jolla, California. Unpublished TS (1 p.) in 2 pp. letter to J.H. Prynne, held by J.H. Prynne, Binder D20 (January 1976–December 1976).

* **Phænominon**—February–March 1976. Published as a broadside (San Francisco & Healdsburg: Zephyrus Image, 1 February & 1 March 1976). The broadside notes that the poem is from *Hello, La Jolla* (1978), but it does not appear there.

* **A Late Luddite Opinion**—Undated. Published in *The* 14, ed. Jack Collom (Boulder, 1977), where it is preceded by the *Hello, La Jolla* poems "A Sense of Place" and "2 Gulls Sittin on the Richmond Bridge" *CP* (pp. 626–627).

* **Drought report from Chlorofluornia**—Undated. Unpublished TS (1 p.) in 2 pp. letter to Gordon Brotherston, 23 December 1976, Healdsburg, California, held by Gordon Brotherston. Noted as being part of *Hello, La Jolla*, which Dorn refers to as: *Hello, La Jolla, Goodbye Gary. Excursions in Chlorofluornia*.

* **LA JOLLA RETURN**—These are most of the additions Dorn wrote into his copy of *Hello, La Jolla* (1978). The title has been applied by the editors.

  * **There is a considerable amount of**—Undated. Appears above "PREFACE" (*Hello, La Jolla*, p. 7; cf. *CP*, p. 599).

  * **PREFACE**—Undated. Version of "PREFACE" with handwritten extension (*HLJ*, p. 7; cf. *CP*, p. 599).

  * **The Brooks Adams Quote**—Undated. Appears beneath "Del Mar" (*HLJ*, p. 17; cf. *CP*, p. 602).

  * **Chicken Relativity**—Undated. Version of "Chicken Relativity" with handwritten extension (*HLJ*, p. 21; cf. *CP*, p. 604).

  * **I was 11 in 1940**—Undated. Appears beneath "Period Westerns" (*HLJ*, p. 42; cf. *CP*, p. 612).

  * **So Far**—Undated. Appears beneath "On the Other Hand" (*HLJ*, p. 44; cf. *CP*, p. 613).

  * **4 July**—4 July 1978, San Francisco. Appears beneath "On Stooping for Money" (*HLJ*, p. 46; cf. *CP*, p. 614).

  * **I spent the winter of 1977–1978 swinging**—4 July 1978, San Francisco. Appears beneath "The Las Tycoon (A Review)" (*HLJ*, p. 50; cf. *CP*, p. 615).

  * **American as Apple Pie**—Undated. Appears beneath "The Sanders Quote" (*HLJ*, p. 55; cf. *CP*, p. 616).

* **But Before That**—Undated. Appears beneath "The Burr Quote" (*HLJ*, p. 84; cf. *CP*, p. 627).

* **Good filing cabinet**—Undated. Appears above the palm trees image (*HLJ*, p. 92).

* **The Gore Vidal quote**—Undated. Appears below the palm trees image (*HLJ*, p. 92).

* **Gotta Hurt Somebody**—Undated. Appears on the verso before the colophon and continues above the colophon (*HLJ*, pp. 94–95). The title has been applied by the editors.

* **Quote followed by example**—Undated. Transcribed from a reading given for the Charles Olson Event at the University of Iowa, 5–11 November 1978, where Dorn notes that it is from *Hello, La Jolla* (though it was not collected there); recording held at the New York Public Library.

* **To Wit**—ca. 2 December 1978. Published with **A Variation on Hobbes** and **It Seems to Me I've Heard that Song Before** in *Tellus* 2, ed. Stephen Bunch (Lawrence, 1979). Dated MS of **It Seems to Me I've Heard that Song Before** (2 pp.), Series B, Folder 577, Notebook 4, EDP-3009.

* **Office Equipment**—August 1979, Boulder. Published as a broadside (Washington, DC: Folger Evening Poetry Series, 1979–1980).

* **Poor Carter**—ca. 1979. Unpublished MS (1 p.), Box 42, Notebook "Pen-tab" (1979), EDP-UConn.

* **In the interest of equality**—ca. 1979. Unpublished MS (1 p.), Box 42, Notebook "Pen-tab" (1979), EDP-UConn.

* **De Characteristic do git inflated**—Undated. Published with **Name for an early American punk group** and **The Country Awards** in *Chicago Review* 30:3, Black Mountain and Since: Objectivist Writing in America, ed. Cheryl Glickfield (Winter 1979).

* **Some free & curious data**—Undated. Published with **Worse than Baden-Baden** in *Sperlonga Manhattan Express*, ed. Franco Beltrametti (Riva San Vitale: Scorribanda Productions, 1980).

* **AN OBSERVATION ON BOULDER'S MALL**—Undated. Published with **HARDBALL SIMILE** and **QUOTATION FROM KIDD** in *Cottonwood Review* 22, eds Denise Low and Robin Tawney (Lawrence, Spring 1980).

* **A Robert Service Bear Flies Imitation**—June 1980, Juneau, Alaska. Published as a broadside, designed and printed by Graham Macintosh (Santa Barbara: Cadmus Editions, 1982). Dated TS with handwritten revisions (1 p.), Series 2:A, Folder 490, EDP-3009. A crossed-out note indicates that this was part of a project called "Alaska Poems".

* **The Democrats**—14 August 1980, Boulder. Unpublished MS (1 p.), Series 2:A, Folder 495, EDP-3009.

* **The Republicans**—14 August 1980, Boulder. Unpublished MS (1 p.), Series 2:A, Folder 495, EDP-3009.

* **The last bumper sticker**—22 December 1980. Unpublished MS (1 p.) written into a copy of *Yellow Lola* (1980).

* **Boulder Blue**—Undated. Unpublished TS (1 p.), Series 2:A, Folder 495, EDP-3009. A note on an MS draft in Folder 495 indicates that this belongs to a project called "The Boulder Book", which is perhaps the same project as the one called "A 2sided Boulder", mentioned in the next note.

* **How Small Can Awesome Get?**—6 April 1981, Boulder. Published with **Further Thoughts on Dogs** and **Let Those People Go** in *Spectacular Diseases* 6, ed. Robert Vas Dias (Cambridge, 1981); in *Wch Way* 4, eds Jed Rasula and Don Byrd (Los Angeles & Albany, Summer 1982); and with **Further Thoughts on Dogs** and **Let Those People Go** in Dorn, *Two Interviews*, eds Gavin Selerie and Justin Katko (Exeter: Shearsman Books, 2012), pp. 98–101. Draft MS entitled "Personage" labelled as belonging to a project called "A 2sided Boulder" (2 pp.), Box 42, Notebook "The Joy of Nothing" (1981–1993), EDP-UConn; published in *Two Interviews* (p. 99).

* **On First Looking into Marsden Hartley**—ca. May 1981, Boulder. Unpublished MS (1 p.), Box 42, Notebook "The Joy of Nothing" (1981–1993), EDP-UConn.

* **Unedible is this Nation's Blessed spirit**—4 January 1982. Unpublished MS (1 p.), Series 2:A, Folder 495, EDP-3009.

* **The Ladder of Opportunity?**—Undated. Published with **Neutre Pronoun** and **Things We Know** in *Ink* 6, eds John Daley & Deborah Daley (Buffalo: Just Buffalo Press, 1983).

FROM THE WRONG SIDE OF THE PARTITION (1980–1981)

These are poems that were not included in *Captain Jack's Chaps or Houston/MLA* (1983); cf. *CP* (pp. 665–680). Note that the cowboy musician R.A. Dillof, referred to as "Dobro Dick" in *Captain Jack's Chaps*, is variously referred to here as "Ricardo Montana" and "Montana Dick".

* **The next morning**—ca. late December 1980. Unpublished TS (1 p.), Series 2:A, Folder 495, EDP-3009.

* **From the Bayou to the ringworm**—ca. late December 1980. Unpublished MS (6 pp.), Series 2:A, Folder 495, EDP-3009.

* **Returning to the Harley**—ca. late December 1980. Unpublished TS (2 pp.), Series 2:A, Folder 495, EDP-3009.

* **The Power of a Word**—13 February 1981, Boulder. Unpublished TS (1 p.), Series 2:A, Folder 495, EDP-3009.

MORE ABHORRENCES (1983–1989)

This is a selection from the extensive reserve supply of unpublished "ABHORRENCES". Cf. *Abhorrences: A Chronicle of the Eighties* (1990); *CP* (pp. 681–772). Dorn's cartoon on the section title-page is taken from a photocopy broadside entitled "Abhorrences poster #2", printed on a 1 p. letter to Gordon Brotherston, 2 May 1986, Boulder, held by Gordon Brotherston; the figures in the poster are from a Cold War-era advertisement for the American Viscose Corporation, the "World's Largest Producer of Man-Made Fibers".

* **There's nothing to do w/ valentine's day**—Undated. Unpublished MS (1 p.), Box 38, Folder 588, EDP-UConn.

* **the bite is sharp**—6 April 1983. Unpublished MS (1 p.), Box 38, Folder 587, EDP-UConn.

* **REVENGE: as an insufficient inducement**—13 May 1983, Boulder. Unpublished TS with handwritten revisions (1 p.), Box 38, Folder 588, EDP-UConn. The photocopy broadside made by Dorn poster is in Box 38, Folder 582, EDP-UConn.

* **Shuffleburger, your name was odd**—May 1983. Unpublished TS with hand-written revisions (1 p.), Box 38, Folder 582, EDP-UConn. Note the three variant drafts TSS with handwritten revisions (3 pp.), Box 38, Folder 582, EDP-UConn. Lieutenant Commander Albert Schaufelberger, deputy Commander of the U.S. Military Group in El Salvador, was assassinated on 25 May 1983.

* **Witnesses say they do not want to be identified**—26 May 1983. Unpublished TS (1 p.), Box 38, Folder 582, EDP-UConn.

* **Not to mention names**—22 November 1983. Unpublished TS with handwritten revisions (1 p.), Box 38, Folder 582, EDP-UConn. In the opening line, "Charles Olson" is written in place of "my master". Seamus Heaney reviewed *The Modern Poetic Sequence: The Genius of Modern Poetry*, by M.L. Rosenthal and Sally M. Gall, for the *New York Times Book Review* in 1983.

* **Public Safety #2**—6 December 1983, Boulder. Unpublished TS, originally titled "Air Bag II", with handwritten revisions (1 p.), Box 38, Folder 582, EDP-UConn.

* **The Hysteria of Left wing Bogey making**—14 December 1983, Boulder. Unpublished MS (1 p.), Box 38, Folder 582, EDP-UConn.

* **Freedom of information**—12 January 1984. Unpublished MS (1 p.), Box 38, Folder 584, EDP-UConn.

* **Anykyn**—17 February 1984, Boulder. Unpublished TS (1 p.), Series 2:A, Folder 490, EDP-3009.

* **Crippled Clerihew**—5 March 1984. Unpublished TS with handwritten revisions (1 p.), Box 38, Folder 582, EDP-UConn. Dating based on a Nightline debate between Pat Boone and Connecticut Senator Lowell Weicker over prayer in school.

* **I'm from Idaho**—15 March 1984. Unpublished TS (1 p.), Box 38, Folder 582, EDP-UConn.

* **A Critique of Recent Developments in Meso-America**—1 May 1984. Unpublished TS (1 p.), Box 38, Folder 582, EDP-UConn.

* **Boulder print-out**—15 June 1984. Unpublished MS (1 p.), Box 42, Notebook "The Joy of Nothing" (1981–1993), EDP-UConn.

* **Property rights are not negotiable**—June 1984, Boulder. Unpublished TS with handwritten revisions (1 p.), Box 38, Folder 582, EDP-UConn. The final line originally read: "its absolutes are truly absolute." Draft MS (1 p.), Folder 582, is dated 26 May 1983, the day after the assassination of Albert Schaufelberger.

* **Going Blind into Restaurants**—4 July 1984. Unpublished MS (1 p.), Box 42, Notebook "The Joy of Nothing" (1981–1993), EDP-UConn.

* **Even I End Up Living in Dogtown**—14 July 1984. Unpublished TS (2 pp.), Box 38, Folder 586, EDP-UConn.

* **Copyright**—21 July 1984. Unpublished TS with handwritten revisions (1 p.), Box 38, Folder 582, EDP-UConn.

* **The Tyranny of Food**—21 July 1984. Unpublished TS (1 p.), Box 38, Folder 586, EDP-UConn.

* **The Tariff Question**—24 July 1984. Unpublished TS (1 p.), Box 38, Folder 585, EDP-UConn.

* **On Rejuvenating the Hotline**—30 July 1984. Unpublished TS (1 p.), Box 38, Folder 586, EDP-UConn.

* **For the Protection of this Whole World**—30 July 1984. Unpublished TS (1 p.), Box 38, Folder 586, EDP-UConn.

* **Kansas City Collapse**—July 1984. Unpublished TS with handwritten revisions (1 p.), Series 2:A, Folder 490, EDP-3009.

* **W.C. WILLIAMS**—ca. July 1984–1987. Unpublished, compiled from two TSS with handwritten revisions (2 pp.) and one MS (3 pp.), Series 2:A, Folder 490, EDP-3009. A handwritten note at the bottom of one of the TS pages reads: "For W.C. Williams series".

* **In Humble Admiration**—1 August 1984. Unpublished TS (1 p.), Box 38, Folder 585, EDP-UConn. Draft TS with handwritten revisions (1 p.), Box 38, Folder 586, EDP-UConn.

* **Of Decadent, Californian Tories**—4 August 1984. Unpublished TS with handwritten revisions (1 p.), Box 38, Folder 586, EDP-UConn.

* **Preposterous Propaganda**—12 August 1984. Unpublished TS (1 p.), Box 38, Folder 586, EDP-UConn.

* **New Matches for the Fall**—September 1984. Unpublished TS (1 p.), Box 38, Folder 582, EDP-UConn.

* **I would say, with all due respect**—4 September 1984. Unpublished TS (1 p.), Box 38, Folder 582, EDP-UConn. A note on the poem dated 7 October 1988 reads: "withheld because | it is beyond the | call of reason".

* **Law & Order**—26 August 1984. Unpublished MS (1 p.), Box 38, Folder 588, EDP-UConn.

* **"Where's the Pork?"**—4 September 1984. Unpublished TS (1 p.), Box 38, Folder 582, EDP-UConn.

* **Shopping List**—23 September 1984. Unpublished MS (1 p.), Series 2:A, Folder 489, EDP-3009. Dorn's note at the bottom of the MS reads: "Sent to Anne Waldman | For Book of Ted".

* **"Paralyzing Affability"**—29 September 1984. Unpublished TS (1 p.), Box 38, Folder 586, EDP-UConn.

* **Contact w/ the Enemy #1**—ca. mid-December 1984. Unpublished MS (1 p.), Box 42, Notebook "Record Abhorrences" (1983–1986), EDP-UConn.

* **A Canadienne View of the Border**—November 1984. Unpublished TS (1 p.), Box 38, Folder 585, EDP-UConn.

* **All the people who were craven**—13 December 1984. Unpublished MS (1 p.), Box 42, Notebook "Abhorrences" (1984–1985), EDP-UConn.

* **Sticking by the duly forgotten**—ca. mid-December 1984. Unpublished MS (1 p.), Box 42, Notebook "Abhorrences" (1984–1985), EDP-UConn.

* **Twice shy**—1984. Unpublished TS (1 p.), Series 2:A, Folder 490, EDP-3009.

* **Dave Rudabaugh for President**—ca. 1984–1985. Unpublished MS (1 p.), Box 42, Notebook "Abhorrences" (1984–1985), EDP-UConn. Image reproduced from the same notebook.

* **Really great lies are expensive**—Undated. Published with **Too Latent for Fascism** and **Anything you can push** in *Infolio* 16, ed. Tom Raworth (Cambridge, Tuesday July 22 1986).

* **Legal Definitions aren't Everything**—14 January 1985. Unpublished MS (1 p.), Box 42, Notebook "Abhorrences" (1984–1985), EDP-UConn.

* **Lemma dilemma**—8 February 1985. Unpublished MS (1 p.), Box 42, Notebook "Abhorrences" (1984–1985), EDP-UConn.

* **The Beginning of Sorrows**—24 February 1985. Unpublished MS (2 pp.), Box 38, Folder 587, EDP-UConn.

* **MEAN QUISINE**—26–27 February 1985. Unpublished TS (1 p.), Box 38, Folder 583, EDP-UConn.

* **the power of good editing**—5 April 1985. Unpublished MS (1 p.), Box 42, Notebook "Abhorrences" (1984–1985), EDP-UConn.

* **Basil Bunting**—Undated. Unpublished MS and TS (1 p.), Box 38, Folder 587, EDP-UConn. Basil Bunting died 17 April 1985.

* **Propositions from Introspection Time**—20 May 1985. Unpublished TS (1 p.), Box 38, Folder 582, EDP-UConn.

* **The speck in the Milky Way**—23 June 1985. Unpublished MS (1 p.), Box 42, Notebook "Abhorrences" (1984–1985), EDP-UConn.

* **RaIsInG BlIsTeRs**—31 August–2 September 1985, Boulder. Unpublished TS (1 p.), Box 38, Folder 582, EDP-UConn.

* **A Drug of greater price than coke**—19 September 1985. Unpublished MS (1 p.), Box 38, Folder 584, EDP-UConn.

* **Letter to Ethiopia**—22 September 1985, Boulder. Unpublished MS (2 pp.), Box 38, Folder 584, EDP-UConn.

* **Summaries and Conclusions of a September Flight**—Fall 1985. Unpublished TS with handwritten revisions (1 p.), Box 38, Folder 582, EDP-UConn.

* **I'm haunted by my past these days**—2 November 1985. Unpublished TS (1 p.), Box 3, Folder 8, EDP-M1460.

* **The Long So-Long**—6 November 1985. Unpublished TS (1 p.), Box 38, Folder 583, EDP-UConn.

* **Being Able**—February 1986. Unpublished TS (1 p.), Box 38, Folder 582, EDP-UConn.

* **What a technical advance**—3 April 1986. Unpublished MS (1 p.), handwritten into an *Abhorrences* pamphlet published by Tom Clark (Berkeley & Boulder: Handmade Books, 1986).

* **That Which is Cute & Sick**—June 1986. Unpublished TS (1 p.), Box 38, Folder 582, EDP-UConn.

* **Republican Form**—14 September 1986, Boulder. Unpublished TS (1 p.), Series 2:A, Folder 490, EDP-3009.

* **Expect to be Ripped Off**—September 1986. Unpublished TS (1 p.), Box 38, Folder 582, EDP-UConn.

* **Forget the Jar Wars**—11 October 1986. Unpublished TS (1 p.), Series 2:A, Folder 490, EDP-3009.

* **Dynamo Tedium**—21 October 1986. Unpublished TS (1 p.), Box 38, Folder 582, EDP-UConn.

* **Rose Bird**—30 October 1986. Unpublished MS (1 p.), Box 38, Folder 582, EDP-UConn.

* **Semiotics for Semidiotics**—Undated. Unpublished MS (1 p.), Box 43, Notebook "Untitled" (1988) #1, EDP-UConn.

* **On the other hand**—10 November 1986. Unpublished MS (1 p.), Series 2:A, Folder 490, EDP-3009.

* **The passing of a Great Bartender**—10 November 1986. Unpublished MS (1 p.), Series 2:A, Folder 490, EDP-3009.

* **Without Title**—13 December 1986. Unpublished MS (1 p.), Series 2:A, Folder 489, EDP-3009.

* **The Church that is Stapleton Aerodrome**—22 December 1986. Unpublished TS with handwritten revisions (1 p.), Box 38, Folder 588, EDP-UConn.

* **Anti-Literacy Campaign**—9 January 1987. Unpublished TS (1 p.), Box 38, Folder 585, EDP-UConn.

* **Where are we now?**—9 January 1987. Unpublished TS (2 pp.), Box 38, Folder 585, EDP-UConn.

* **EASTER SUNDAY**—19 April 1987. Unpublished TS (1 p.), Series 2:A, Folder 490, EDP-3009.

* **ON PRINCIPLE**—2 April 1987. Unpublished TS with handwritten revisions (2 pp.), Series 2:A, Folder 490, EDP-3009.

* **OUTSIDE GART BROTHERS**—June 1987. Unpublished TS (1 p.), Series 2:A, Folder 490, EDP-3009.

* **The Ollie Predicament**—8 July 1987. Unpublished TS (1 p.), Series 2:A, Folder 490, EDP-3009.

* **Old quotes are the best**—22 July 1987. Unpublished MS (2 pp.), Series 2:A, Folder 490, EDP-3009.

* **That the american people**—3 January 1987. Unpublished MS (1 p.), Box 38, Folder 582, EDP-UConn.

* **Supreme Abhorrence**—3 January 1987. Unpublished MS (1 p.), Box 38, Folder 588, EDP-UConn.

* **Paul Simon, answering**—16 December 1987. Unpublished MS (1 p.), Series 2:A, Folder 489, EDP-3009.

* **The tighter the orbit, the more power**—July 1987. Unpublished MS (1 p.), Box 38, Folder 582, EDP-UConn.

* **Don't Forget the Mortgage**—15 February 1988. Unpublished TS with handwritten revisions (1 p.), Box 38, Folder 583, EDP-UConn.

* **Motel Superbo**—19 July 1988. Unpublished TS with handwritten revisions (1 p.), Box 38, Folder 582, EDP-UConn.

* **Platinum parachute**—15 August 1988. Unpublished TS with handwritten revisions (1 p.), Box 38, Folder 582, EDP-UConn.

* **Co-opted by the Axis**—September 1988. Unpublished MS (1 p.), Box 43, Notebook "Untitled" (1988) #1, EDP-UConn.

* A vast gisting of the 80ies—Mayday 1989. Unpublished TS (2 pp.), Box 38, Folder 587, EDP-UConn.
* Would you buy a Used Car from this Century?—Undated. Unpublished TS with handwritten revisions (1 p.), Box 38, Folder 588, EDP-UConn.

ABOMINATIÓNES (1991)

January–Spring 1991. Unpublished MSS (8 pp.), Box 42, Notebook "Hotel Anthony Wayne", EDP-UConn. These poems represent work that Dorn made towards a chronicle of the nineties. Though not all of the poems in this section originally bore the heading "Abominatiónes", we have applied it to poems of a similar theme found in the same notebook.

THE CONNECTION TO NOWHERE (1992–1999)

* The germ of failure resides—ca. 1978–1979/February 1996. Unpublished MS (1 p.), Series B, Folder 577, Notebook 4, EDP-3009. The first couplet appears to have been written 1978–1979, the date-range covered by most of the notebook; the second couplet is dated February 1996.
* AN ACCOUNT OF A TRIP WITH JEREMY PRYNNE—January 1992. Unpublished TS (2 pp.), held by Jennifer Dunbar Dorn.
* Thinking of my life as a teacher—Undated. Unpublished MS (1 p.), Series B, Notebook, EDP-3009.
* Prosaic Justice—ca. June 1994. Unpublished TS (1 p.), Series 2:A, Folder 500, EDP-3009. Draft TS with handwritten revisions (1 p.), Series 2:A, Folder 551, EDP-3009, labelled as belonging to "Rocky Mountain Spine", for which cf. CP (pp. 869–878).
* Intervention Alley—ca. 1995. Unpublished TS with handwritten revisions (1 p.), Series 2:A, Folder 551, EDP-3009.
* Sub Coupe—Undated. This and the five poems that follow (ending with MO COUPS) are unpublished TSS with handwritten revisions (7 pp.), Series 2:A, Folder 542, EDP-3009. These are poems that were not published in Low Coups and Haut Coups (1995–1998); CP (pp. 861–868). The original title of MO COUPS was "WON COUPS", and its sixth stanza is taken from a draft of "Early Modern" (1 p.), Series 2:A, Folder 542, EDP-3009; CP (p. 865).
* The Jaw is there—11 August 1998. Unpublished MS (2 pp.), Series B, Folder 605, Notebook 7, EDP-3009.
* Remember the Starling Show—18 December 1998, Rome. Unpublished MS (3 pp.), Series B, Folder 605, Notebook 7, EDP-3009.
* Blown fuse—20 December 1998, Rome. Unpublished MS (2 pp.), Series B, Folder 605, Notebook 7, EDP-3009.
* On first looking into Shakespeare's Folios—ca. late December 1998. Unpublished TS (1 p.), held by Jennifer Dunbar Dorn.
* Open Letter to the Apache Nation (unrevised)—28 April 1999, Denver. Unpublished TS with handwritten revisions (4 pp.), Series 2:A, Folder 551, EDP-3009. A revised version is published in CP (pp. 886–887). There are two

other drafts. Unpublished MS (3 pp.), 18 April 1999, Series B, Folder 605, Notebook 7, EDP-3009. Unpublished TS with handwritten revisions (1 p.), Box 2, Folder 3, EDP-M1460. Some minor revisions are taken from the Stanford text.

* **Notes on Olson**—14 October 1999. Published in Tom Clark, *Charles Olson: The Allegory of a Poet's Life*, Second edition (Berkeley: North Atlantic Books, 2000), pp. 351–352.

DENVER SKYLINE (1993–1999)

Denver Skyline is the name of a series of "local poems" which includes "Sketches from Edgewater" (*CP*, pp. 891–893).

* **On Seeing Kidd Onto the London Suborbital at Stapleton**—17 March 1993, Denver. Unpublished TS (1 p.), held by Jennifer Dunbar Dorn.

* **SUMMER CRITIQUE**—ca. 23 July 1994, Denver. Unpublished TS (1 p.), Series 2:A, Folder 551, EDP-3009.

* **REPULSION—Superbowl '95**—30 January 1995, Denver. Unpublished TS (1 p.), Box 1, Folder 9, EDP-M1460.

* **St. George Drops Dead at the Denver Zoo**—ca. 1995, Denver. Unpublished TS (1 p.), Series 2:A, Folder 551, EDP-3009.

* **West of the Platte on a Saturday Naitte**—ca. 1995, Denver. Unpublished TS with handwritten revisions (2 pp.), Series 2:A, Folder 551, EDP-3009.

* **The Screwball**—8 February 1996, Denver. Unpublished TS with handwritten revisions (1 p.), Series 2:A, Folder 551, EDP-3009.

* **Repulsion II: at the snack-crazed Safeway**—31 January 1999, Denver. Unpublished TS with handwritten revisions (1 p.), Series 2:A, Folder 551, EDP-3009.

PLUS DE LANGUEDOC VARIORUM (1992–1999)

As demonstrated in *CP* (pp. 811–860), *Languedoc Variorum: A Defense of Heresy & Heretics* has a three-tiered textual structure: the main text of the poems runs along the top half of each page, while the "Subtexts" and "NAZDAKS" run along the bottom half. There is no authoritative publication of the entire project, and so there is some uncertainty about the inclusion and order of the seven texts which begin this section. Note that at different stages in the project, both the "Subtexts" and "NAZDAKS" bore the title "The Moses Mosaics".

* **1099—one hundred years after Andromeda blew up**—1995. Unpublished TS with handwritten revisions (1 p.), Series 2:A, Folder 551, EDP-3009.

* **Aum: Heresy Automatic Designation Cult**—ca. mid-1995. Unpublished TS (1 p.), Series 2:A, Folder 538, EDP-3009.

* **Unabomber as Heretic**—ca. 1996. Unpublished TS (1 p.), Series 2:A, Folder 538, EDP-3009.

* **A Review of Volume Ten of the Olson/Creeley Correspondence**—ca. after 1996. Unpublished TS with handwritten revisions (1 p.), Series 2:A, Folder 538, EDP-3009.

* **Monotheism**—ca. after 1996. Unpublished TS with handwritten revisions (1 p.), Series 2:A, Folder 538, EDP-3009.

* **JESUS—HE WAS A HANDSOME MAN**—ca. after 1996. Unpublished TS (1 p.), Box 3, Folder 8, EDP-M1460.

* **Another Heretic takes wing**—ca. late 1998. Unpublished TS (1 p.), Series 2:A, Folder 532, EDP-3009. Loyalist paramilitary leader Billy Wright was assassinated on 27 December 1997.

* **SUBTEXTS**—The forty published "Subtexts" (CP, pp. 813–831) have not been included here. For the most part, the order of the texts printed here reflects the main sequence of the TS with handwritten revisions (9 pp.), Series 2:A, Folder 538, EDP-3009. What follows are notes on texts that have been edited or interpolated into the main sequence. The text beginning "The Mormans are not part of the problem . . ." is from earlier in the "Subtexts" sequence, meant to follow the published text beginning "A Business passing itself off . . ." (CP, p. 823). The text beginning "Christian Criminals ignore the code . . ." is from TS (2 pp.), Series 2:A, Folder 538, EDP-3009; virgules have been added to indicate potential line breaks, as transcribed from an original MS by Maya Dorn. The text beginning "Sanctimony follows the money" is separate from the main sequence, and is found on the final page of the above-mentioned 9 pp. TS beneath "Aum: Heresy Automatic Designation Cult". The text beginning "Intellectual workers are poorly paid . . ." is from the above-mentioned 2 pp. TS; virgules have been added to indicate potential line breaks, as transcribed from an original MS by Maya Dorn. The text beginning "The Catharans shared a fundamental conception . . ." appears to be incomplete and has been edited for continuity. The text beginning "Northern Ireland Protestants . . ." is from the above-mentioned 2 pp. TS; virgules have been added to indicate potential line breaks, as transcribed from an original MS by Maya Dorn.

* **NAZDAKS**—Mostly unpublished TS (15 pp.), held by Jennifer Dunbar Dorn. The "NAZDAKS" up to ". . . STRIPPED THE REPUBLIC OF ITS PILFERED ASSETS" are published in CP (pp. 813–831). Revisions adopted from incomplete TSS with handwritten revisions (40 pp.), Series 2:A, Folder 537, EDP-3009. After "POPE, BISHOPS, PRIEST, PEOPLE", all "NAZDAKS" are from TS (2 pp.), Series 2:A, Folder 538, EDP-3009; as transcribed from an original MS by Maya Dorn.

INDEX OF TITLES OR FIRST LINES

EDWARD MERTON DORN (1929–1999) was born in Villa Grove, Illinois, on the day after April Fools'. He studied the American West with Charles Olson at Black Mountain College in the early fifties, and throughout that decade worked as a day labourer across the western United States. He was married to Helene Buck for over a decade, with whom he had a son, Paul, and was stepfather to Helene's children Fred and Chansonette. Dorn first met his own father at the age of thirty-two. Living in a refurbished chicken coop for much of the early sixties, Dorn worked as a university teacher in Idaho, publishing two books of poetry, a novel, and an anthropological work, *The Shoshoneans*. Promoted in the late fifties and early sixties by such writers as Denise Levertov, Robert Creeley, Amiri Baraka, Tom Raworth, and J.H. Prynne, his first consistent publisher was Fulcrum Press in London. Dorn moved to Colchester on a Fulbright teaching fellowship in 1965, and stayed until 1968, after which point he followed teaching gigs and reading tours between England and North America until the late seventies. With his second wife Jennifer Dunbar and their children Kidd and Maya, Dorn settled in Colorado, where he continued to teach for the rest of his life. In the early nineties, he spent a year in Languedoc teaching and studying the history of the Inquisition. In 1997, he was diagnosed with cancer and continued to write through bouts of chemotherapy until his death on 10 December 1999. Edward Dorn is probably best known for work that he published during the late sixties and early seventies, during which time he worked on significant collaborations with Gordon Brotherston, and helped to imagine and produce a number of radical and experimental publications with Frontier Press and Zephyrus Image. As an editor, he co-founded the magazine *Wild Dog* in the early sixties, ran the short-lived satirical newspaper *Bean News* in the early seventies, and co-edited the newspaper *Rolling Stock* through the eighties and nineties. The first comprehensive collection of his poetry was published in 1975, and his posthumous *Collected Poems* was published by Carcanet Press in 2012.

JUSTIN KATKO, born 1984 in Kentucky, lives in London, where he runs Critical Documents and is the author of such books as *Nine out of Ten Terrorists Agree that Brini Maxwell is the Next Martha Stewart* (2004), *The Death of Pringle* (2011), and *Basic Middle Finger* (forthcoming).

KYLE WAUGH, born 1979 in Kansas City, lives in Brooklyn, where he is a PhD student at the Graduate Center, CUNY. He is co-editor, with Cyrus Console, of Kenneth Irby's *The Intent On: Collected Poems, 1962–2006* (North Atlantic Books, 2009).